The DOORS *Companion*

The DOORS *Companion*

Four Decades of Commentary

Edited by
JOHN M. ROCCO

SCHIRMER BOOKS
An Imprint of
Simon & Schuster Macmillan
New York

Prentice Hall International
London Mexico City New Delhi Singapore Sydne
Toronto

Copyright © 1997 by Schirmer Books

Schirmer Books
An Imprint of Simon & Schuster Macmillan
1633 Broadway
New York, NY 10019

Library of Congress Catalog Card Number: 96-45692

Printed in the United States of America

Printing number
1 2 3 4 5 6 7 8 9 10

Library of Congress Cataloging-in-Publication Data

The Doors companion : four decades of commentary / edited by John M. Rocco.
    p. cm.
  Includes bibliographical references (p.) and index.
  ISBN 0-02-864661-4 (alk. paper)
  1. Doors (Musical group) I. Rocco, John (John M.)
ML421.D66D65 1997
782.42166'092'2—dc21   96-45692
                                                                        CIP
                                                                        MN

This paper meets the requirements of ANSI/MOSP 739.48-1992 {Permanence of Paper}.

for Brian Rocco
Stronger Than Dirt

We're erotic politicians.

—JIM MORRISON

If the doors of perception were cleansed every thing would
appear to man as it is, infinite.

—WILLIAM BLAKE, *The Marriage
of Heaven and Hell*

America always gives me the feeling of real asceticism.
Culture, politics—and sexuality too—are seen exclusively in terms
of the desert, which here assumes the status of a primal scene.
Everything disappears before that desert vision. Even the body,
by an ensuing effect of undernourishment takes on a transparent
form, a lightness near to complete disappearance. Everything
around me suffers this same desertification. But this radical
experimentation is the only thing that enables me to get through
and produces that astral quality I have not found anywhere else.

—JEAN BAUDRILLARD, *America*
(trans. Chris Turner)

In music the passions enjoy themselves.

—FRIEDRICH NIETZSCHE, *Beyond Good and Evil*
(trans. Walter Kaufmann)

Contents

Acknowledgments

I need to give thanks to the following people who were there before, during and after: Thanks to Richard Carlin for commissioning this book and for Alicia Williamson for always being on the other end of the phone at Schirmer Books; thanks to Richard Goldstein for writing all these years in the *Voice;* thanks to Dr. John Morgan for opening up his correspondence with Albert Goldman and thanks to Jane Krupp of Shpritzgun Productions who allowed me to reprint Goldman's words; thanks to James Riordan for helping me reprint two big selections from the great book he wrote with Jerry Prochnicky; and thanks to Vicki Chamlee for her patience and her belief in the Packers.

Jerry Hopkins wrote me long and helpful letters from Bangkok and without his kindness and advice this would be a poorer book. And my last and most important literary thanks goes to the man who got me this job and who taught me how to look at the avant-garde in art and life: Richard Kostelanetz.

Patricia Kennealy Morrison not only shared her writing with me, she shared her memories and Jim Morrison's words. I owe her a great debt and so does everyone who is interested in the life and work of Jim Morrison. Her kindness, generosity, and depth of spirit made this a better book and me a better reader of Jim Morrison's legacy.

On a personal note I have to thank the people who drank beer and listened to the Doors with me: Kev, Vin, Tom, Fran, Jerry, and Bill; and the guys who bought me all those dinners all those nights: Mark Daly and Steve Danesghar. Thanks to Frank and Biff and thanks to Mary Clancy to whom I owe more than I can say. And thanks to Dana for the love *because the mountain grass cannot but keep the form where the mountain hare has lain.* This book is dedicated to my brother, Brian, who drank lots of beer and listened to lots of Doors albums with me; he also read through the manuscript and told me where I got boring.

Introduction: The Haunting of the Doors

He felt a swelling ache in his chest, and knew that the Red Death was
already inside him, specking his blackened organs with carmin and scar-
let. It was unbearable; he needed a drink. His hands searched eagerly in
his pocket and found a penny; he went into a tavern and had a glass of
wine, and his face flushed and he determined to seek out the Grave of
Lost Stories and set those poor souls free; for he knew where it was,
and though the task scarcely be safe or easy, he thought that he had
sufficient boldness to undertake it.

—WILLIAM T. VOLLMANN, "The Grave of Lost Stories"

The smell of old leather and the crack of a whiskey bottle opening; rolling
mist and headlights coming through it and a crowd somewhere rushing
the stage; an empty green wine bottle falling and rolling across tile; a zip-
per being pulled down and a cymbal dropped as the apparition appears
was always there and leans against my desk. Sibilant voices echo and call.
The ghost of Jim Morrison leans over me and the smell of a thousand
drinking nights comes from him among the odor of wetted ashes.

The Ghost: So what is this here? Freedom within the pages of a school
book? Or just another asshole making money off of my days and nights
and the things we tried? Get a brain pan, man.

From everywhere a thousand half-empty whiskey bottles appear and
the ghost is momentarily distracted. The ghost ponders labels with his
head slightly tilted to the left.

The Editor: No, Jim. Yes, Jim. No, Mr. Morrison. I mean no disrespect,
but it's just that you and that band won't go away. You are everywhere.
They want to read about you. They want to come to some understanding

about those days and nights and why the music still pulls at them. The music is not over. The lights are still on.

The Ghost *(waves at the whiskey bottles and they fall into the eagerly awaiting sea):* Valéry once said that a poem is never finished, it is only abandoned. I have abandoned. It is finished.

The Whiskey a Go-Go appears only to be swallowed up by a court-room which is quickly torn apart by a film crew weighed down with cameras, microphones, scripts, lights, computer screens, Oliver Stone. The Ghost picks up this book and its pages open, close, open.

The Editor: It's only words.

The Ghost: I've been down so long that anything looks up to me. Why do they care?

Phantom policemen rush the desk and struggle with the Ghost. The Ghost throws a policeman's hat into the audience. The cops fall back and lick ghost wounds and hold hands and light skull-shaped candles. An old bluesman clears his throat, spits, and picks up his battered guitar. A woman laughs until she cries. A dark forest grows and a poet has lost his way. The woods decay, the woods decay and fall.

The Editor: You have touched them. The Doors have touched them. They cannot be the same again.

The Ghost *(not touching the earth):* I need someone who doesn't need me. I need my poetry. My poetry is here.

Cameras erupt from the floor. Mr. Mojo Rises above the lights covering the room in white, blind light. Movies run through projectors and people hitchhike all over America knowing that there is a killer on the road. A black sun falls and consumes everything. There is feedback from an amp.

The Ghost: Why all this? Crawl all over me. This writing and the writing all over my grave. Why can't they just stop writing and just listen. Forget the night.

The Editor: But they need to understand why and how. Or just how. You and the music have become a part of their consciousness and they need to understand themselves. They want to read about themselves so they read about you. One conversation on one beach has led them all talking across the beaches of the world. Under the pavement, the beach!

The Ghost picks up a handful of sand and drops stars. Bushmills and cigar smoke. Flashbulbs explode. Warhol's golden telephone rings. Verlaine reels like an indignant desert bird and shoots Rimbaud.

The Ghost: But it was all just about freedom. That's all I was interested in.

The Ghost rubs his eyes and the ocean waves roar in silence.

Jim Morrison has haunted me. During the long process of putting this book together—the research, the letter writing, the phone calls—the ghost of Jim Morrison has ruffled my pages, freaked out my computer, and spilled (ghost gulped) my drinks. (My water and coffee remained standing, but my beer and whiskey flowed. . . .) But this is not only because I reread the book which first turned my generation onto the facts and myths behind the Doors (*No One Here Gets Out Alive* was passed around my junior high school class like the Shroud of Turin). And I wasn't haunted because I again watched the show at the Hollywood Bowl (Mick Jagger called it boring!) or compared my scratchy but warm albums to newly opened CDs. And it wasn't because I read through over a hundred pieces of writing on the Doors and Jim Morrison—over a hundred different takes on the music and over a hundred different looks at the band. The Doors have provoked an industry of criticism, gossip, and biography that still flourishes twenty-five years after Morrison's death. There is a great deal of material to read about the Doors and this caused Oliver Stone to describe the research involved behind his depiction of Morrison as reminiscent of *Citizen Kane*: "He was everything to everybody, and no one will quite agree on all the events." But it wasn't because I read through all this writing and edited this book: the ghost came to me as it does to everybody who has listened to the strange, dark, mesmerizing music that the Doors produced. He was everything to everybody, *they* were everything to everybody. Jim Morrison and the Doors haunt us and the haunting only increases with each year, with each new book, with each time one of the songs is played on the radio.

When Val Kilmer was studying for his role as the Lizard King, his dreams were disturbed by a figure Morrison described in "Queen of the Highway": a monster dressed in black leather. But like all artists, Jim Morrison was a collection of several different people battling for dominance in one body and through one art. As Lester Bangs put it:

[W]hat it came down to fairly early for me, actually, was accepting the Doors' limitations and that Morrison would never be so much Baudelaire, Rimbaud and Villon as he was a Bozo Prince. Surely he was one father of new wave, as transmitted through Iggy and Patti Smith. . . . One thing that can not be denied Morrison is that at his best . . . he had style, and as he was at his best as a poet of dread, desire and psychic dislocation, so he was also at his best as a clown. So it's no wonder our responses got, and remain, a little confused.

He was a monster in black leather, but he was also a great rock and roll singer, an acute cultural critic, a poet, a filmmaker and film theorist, a "Bozo Dionysus" as Bangs calls him, and probably the most effective popularizer of Nietzsche in the twentieth century. The music this man helped create with Ray Manzarek, Robby Krieger, and John Densmore has gotten into the consciousness of America. The aim of this book is to provide an entrance into reading about this provocative, complex, and important cultural phenomenon. The Doors are an important influence on contemporary rock and roll and thus an important influence on postmodern American culture. This book is designed to help the reader approach the wealth of writing there is out there on the band and on Morrison's life and myth. This book will help the reader get behind the Doors; and it works in the same way the novelist Toni Morrison described her novel *The Bluest Eye:* "There is nothing more to say—except why. But since *why* is difficult to handle, one must take refuge in *how.*" This book describes some of the ways the Doors can be read—*how* they can be read, seen, listened to, written about, understood. This book is about the *how* of a ghost.

> In a dream, silently, she had come to him, her wasted body within
> its loose graveclothes giving off an odour of wax and rosewood,
> her breath, bent over him with mute secret words, a faint odour of
> wetted ashes.
>
> —JAMES JOYCE, *Ulysses*

The story has become a myth. As with all myths, this story is retold over and over again. We hear the story in the books (there are at least two a year), on the screen, and in places like Manhattan's Wetlands where the Doors tribute band The Soft Parade takes a clubful of kids back in time every other weekend. The myth gains its power and its influence with each retelling and each retelling tells us something else. Here it is again.

A precocious high school student in Florida reads everything he can get his hands on—Kerouac, Blake, Rimbaud, Joyce, Nietzsche—and stuns his teachers with his grasp of literature and arcane subjects. Instead of excelling academically, he becomes rebellious and always seems to be looking for something else. His father is a high-ranking navy officer who will later become the navy's youngest rear admiral. This turns out to be the greatest irony in rock and roll history: Jim Morrison, the first rock singer to be arrested *on stage,* the symbol of personal rebellion for an entire culture, was the son of a man who had a prominent role in the Tonkin Gulf incident that officially began U.S. military involvement in Vietnam. One of the things Morrison did when he was first faced with media attention was to declare himself an orphan.

But before Morrison symbolically kills off his family, he attends Florida State and then quickly transfers to the film school at UCLA. He learns about film and drugs. He drinks. He keeps a notebook of poems on film aesthetics that will later turn into his first book, *The Lords: Notes on Vision*. He spends the summer after graduating on a rooftop overlooking the beach; he fasts and drops acid. He writes constantly ("I slept on a roof./At night the moon became/a woman's face"). After this experience on the roof (Verlaine: "Le ciel est, par-dessus le toit, /Si blue, si calme!") he will form a band with three musicians and they will call themselves the Doors after Huxley's investigations into transforming reality with mescaline in *The Doors of Perception*. Morrison knew that Huxley got his title from Blake's *The Marriage of Heaven and Hell* and on that rooftop overlooking Venice beach he asks the same question Blake's poem asks:

> How do you know but ev'ry Bird that cuts the airy way,
> Is an immense world of delight, clos'd by your senses five?

But before he met what he called "the Spirit of Music" on the roof, Morrison met Ray Manzarek, a fellow film student and keyboard player for a band called Rick and the Ravens. (Ravens. A foreshadowing of the ghost to come; Poe's Raven: "And his eyes have all the seeming of a demon's that is/dreaming.") Manzarek gave Morrison his first music job: he was paid $25 to stand with the band and pretend to play guitar. It was with Manzarek that Morrison would have the famous conversation on the beach. Morrison was down from the roof and he accidentally bumped into Manzarek. Morrison was supposed to have been in New York and Manzarek was surprised to see him on the beach. He asked Morrison what he had been up to and Morrison sang him "Moonlight Drive." It was the first Doors performance and Manzarek was the first audience. Jerry Hopkins describes this as a "perfect rock and roll myth, a Horatio Alger cliché." And so it goes: Manzarek was taking a meditation class at the time and in it were John Densmore and Robby Krieger. The drummer and the guitarist Manzarek meditated with were members of a band called the Psychedelic Rangers. They soon became the members of a different band. Ravens on acid: "Take thy beak from out my heart, and take thy form/from off my door!"

The myth rolls on through the London Fog and the Whiskey a Go-Go and into the night Morrison ate a giant quantity of acid and spontaneously composed the Oedipal section of "The End" in front of a stunned, mesmerized crowd. The Doors are promptly fired as the Whiskey's house band. But they get signed by Elektra and after Morrison destroys a studio the first album is released. *The Doors* reflects the interests the band will pursue throughout their career: from the Brechtian "Alabama Song (Whiskey Bar)" to Willie Dixon's "Back Door Man" to the Oedipal nightmare of "The End" the first album is a concentrated attack upon conventional rock and, at the same time, it roots them in a tradition of radical art. In July of '67, "Light My Fire" hits number one. Five years later Jim Morrison is found dead in Paris. His headstone in the Père-Lachaise Cemetery reads "Kata ton daimona eay toy"—Greek for "True to his own spirit."

Many things happened during the strange days between "Light My Fire" being played on every radio station in America and Morrison's last bath. But that, in part, is the aim of this book: to fill in the missing pieces, to lead to other reading about the band called the Doors. And if I have described writing and reading about the Doors as a ghost experience, it is only because others have done so before me. In his fascinating and often touching account of his life with the band, *Riders on the Storm,* John Densmore speaks to a Morrison who is not there. When writing about one of the incidents I left out in my account of the myth—the time when Manzarek, Densmore, and Krieger almost sold the rights to "Light My Fire" for a commercial—Densmore tells the long-gone but ever-present Morrison:

> *. . . You were furious when you got back, weren't you? Mind you, you didn't write "Light My Fire," Robby did. All I can say is that, looking back, I am touched that you cared enough about one of our creations to stand up for it not being bastardized. We weren't businessmen when we got together in Venice, but we were on our way there. Me, Ray, and Robby, at least. . . . You, of course, didn't say much of anything directly to any of us about this incident, keeping in line with the Doors' unspoken credo not to confront each other. But your message was to confront!*

The message still lives and this book will help the reader confront the myths, the facts, and the music.

Boredom is no longer my love. Rage, debauchery, madness—
I know all their aspirations and disasters—all my burden is
laid aside.

—ARTHUR RIMBAUD, "Bad Blood" (from *Une Saison
en enfer,* trans. Louise Varèse)

The officials who run the Père-Lachaise Cemetery in Paris say that in 2001 they will not renew the thirty-year lease taken out on Morrison's grave. It seems that Morrison's ghost has been disturbing the ghosts of Edith Piaf, Balzac, and Proust (but Oscar Wilde seems to enjoy the company: "Pleasure is the only thing one should live for. Nothing ages like happiness.") There is too much traffic and too much graffiti for the cemetery's owners and they say that Morrison's remains will have to be removed. What the cemetery owners do not understand is that even if they do have Morrison's skeleton removed—in what posture do the bones lay? Hands on crotch and heart or is the legend true that he was buried with a bottle of Irish whiskey? Everybody has fun at *Finnegans Wake!*—and even if they eradicate all the evidence of the site, the people will still come and they will still sit around and smoke and drink and cry and sing and dance and write all over the other tombs. They will still feel the ancient shape all around them. The ghost laughs at exorcism.

Jim Morrison and the Doors will not leave us that easily. As Mikal Gilmore pointed out in *Rolling Stone,* the Doors began a split in popular culture, a schism that has formed the basis of modern rock:

> While groups like the Beatles or the many bands emerging from the Bay
> Area were earnestly touting a fusion of music, drugs and idealism that
> they hoped would reform and redeem—a troubled age, the Doors had
> fashioned an album that looked at prospects of hedonism and violence, of
> revolt and chaos, and embraced those prospects unflinchingly.

And from their first album each Doors production—album, concert, interview, book, film, Morrison arrest—was a deeper rip in the social construction we call rock and roll. Early in his career, Morrison mixed together Blake's prophesies and Huxley's recipes for mind expansion and said: "There are things known and unknown and in between are the Doors." This "in between" world that the Doors gave us was the beginning of the dark forces behind new wave and punk; and people and groups like Iggy Pop, Alice Cooper, the Stranglers, Joy Division, and Patti Smith were members of the first generation to take up the Doors' legacy. Morrison died in 1971 and the music of the '70s was colored by the angst, the re-evaluation of all values, and the primitive rush to destroy conventions that were his trademarks. The Beatles told us that all we needed was love, but Morrison and the Doors denied this and they demanded the entire world and they backed up their demand with the arrogance of asking for it *now*. *Now* became the watchcry for the jaded '70s, a period of Vietnam burnout and the rise of political and social conservatism.

One woman from New Jersey may be pointed to as the catalyst between the ghost in Père-Lachaise and the punk movement. By 1974, Patti Smith had published poetry and worked in the theater with Sam Shepard. In that year she also released her first music. In *England's Dreaming: Anarchy, Sex Pistols, Punk Rock, and Beyond,* Jon Savage points to two of her early songs as emblematic of her role in the forma-tion of punk:

> "Piss Factory" both celebrated her escape from New Jersey and laid down the script for the autobiography in which she was now starring. Despite the addition of musicians, Smith was the focus. Each performance would see her launch into the unknown, through her improvisations on songs like the Punk classic "Gloria." Androgynous, she would invoke Rimbaud, Reich, even the CBGBs dog, in her attempt to achieve unconsciousness, to dissolve, as she sang on her centerpiece, "Land," into "the sea of possi-bility."

With Morrison she shared an admiration for Rimbaud and the Beats. Her rendition of "Gloria" that appears on *Horses* (an album produced by John Cale and featuring the photographs of Robert Mapplethorpe) owes a debt to the Doors' live performance of the song: Morrison's improvisation of the song invites the song's namesake up to his room, while Smith's take on the song begins with a meditation on personal salvation ("Jesus died for somebody's sins, but not mine"). In 1975, the year before punk broke, Smith did guest vocals on Ray Manzarek's *The Whole Thing Started with Rock & Roll*. In 1979, at the tail end of the punk explosion, Smith reviewed *An American Prayer* for *Creem* and she asked:

> And what will be done with him, his prayer? Where does a guy like him fit in? He stood on a tradition of men who could not be bought. Men that disintegrated fast, when borrowed, like salt in the rain. Will they sand-

wich a section of Jim Morrison sacrificing his cock on the altar of silence between Abba and Boston?

But Patti Smith herself is one of the answers to this question: Morrison does not fit in between Abba and Boston on the radio. She makes this clear when she pointed out their similar aesthetic stances: "Tell them james how we pray screaming."

One of the roads leading to punk stems from Morrison's injunction to "Wrap your legs around my neck" in his version of "Gloria." One of the people who saw Patti Smith dig into her subconscious at CBGBs while she sang her version of "Gloria" was Malcolm McLaren, the proprietor of SEX, a London shop catering to anti-fashion and marital aids. McLaren was also interested in managing a rock band. The same year he saw Patti Smith in New York, his store was selling a T-shirt that he and his wife, Vivienne Westwood, designed. The shirt read: "You're gonna wake up one morning and *know* what side of the bed you've been lying on!" Also printed on the shirt were two long lists: one of "Hates" (Mick Jagger, The Liberal Party, Andy Warhol, Parking Tickets, a passive audience) and one of "Loves" (Eddie Cochran, Strange Death of Liberal England, Raw Power, Marianne Faithful, Iggy Pop, Jamaican Rude Boys). As Jon Savage points out, the T-shirt is important because it is the first printed mention of the Sex Pistols. Under "Loves" is listed the band Steve Jones and McLaren were forming: "Kutie Jones and his SEX PISTOLS." Also listed under "Loves" is Jim Morrison. And so the story goes: McLaren takes a violent punk with green hair and bad teeth off the street and has him sing in front of a jukebox playing Alice Cooper's "Eighteen." Johnny Rotten is named, the rest of the band hates him, and the Sex Pistols are born.

Punk was a posture that turned into a way of life; punk was a living statement of resistance against the face of stultifying Thatcherism and economic and social disenfranchisement. Eight years after the Doors played the London Roundhouse, the Clash stood on the same stage and Joe Strummer spoke to the audience:

I've been trying to go out recently, but I've had to stay in. And the only thing I've got at home is a TV that hasn't got any sound on it. So I'm staying in, right, and I just want to hear sounds, I don't want to see no visuals, I want to go out and see some groups. But there ain't anything to go out and see. I've seen it all before. So I have to stay at home and watch TV without sound and lip-read my way through it. I'd just like to protest about this state of affairs. So if there's any of you people in the audience who aren't past it yet, and if you can do anything, why don't you get up and do it, instead of, like, lying around?

This is a call for revolution or negation of the status quo from a *personal* stance ("I've had to stay in" or, as Johnny Rotten says at the beginning of a live version of "Substitute": "You don't need permission for anything"). This was a call that Morrison began with the help of Nietzsche who taught him that "facts are precisely what there is not, only interpretations." This emphasis on "interpretations" led Morrison to experiment with his own interpretations, with his own unconscious visions of the world. Savage points to the Doors' influence as "the start of pop's fantastic voyage into the subconscious." The Doors pointed to the dark mirror reflecting a culture gone mad through war and self-righteous morality; and the punks attempted to smash the mirror and grind its jagged pieces into the face of a complacent and hypocritical society (John Lydon in *Rotten: No Irish, No Dogs, No Blacks:* "Our interest in politics at the time was zero. . . . [D]uring the Pistols, I was too young. I couldn't even vote. I just knew they were all corrupt—like the people who would run off with the money and fake their own deaths"). The Doors were the first rock band to inject theater into their work and they were immediately spoken of as practitioners of performance art by critics. Richard Goldstein was one of the first to write about their dark theatrics and he called them "an inner theatre of cruelty." Morrison earned his place on the punk "Loves" list because he embodied the theatrics of rebellion and he pointed this out early in a famous comment: "I'm interested in anything about revolt, disorder, chaos, especially activity that appears to have no meaning. It seems to me to be the road toward freedom." This road to freedom led to Steve Jones saying to an interviewer after one of the early Sex Pistols' shows: "Actually we're not into music. . . . We're into chaos." It also led to Johnny Rotten screaming "I AM AN ANTICHRIST!"

The split—the gaping crack into the black heart of America—Morrison and the Doors caused in rock is one of the reasons their influence can be seen in such diverse bands as Pearl Jam (Eddie Vedder's tormented pose and the lyrics dripping with inner turmoil), Guns N' Roses (the collective trip to the edge complete with Slash and Duff waving bottles at award shows and behind it all the shadow of Mr. Brownstone), and Nine Inch Nails (Trent Rexnor's leathers and Bataille's "The Solar Anus": "I want to have my throat slashed while violating the girl to whom I will have been able to say: you are the night"). But if the crack gave birth to punk, new wave, and grunge, it also demanded lives. Jimi Hendrix and Janis Joplin went first before Morrison saw his last movie— *The Pursued* starring Robert Mitchum—and took his last bath. Sid Vicious, GIMME A FIX written across the scars on his chest, didn't even blink when it came for him. When Kurt Cobain was growing up in the small city of Aberdeen, Washington, he could not get any Sex Pistols records so he just played three chords and screamed a lot. Later, when Nirvana was Nirvana, Cobain used Sid Vicious's real name—Simon Ritchie—when he traveled. The trip took him to 1994. Michael Azerrad, in *Come as You Are: The Story of Nirvana,* traces the edge of the crack Cobain skipped across:

> Much was made of the fact that Kurt died at precisely the same age as Joplin, Hendrix, and Morrison, but Kurt didn't act out some hackneyed rock truism about living fast and dying young. When he said in his suicide note that 'it's better to burn out than fade away,' it was his sarcastic way of showing that he knew full well how his death would look.

Looking at death and playing with the ghosts of the past was a Doors legacy and a Doors curse.

> *When you are actually in America, America hurts, because it has a pow-*
> *erful disintegrative influence upon the white psyche. It is full of grin-*
> *ning, unappeased aboriginal demons, too, ghosts, and it persecutes the*
> *white men, like some Eumenides, until the white men give up their*
> *absolute whiteness. America is tense with latent violence and resistance.*
> *The very common sense of white Americans has a tinge of helplessness*
> *in it, and deep fear of what might be if they were not common-sensical.*
>
> —D. H. LAWRENCE, *Studies in Classic American Literature*

Lawrence describes here the symbolic and cultural background for the settling and taming of wild America. This symbolic force presents itself in early American literature: the white Europeans used their "common sense" to battle the "primitive" magic and forest power of Native Americans. Ralph Ellison describes this need to fall back upon "common sense" as the pathology behind racism: "Color prejudice springs not from the stereotype alone, but from an internal psychological state; not from misinformation alone, but from an inner need to believe." The white Europeans needed to believe that the Indians were "ghosts" from a lost world; the settlers needed to fight these phantasms with every logical weapon in their arsenal. (Lawrence describes the "essential American soul" as "hard, isolate, stoic, and a killer." He forgot to add that his brain squirms like a toad.) And after the initial contact with the ghost people of the woods and the plains, the problem facing the European was compounded by the interaction with African-Americans and *their* culture. This kind of thinking is still representative of American ideology: our common sense will defeat their "savage" words and their magical arts.

But their magical arts are very much alive. American music was founded upon African rhythms and the blues were the first original sounds America gave the world. What the Doors did in a very self-conscious manner was to acknowledge their debt to the blues while they invoked the ceremonies and belief systems of the Native Americans. Morrison embraced the role of shaman and he believed there was an ancient spirit animating his power, his words, and his life. In *Mystery Train,* his study of how America is depicted in rock, Greil Marcus describes the early blues singer Robert Johnson in a way that is perfectly appropriate for a description of Morrison: "Like a good American, Johnson lived for the moment and died for the past." Many think Morrison died for the past: he met the Devil at the crossroads and watched as several Indian souls leaped into his body after being scattered across dawn's highway bleeding. Jim Morrison haunts us because he was haunted by America. He was the ghost god himself.

Morrison may have died for the past, but he did live for the moment; and this moment was first given to him in the literature that was closest to the energy behind the music of the Doors. The Beats put the "Beat" in the Beatles, and they also gave rock its strength and its edge. Ray Manzarek once said that if *On the Road* had never been written, the Doors would never have been formed. Kerouac's novel was particularly important for Morrison's writing. Joyce may have perfected the stream-of-consciousness technique of depicting the inner workings of a mind, but it was Kerouac who connected it with jazz and made his own prose sing with a new American voice. It was Kerouac's method of composition that influenced Morrison's poetry, especially the epics "The End," "The Music's Over," "The Celebration of the Lizard," and "The Soft Parade." When Allen Ginsberg and William Burroughs asked Kerouac to define his method, he wrote a kind of manifesto called "Essentials of Spontaneous

Prose" that pointed to his intent: "Time being of the essence in the purity of speech, sketching language is undisturbed flow from the mind of personal secret idea-words, *blowing* (as per jazz musician) on subject of image." Kerouac led the Beats into thinking of writing as music, as the music of an everyday America. The Beats conjured up the ghosts of the past and refashioned them into new forms, but the past was always there and Ginsberg knew it when he wrote in a poem called "America": "It occurs to me that I am America./I am talking to myself again." The great example the Beats supplied for Morrison and the Doors was that the personal was the political, and the personal was the American past, and the dark of the American night.

America haunted Morrison, but it also haunted Europe. The American Revolution set the stage for the French Revolution and the overall modern revolt against old forms of religious and social authority. Blake describes this force behind America in a prophecy: "Thou art the image of God who dwells in darkness of/Africa;/And thou art fall'n to give me life in regions of dark/death." Morrison was attracted to the European poets who reveled in the dark energy of visions such as this; he read the English Romantics (he used Blake and Shelley to teach Nico how to write songs) and the French Symbolists. But as Wallace Fowlie has demonstrated in *Rimbaud and Jim Morrison: The Rebel as Poet,* Arthur Rimbaud was the single most important poet in Morrison's life. The reason for this is that Rimbaud's visionary poetry attracted Morrison's artistic side while the example of Rimbaud's life provoked Morrison's thirst for rebellion. Antonin Artaud would later adapt Rimbaud's violent visions for the theater, but no one in the history of literature has come close to Rimbaud's intense approach to life and art. In a famous letter, Rimbaud pointed to his goal as a poet: "One must, I say, be a *visionary,* make oneself a *visionary.* The poet makes himself a *visionary* through a long, a prodigious and rational disordering of *all* the senses." The poet becomes the subject and the vehicle for his art. This approach to dismantling how we normally see the world was Morrison's way of combating the haunting of America. But, as F. Scott Fitzgerald once said, "There are no second acts in American lives." Morrison died, but he is with us more than ever. Our task is to understand the haunting of Morrison and the way the music still reaches us. Morrison haunts us because he brought up the great questions about life and death and we watched him get his kicks before the whole shit house went up in flames. These were the same questions Van Gogh asked his brother in a discussion of a painting he had just finished called "Starry Night":

This picture raises the eternal question whether we can see the whole of life or only know a hemisphere of it before death. I've no idea of the answer myself. But the sight of stars always sets me dreaming of towns and villages. Why should those points of light in the firmament, I wonder, be less accessible than the dark ones on the map of France? We take the train to go to Tarascon or Rouen and we take death to go to a star. What is certainly true about this argument is that as long as we're alive we can't visit a star any more than when we are dead we can take a train. Anyhow, I don't see why cholera, the stone, phthisis and cancer should not be heavenly modes of locomotion like ships, buses and trains here below, while if we die peacefully of old age we make the journey on foot.

Open
the

If you're working with words, it's got to be poetry. I grew up with Kerouac. If he hadn't written On the Road, *the Doors would never have existed. Morrison read* On the Road *down in Florida, and I read it in Chicago. That sense of freedom, spirituality, and intellectuality in* On the Road—*that's what I wanted in my work.*

—RAY MANZAREK

But then they danced down the streets like dingledodies, and I shambled after as I've been doing all my life after people who interest me, because the only people for me are the mad ones, the ones who are mad to live, mad to talk, mad to be saved, desirous of everything at the same time, the ones who never yawn or say a commonplace thing, but burn, burn, burn like fabulous yellow roman candles exploding like spiders across the stars and in the middle you see the blue centerlight pop and every-body goes "Awww!"

—JACK KEROUAC, On the Road

Those first five or six songs I wrote, I was just taking notes at a fantastic rock concert that was going on inside my head. And once I had written the songs, I had to sing them.

—JIM MORRISON

A Doors concert is a McLuhanist football game.
—*Ellen Sander*

The five years that the Doors were together produced all of their music, all of their myths, all of their troubles, and all of our fascination. The movement from their first album of Brechtian celebration and Freudian nightmares to the deep blues of *L.A. Woman* took so little time that it has taken us twenty-five years to digest it all. It has been twenty-five years since Morrison streaked across the sky of our collective consciousness and we still listen to him and read and write about him. And this book is representative of the eclectic nature of the writing on the Doors: from personal remembrances like that of Jac Holzman—the man who signed the Doors to Elektra—to academic analysis of Morrison's poetics and the band's place in American culture.

To begin this book, this section opens the Doors by featuring two of the most famous pieces written on the band. Richard Goldstein, one of the most influential of all of our rock critics, interviewed Morrison in 1968 and wrote "The Shaman as Superstar." As Jerry Hopkins has described it in *The Lizard King: The Essential Jim Morrison,* "He was smart and the interviewer was smart, so Jim gave the interviewer smart stuff." This "smart stuff" was the first full-length portrait of Morrison to gain wide circulation and it set the tone for all subsequent evaluations of the Doors. In the third section of this book, Goldstein looks across the abyss of over twenty years to look again into the abyss of Morrison. Joan Didion's "Waiting for Morrison" of the same year as Goldstein's first meeting with Morrison is important because it is one of the first published accounts of the tensions within the band. And the larger Didion essay this piece found its way into, "The White Album," placed the Doors squarely in the tumultuous events of the '60s. Michael Cuscuna's later visit with Morrison (1970) describes the discontent over the band's middle period—and particularly *The Soft Parade*—and Morrison's interest in the blues.

The critic, poet, and anthologist Richard Kostelanetz saw the Doors in 1968 and his impressions are reprinted here; it is a firsthand account of the band's performance at one of the historically important rock venues, the Fillmore East. In contrast to this firsthand account, David Dalton reconstructs the early performances of the Doors in the light of their aesthetic interests and their historical context. Also reprinted here is an article from *The New York Times* that describes the night Morrison became the first rock performer to be arrested on stage.

In a fascinating piece glowing with the glorious/maddening chaos that was the late '60s, Stephanie Harrington gives us an account of one of the most famous rock shows in the history of modern music: the infamous Miami show. James Riordan and Jerry Prochnicky describe Morrison's interest in shamanism, which Morrison first indicated back in '68 when he talked to Goldstein. And Goldstein was also the first critic to point to the influence of the writer Antonin Artaud, who attacked a stultifying conception of theater with the anger of a madman and the cruelty of a poet.

IN THAT YEAR
JIM MORRISON

In that year there was
an intense visitation
of energy.
I left school & went down
to the beach to live.
I slept on a roof.
At night the moon became
a woman's face.
I met the Spirit of Music.

THE SHAMAN AS SUPERSTAR

RICHARD GOLDSTEIN

*The shaman . . . he was a man who would intoxicate himself. See, he was
probably already an . . . uh . . . unusual individual. And, he would put himself
into a trance by dancing, whirling around, drinking, taking drugs—however.
Then, he would go on a mental travel and . . . uh . . . describe his journey to the
rest of the tribe.*

—Jim Morrison

He comes to meet you in superstar fatigues: a slept-in pullover and the
inevitable leather pants. A lumpy hat covers most of his mane. You mut-
ter "groovy" at each other in greeting, and split for the beach. His most
recent song comes on the radio. You both laugh as he turns up the volume,
and fiddles with the bass controls. It's a perfect afternoon, so he picks up
his girl. She says, "Your hat makes you look like a Rembrandt, Jim," and
he whispers, "Oh, wow," riding the image as though it were a breaking
wave.

Between freeways, you talk about his bust in New Haven (the charge:
indecent and immoral exhibition), the war, psychoanalysis, and his new
album. He wants to call it "The Celebration of the Lizard" after a 24-
minute "drama" which he has just composed. He is very much into reptiles. He wants the album's jacket printed in pseudo-snakeskin, with its
title embossed in gold.

The official interview takes place in a sequestered inlet at the Garden
of Self-Realization, an ashram Hollywood style. You sit not far from an
urn certified to contain Mahatma Gandhi's ashes. Music is piped in from
speakers at the top of a stucco arch with cupolas sprayed gold. The
ground on which you are assembling your tape recorder is filled with
worms. They seem to be surfacing around his hands, and he examines one
as you set the mike in place. A willing suppliant, it lies prone upon his
palm. Does it know him as a serpent-king?

Amid a burst of strings from the hidden speakers, you ask the trial
question. Jim answers in a slithering baritone. "I dunno . . . I haven't
thought about it." The garden supplies Muzak hosannas.

"When you started, did you anticipate your image?"

"Nahhh. It just sort of happened . . . unconsciously."

"How did you prepare yourself for stardom?"

"Uh . . . about the only thing I did was . . . I stopped getting haircuts."

"How has your behavior onstage changed?"

"See, it used to be . . . I'd just stand still and sing. Now, I . . . uh . . . exaggerate a little bit."

His voice drops an octave at the sight of a tape recorder, and the surrogate audience it represents. He gives a cautious mischievous interview, contemplating each question as though it were a hangnail, and answering with just a trace of smile in the corners of his quotation marks. But he gets his scene across.

"I'm beginning to think it's easier to scare people than to make them laugh."

"I wonder why people like to believe I'm high all the time. I guess . . . maybe they think someone else can take their trip for them."

"A game is a closed field . . . a ring of death with . . . uh . . . sex at the center. Performing is the only game I've got, so . . . I guess it's my life."

His statements, like his songs, are unpunctuated puzzles. You connect the dots between images, and become involved. "I'm a word man," he exults. In discussing his craft, he sputters with esthetic energy. "See, there's this theory about the nature of tragedy, that Aristotle didn't mean catharsis for the audience, but a purgation of emotions for the actors themselves. The audience is just a witness to the event taking place onstage."

He suggests you read Nietzsche on the nature of tragedy to understand where he is really at. His eyes glow as he launches into a discussion of the Apollonian-Dionysian struggle for control of the life force. No need to guess which side he's on.

"See, singing has all the things I like," he explains. "It's involved with writing and with music. There's a lot of acting. And it has this one other thing . . . a physical element . . . a sense of the immediate. When I sing, I create characters."

"What kind of characters?"

"Oh . . . hundreds. Hundreds of 'em."

I like to think he just arrived—you know, came out of nowhere.
—A Fan

He was born James Douglas Morrison, under the sign of Sagittarius the hunter, in Melbourne, Florida, 24 years ago. He once told a reporter, "You could say I was ideally suited for the work I'm doing. It's the feeling of a bow string being pulled back for 22 years and suddenly let go."

But he won't discuss those years on the taut end of existence. He would like you to accept his appearance as a case of spontaneous generation—America's love-lion spurting full grown from the neon lions of the '60s. "They claim everyone was born, but I don't remember it," he insists. "Maybe I was having one of my blackouts."

To accept the thumbnail sketch he offers, there is little in Jim's past to account for his presence. His father is an admiral, but he doesn't think that explains his fascination with authority or his devotion to its overthrow. His family moved so often that his most immediate childhood memories are of landscapes. But that suggests nothing to him about his current shiftlessness. (He lives in motels, or with friends.)

Jim parries questions about his personal experience with acrobatic agility. You find yourself wondering whether he can manipulate his soul with the same consummate ease. Does he choose to show an amiable crescent of himself for this interview? Does his dark side appear at random, or can he summon the lunatic within the way most of us put on a telephone voice? You keep trying to catch him in a moment of prefabricated magic (he wouldn't be the first shaman to take refuge in ritual). But any attempt to grasp the corporeal essence of Jim Morrison is repelled by that fortress of ego, which is yet another of his persona. Behind the walls, however, you sense a soft, slippery kid, who was probably lonely and certainly bored.

"I was a good student. Read a lot. But I was always . . . uh . . . talking when I wasn't supposed to. They made me sit at a special table . . . nothing bad enough to get kicked out, of course. I got through school. . . . Went to Florida State University . . . mainly because . . . I couldn't think of anything else to do."

He came west after college to attend the U.C.L.A. film school. He lived alone in Venice, among the muddy canals and peeling colonnades. The roof of a deserted warehouse was his office. He spent most of his free time there, writing and planning a career in the literary underground. He was brooding (now they say "intense") and shy (in the fan magazines, "sensitive"). A classmate recalls: "He was a lot like he is now, but nobody paid much attention then."

At U.C.L.A., Morrison met Ray Manzarek, a young filmmaker and a jazz pianist on the side. For a while they shared a tiny flat, and Jim began to share his poems as well. It was Manzarek who thought of setting them to music. And though he had never sung before, Jim spent the next few months exploring his voice, and transmitting his vision to drummer John Densmore and guitarist Robbie Krieger. They added sturdy hinges to the sound of the Doors. With Manzarek skimming the keyboard of an electric organ like a flat pebble on water, the new group was tight and sinewy from the start. They did bread-gigs at small clubs along the Sunset Strip, reworking rock-blues standards and staking out a milieu for themselves. But they spent most of their dormant period implementing the controlled insanity that Jim Morrison was soon to loose on modern rock. Long before the three musical Doors ever saw the inside of a recording studio, they had distilled the essence of Jim's screaming "recitatif" into vibrant rhythms and riffs.

"We all play a lead and subjugation things with each other," explains Ray. "When Jim gets into something, I'm able to give of that area within myself. We may look cool, but we are really evil, insidious cats behind Jim. We instigate the violence in him. A lot of times he doesn't feel particularly angry but the music just drives him to it."

This total immersion of sentiment in sound amplifies Morrison's lyrics, transforming them into something more like pageant than poetry. Jim himself is ennobled by the sound. Onstage, his voice becomes a fierce rattle, and all his games are magic spells. In a tiny sweat-cellar like Ondine, where they first played in New York: magic. In the Singer Bowl in Flushing, where they play on August 2. On the radio. In stereophonic sound: magic. They put a spell on you.

> Think of us as erotic politicians.
> —JIM MORRISON to Newsweek

Elvis Presley was the Rasputin of Rock. He ground country funk into the nation's consciousness by playing music as though it were motion. Even with his famous hips obscured on television, there was magic in every quiver of his voice. .

Presley's hillbilly grace is now a patriarchal paunch. But none of the rock titans who followed him has inherited his crown. Even the Beatles built their empire on clean energy ("Yeah, yeah, yeah") and later refined that base through the safe profundity of artsong. The Rolling Stones came close. Their message was the ecstasy of straight potent sex, and their medium was honest ugliness. But the Stones were after mere rape, not soul plunder.

The Doors, however, are an inner theatre of cruelty. Their musical dramas have made fear and trembling part of the rock lexicon. These days every band worth its psychedelic salt has a local lunatic singing lead. But the Doors have already transcended their own image. Now, they are in search of total sensual contact with an audience. They may yet appear at a future concert in masks. As Ray Manzarek explains: "We want our music to shortcircuit the conscious mind and allow the subconscious to flow free."

That goal is a realization of all that was implicit in Elvis Presley's sacred wiggle. But if Elvis was an unquestioning participant in his own hysteria, the Doors celebrate their myth as a creative accomplishment. Playing sorcerer is Jim's thing—not a job, or a hobby, or even one of those terribly necessary rituals we sanctify with the name Role. Jim calls it "play":

"Play is not the same thing as a game," he explains. "A game involves rules. But play is an open event. It's free. Like, you know how people walk to where they're going—very orderly, right? But little kids . . . they're like dogs. They run around, touch things, sing a song. Well, actors play like that. Also, musicians. And you dig watching somebody play, because that's the way human beings are supposed to be . . . free. Like animals."

Words are Jim's playpen. He jots stanzas, images, and allusions into a leather bound notebook, as they occur to him. These are shaped and sifted into the thought-collages which are the Doors' finished lyrics. . . .

"See, this song is called 'Horse Latitudes' because it's about the Doldrums, where sailing ships from Spain would get stuck. In order to lighten the vessel, they had to throw things overboard. Their major cargo was working horses for the New World. And this song is about that moment when the horse is in air. I imagine it must have been hard to get them over the side. When they got to the edge, they probably started chucking and kicking. And it must have been hell for the men to watch, too. Because horses can swim for a while, but then they lose their strength and just go down . . . slowly sink away."

Even when Jim writes about impersonal situations they become charged with the tension of imminent explosion. Violence is his major motif. It permeates to the core of his work. His central symbol, the Great Snake, appears throughout the repertory of the Doors. Sometimes it is a phallic liberator, extolling an act of creative desecration. Sometimes it is a handy fetish to wave in the breeze, instead of the real thing. But most often, it is the agent of self-knowledge, residing in our imaginations, and slinking toward consciousness to be born. Most Doors songs plead with us to reject all repressive authority and embrace the Great Snake, with its slippery equation of freedom and violence. It is an equation we are eager to make, rendering holy what is simply unrestrained.

Robbie and I were sittin' on a plane an' like it's first class, so you get a couple o' drinks, an' I said to Robbie, "Y'know, there are these Apollonian people . . . like, very formal, rational dreamers. An' then there's the Dionysian thing . . . the insanity trip . . . way inside." An' I said, "You're an Apollonian . . . up there with your guitar . . . all neat an' thought out . . . y'know . . . an' you should get into the Dionysian thing."

An' he looks up at me an' says, "Oh, yeah, right Jim."

The Lizard King slithers down Sunset Strip in a genuine snakeskin jacket and leather tights. Bands of teenyboppers flutter about like neon butterflies, but he is oblivious to their scene. He moves past ticky-tacoramas and used-head shops into the open arms of recording studio B, where his true subjects wait.

He greets us with a grin out of "Thus Spake Zarathustra," and we realize instantly that Jim is loaded. Juiced. Stoned—the old way. Booze. No one is surprised; Jim is black Irish to the breath. He deposits a half-empty quart bottle of wine on top of the control panel and downs the remnants of somebody's beer.

"Hafta' break it in," he mutters, caressing the sleeves of his jacket. It sits green and scaly on his shoulders, and crinkles like tinfoil whenever he moves.

"It's—very Tennessee Williams, Jim."

Grunt. He turns to producer Paul Rothchild with a spacious grin that says, "I'm here, so you can start." But Rothchild makes little clicking noises with his tongue. He is absorbed in a musical problem, and he offers only a perfunctory nod to the tipsy titan at his side.

Behind a glass partition three musical Doors hunch over their instruments, intent on a rhythm line that refuses to render itself whole. The gap between Morrison and the other Doors is vast in the studio, where the enforced cohesion of live performance is missing. On their own, they are methodic musicians. Densmore drums in sharp, precise strokes. Krieger's guitar undulates like a belly dancer—sinuous but sober. And at the organ, Manzarek is cultivated and crisp. With his shaggy head atop a pair of plywood shoulders, he looks like a hip undertaker.

Jim walks into the studio and accosts a vacant mike. He writhes in languid agony, jubilant at the excuse to move in his new jacket. But Rothchild keeps the vocal mike dead, to assure maximum concentration on the problem at hand. From behind the glass partition, Jim looks like a silent movie of himself, speeded up for laughs. The musicians barely bother to notice.

When he is drinking, they work around him. Only Ray is solicitous enough to smile. The others tolerate him, as a pungent but necessary prop.

"I'm the square of the Western hemisphere," he says, returning to his wine. "Man . . . whenever somebody'd say something groovy . . . it'd blow my mind. Now, I'm learnin' . . . You like people? I hate 'em . . . screw 'em . . . I don't need 'em . . . Oh, I need 'em . . . to grow potatoes."

He teeters about the tiny room, digging his boots into the carpeting. Between belches, he gazes at each of us, smirking as though he has found something vaguely amusing behind our eyes. But the séance is interrupted when Rothchild summons him. While Jim squats behind the control panel, a roughly recorded dub of his "Celebration of the Lizard" comes over the loudspeakers.

Gently, almost apologetically, Ray tells him the thing doesn't work. Too diffuse, too mangy. Jim's face sinks beneath his scaly collar. Right then, you can sense that "The Celebration of the Lizard" will never appear on record—certainly not on the new Doors album. There will be eleven driving songs, and snatches of poetry, read aloud the way they do it at the 92nd St. Y. But no Lizard-King. No Monarch crowned with love beads and holding the phallic scepter in his hand.

"Hey, bring your notebook to my house tomorrow morning, okay?" Rothchild offers.

"Yeah." Jim answers with the look of a dog who's just been told he's missed his walk. "Sure."

Defeated, the Lizard King seeks refuge within his scales. He disappears for ten minutes and returns with a bottle of brandy. Thus fortified, he closets himself inside an anteroom used to record isolated vocals. He turns the lights out, fits himself with earphones, and begins his game.

Crescendos of breath between the syllables. His song is half threat, and half plea: "five to one. . . ."

Everyone in the room tries to bury Jim's presence in conversation. But his voice intrudes, bigger and blacker than life, over the loudspeakers. Each trace of sound is magnified, so we can hear him guzzling and belching away. Suddenly, he emerges from his formica cell, inflicting his back upon a wall, as though he were being impaled. He is sweat-drunk, but still coherent, and he mutters so everyone can hear: "If I had an axe . . . man, I'd kill everybody . . .'cept . . . uh . . . my friends."

Sagittarius the hunter stalks us with his glance. We sit frozen, waiting for him to spring.

"Ah—I hafta get one o' them Mexican wedding shirts," he sighs.

Robbie's girl, Donna, takes him on: "I don't know if they come in your size."

"I'm a medium . . . with a large neck."

"We'll have to get you measured, then."

"Uh-uh . . . I don't like to be measured." His eyes glow with sleep and swagger.

"Oh Jim, we're not gonna measure all of you. Just your shoulders."

WAITING FOR MORRISON FROM *THE WHITE ALBUM*
JOAN DIDION

It was six, seven o'clock of an early spring evening in 1968 and I was sitting on the cold vinyl floor of a sound studio on Sunset Boulevard, watching a band called The Doors record a rhythm track. On the whole my attention was only minimally engaged by the preoccupations of rock-and-roll bands (I had already heard about acid as a transitional stage and also about the Maharishi and even about Universal Love, and after a while it all sounded like marmalade skies to me), but The Doors were different, The Doors interested me. The Doors seemed unconvinced that love was brotherhood and the *Kama Sutra*. The Doors' music insisted that love was sex and sex was death and therein lay salvation. The Doors were the Norman Mailers of the Top Forty, missionaries of apocalyptic sex. *Break on through,* their lyrics urged, and *Light my fire.* . . .

On this evening in 1968 they were gathered together in uneasy symbiosis to make their third album, and the studio was too cold and the lights were too bright and there were masses of wires and banks of the ominous blinking electronic circuitry with which musicians live so easily. There were three of the four Doors. There was a bass player borrowed from a band called Clear Light. There were the producer and the engineer and the road manager and a couple of girls and a Siberian husky named Nikki with one gray eye and one gold. There were paper bags half filled with hard-boiled eggs and chicken livers and cheeseburgers and empty bottles of apple juice and California rosé. There was everything and everybody The Doors needed to cut the rest of this third album except one thing, the fourth Door, the lead singer, Jim Morrison, a 24-year-old graduate of U.C.L.A. who wore black vinyl pants and no underwear and tended to suggest some range of the possible just beyond a suicide pact. It was Morrison who had described The Doors as "erotic politicians." It was

Morrison who had defined the group's interests as "anything about revolt, disorder, chaos, about activity that appears to have no meaning." It was Morrison who got arrested in Miami in December of 1967 for giving an "indecent" performance. It was Morrison who wrote most of The Doors' lyrics, the peculiar character of which was to reflect either an ambiguous paranoia or a quite unambiguous insistence upon love-death as the ultimate high. And it was Morrison who was missing. It was Ray Manzarek and Robby Krieger and John Densmore who made The Doors sound the way they sounded, and maybe it was Manzarek and Krieger and Densmore who made seventeen out of twenty interviewees on *American Bandstand* prefer The Doors over all other bands, but it was Morrison who got up there in his black vinyl pants with no underwear and projected the idea, and it was Morrison they were waiting for now.

"Hey listen," the engineer said. "I was listening to an FM station on the way over here, they played three Doors songs, first they played 'Back Door Man' and then 'Love Me Two Times' and 'Light My Fire.'"

"I heard it," Densmore muttered. "I heard it."

"So what's wrong with somebody playing three of your songs?"

"This cat dedicates it to his family."

"Yeah? To his family?"

"To his family. Really crass."

Ray Manzarek was hunched over a Gibson keyboard. "You think *Morrison*'s going to come back?" he asked to no one in particular.

No one answered.

"So we can do some *vocals?*" Manzarek said.

The producer was working with the tape of the rhythm track they had just recorded. "I hope so," he said without looking up.

"Yeah," Manzarek said. "So do I."

My leg had gone to sleep, but I did not stand up; unspecific tensions seemed to be rendering everyone in the room catatonic. The producer played back the rhythm track. The engineer said that he wanted to do his deep-breathing exercises. Manzarek ate a hard-boiled egg. "Tennyson made a mantra out of his own name," he said to the engineer. "I don't know if he said 'Tennyson Tennyson Tennyson' or 'Alfred Alfred Alfred' or 'Alfred Lord Tennyson,' but anyway, he did it. Maybe he just said 'Lord Lord Lord.'"

"Groovy," the Clear Light bass player said. He was an amiable enthusiast, not at all a Door in spirit.

"I wonder what Blake said," Manzarek mused. "Too bad *Morrison*'s not here. *Morrison* would know."

It was a long while later. Morrison arrived. He had on his black vinyl pants and he sat down on a leather couch in front of the four big blank speakers and he closed his eyes. The curious aspect of Morrison's arrival was this: no one acknowledged it. Robby Krieger continued working out a guitar passage. John Densmore tuned his drums. Manzarek sat at the control console and twirled a corkscrew and let a girl rub his shoulders. The girl did not look at Morrison, although he was in her direct line of sight. An hour or so passed, and still no one had spoken to Morrison. Then Morrison spoke to Manzarek. He spoke almost in a whisper, as if he were wresting the words from behind some disabling aphasia.

"It's an hour to West Covina," he said. "I was thinking maybe we should spend the night out there after we play."

Manzarek put down the corkscrew. "Why?" he said.

"Instead of coming back."

Manzarek shrugged. "We were planning to come back."

"Well, I was thinking, we could rehearse out there."

Manzarek said nothing.

"We could get in a rehearsal, there's a Holiday Inn next door."

"We could do that," Manzarek said. "Or we could rehearse Sunday, in town."

"I guess so." Morrison paused. "Will the place be ready to rehearse Sunday?"

Manzarek looked at him for a while. "No," he said then.

I counted the control knobs on the electronic console. There were seventy-six. I was unsure in whose favor the dialogue had been resolved, or if it had been resolved at all. Robby Krieger picked at his guitar, and said that he needed a fuzz box. The producer suggested that he borrow one from the Buffalo Springfield, who were recording in the next studio. Krieger shrugged. Morrison sat down again on the leather couch and leaned back. He lit a match. He studied the flame awhile and then very slowly, very deliberately, lowered it to the fly of his black vinyl pants. Manzarek watched him. The girl who was rubbing Manzarek's shoulders did not look at anyone. There was a sense that no one was going to leave the room, ever. It would be some weeks before The Doors finished recording this album. I did not see it through.

Several months ago, I received a call from the publicity department at Elektra records.

"Are you still writing for **down beat?** Good, because Jim Morrison wants to be written up in that magazine. He'll be in Philadelphia for a concert soon, and you can talk to him then."

Dismayed at the prospect of encountering another rock ego, yet curious to meet the well-publicized leader of a group that had undergone so many changes in style, I set out to meet Morrison in his motel room prior to his Philadelphia appearance.

The Doors—with Love, Country Joe and the Fish, and Jefferson Airplane—were among those who created the rock underground, and turned the deaf, overconfident recording industry around. Without hit singles, these groups sold thousands of albums on the basis of the quality of their music and the power of word-of-mouth.

With their first album, the Doors brought many innovations to rock. Essentially, it was the first successful synthesis of jazz and rock. No one wrote about it; there were no posters or ads to that effect. Nevertheless, organist Ray Manzarek, guitarist Robby Krieger, and drummer John Densmore comprise a tight musical unit that is equally rooted in the spirit of rock and the feeling of jazz.

The Doors were the first group to introduce the theater song and its derivatives into the realm of current popular music. Listen to their *The End* and Morrison's version of Kurt Weill and Bertold Brecht's *Alabama Song*. Morrison delivers such material with a passion for theater. Indirectly, the Doors opened up the public's ears for the later work of Judy Collins, David Ackles, Van Dyke Parks and Randy Newman.

The inclusion in the Doors' repertoire of Willie Dixon and Howling Wolf's *Back Door Man* foreshadowed the white blues revival that was to dominate the rock scene for well over a year.

The group's second album, *Strange Days,* was one of the first concept albums in the underground, and certainly the most subtle. It strongly resembled the first album in quality and style.

The third disc, *Waiting for the Sun,* sounded as if the now successful Doors were trying to imitate themselves. *The Soft Parade* was an over-produced and over-arranged collection of obvious songs. The spirit of the Doors had all but disappeared.

Jim Morrison rested on his motel bed. "I am not an avid or knowledgeable jazz fan, but I do read **down beat** regularly, because it deals with music. Most of the so-called music magazines cover everything but music. They are fan magazines and sensation-seekers. I have been written about in all of them—but so what," he said.

The antithesis of his extroverted stage personality, the private Morrison speaks slowly and quietly with little evident emotion, reflectively collecting his thoughts before he talks. No ego, no pretensions.

I expressed my feelings about the evolution of the Doors. With a half smile, he said: "Really? Hmm. I like all four albums equally. But I really am proud of our second record because it tells a story, it is a whole effort. Someday it will get the recognition that it deserves. I don't think many people were aware of what we were doing."

In response to my statement that the Doors had lost much of their spirit and creativity on the third and fourth albums, he explained: "Most of the songs on the first two records had been written when we were still playing clubs six nights a week. When it came time for the recording of *Waiting for the Sun,* we were just working concerts and had no chance to work out new material. In fact, some of the songs on that album were written right in the studio. One thing about the fourth album that I am very proud of, is that *Touch Me,* which was also a single, was the first rock hit to have a jazz solo in it, by Curtis Amy on tenor saxophone. I guess *Tell All the People* was a dumb song, but everyone wanted me to do it, so I did. Soon we are going to put out a live concert album, and they may bring back the feeling that you were talking about."

The live album has been delayed in deference to the new *Morrison Hotel,* an intriguing and unusual collection of Morrison originals performed by the Doors with such guest artists as John Sebastian on harmonica and Lonnie Mack on bass. It is not the old Doors, nor is it the current commercial Doors; it is Jim Morrison singing some excellent songs, covering territory that the group had not heretofore explored.

As we conversed, Morrison's opinions of the Doors' music fluctuated, but he remained constant in his lamentation of the group's situation.

"When we were working clubs," he explained, "we had a lot of fun and could play a lot of songs. A lot of things were going on. Now we just play concert after concert, and we have to play the things the audience wants to hear. Then we record and go out into the concert halls again. The people are very demanding, and we don't get to do a lot of new or different things.

"I really want to develop my singing. You know, I love the blues, like Joe Turner and Freddie King. I would like to get into that feeling and sing some old standards like *St. James Infirmary.*"

Morrison has interests outside of music. He became most animated during our conversation when the subject of film was brought up. The Doors' 40-minute *Feast of Friends* has already been shown, to mixed critical and audience reactions. Morrison is also producing and starring in *Hiway,* a color film now nearing completion. He is a former U.C.L.A. film student and has a real passion for the cinema.

Thus the remainder of the interview consisted of our exchanging accolades for Buñuel, Fellini, and other outstanding directors. After dinner, we parted so the group could prepare for the concert.

A few hours later, the Doors appeared on stage, greeted by a mass of screaming fans, and began an exciting set of jazz-rock. The rhythm section was burning as the stage Morrison (loud, mystical, dramatic) belted out some of the group's better known songs. Shades of the exciting and innovative Doors of old!

In Jim Morrison, I found to my surprise a beautiful human being who, not unlike Charles Mingus, has been a victim of sensational publicity and harassment by silly journalists. This same Jim Morrison seems trapped in the routine of success, with a public image to live up to, while his best musical and cinematic talents and ambitions remain stifled and/or untapped.

Whatever part of their musical history appeals to you—if any—the Doors are one of the most important forces in rock. Without the demands that success and hit records make on a group, they might have continued their truly creative work.

The promise shown in their new album could indicate a return to the development of music for the Doors' sake, not for the hit-conscious public's sake.

Meanwhile, Morrison was eagerly awaiting publication of his book of poetry, *The Lords and the New Creatures,* issued by Simon and Schuster this spring. And meanwhile, dedicated rock fans go back nostalgically to the startling, dynamic album that a then unknown Los Angeles rock group quietly released some four years ago on a relatively small folk label called Elektra.

MEMORIES OF MORRISON

JAC HOLZMAN

I dragged my tired tail off an American Airlines 707 in the late spring of 1966 to greet Los Angeles at 11:00 P.M. Pacific time, 2:00 A.M. New York metabolism time, and dashed for the Whisky-a-Go-Go where Love was performing. Love was one of the great underground rock acts of L.A.—in fact, the only good unsigned act when I began foraging for new groups on behalf of Elektra in the mid-'60s.

The Whisky-a-Go-Go was a dark and cavernous club, not unlike the black hole of Calcutta, but with a cover charge. Near the entrance to the stage stood Love's lead singer, Arthur Lee, who, being *numero uno* on the underground scene, was enjoying his celebrity by granting his imprimatur to a new group he found worthy. I had never heard of this group, but I stayed through Arthur's set and into the Doors'.

Morrison made no impression whatsoever. I was more drawn to the classical figurings of keyboardist Ray Manzarek and was attracted to the leanness of the music. The lead singer seemed reclusive and tentative, as if preserving himself. There was nothing that tagged him as special, but there was a subtle invitation to "play," if you were willing to do so on his terms. It was only later that I sensed Jim's "game." I was being tested to see if my interest was real or ephemeral. The Doors had been loosely signed to Columbia and then, after a string of broken promises, let go. It was a real downer.

Clearly I chose to play, because I kept going back every evening for the entire week, and on the fifth night, Morrison really moved out in front, and on "The Alabama Song" and "The End" it all came together—so much so that I immediately offered the group a contract and went through the agony of a summer trying to nurse them toward signing it, which did not occur until several months later.

My memories of Morrison are distinctly different from my memories of the band, because although on record they were totally integrated, in life there were really two entities—Ray Manzarek–Robby Krieger–John Densmore and Jim Morrison, separate and apart.

Jim and I were never really close friends, but there was a fundamental trust between us. He sensed that I would serve him and the band best by not being a part of the entourage, by preserving my objectivity, and by being available as needed "in the clutch."

During the making of the famous first album I would come by the studio most every evening, after things had well settled in. The band was playing in the large open studio space of Sunset Sound, with Jim in an isolation booth to prevent voice leakage onto the instrumental tracks. It was a perfect metaphor.

By the standards of 1966, the sessions were expensive. I had signed the group for an advance of $5,000—high in those days—and lavished almost another $5,000 in recording costs, but it was clear from what was happening musically, under the superlative guidance of Paul Rothchild and Bruce Botnick, that important music was being made. I slipped into the studio during the middle of "The End," becoming totally caught up in that transcendent moment. As the song came to *its* end and the final notes shimmered into silence, the tension in the control room was palpable. God forbid anybody knock over a mike stand or make a noise. We knew magic when it happened.

Morrison was extraordinarily well read, thoughtful, funny, and an absolute devil. He is the only guy I ever knew who could hit a police car—drunk and without a driver's license—and get away with it. There was, in him, an inherent boyish innocence not unlike that of an Andy Hardy who hits a baseball through the parish window and because of an inner glow is forgiven. And Jim's friends would forgive him most anything. His demons were so near the surface that to call Jim on behavior you would not tolerate in anyone else was to *feel* you were adding more pressure than he could handle.

I remember sitting with Jim in a bar near the Elektra studios just schmoozing about life and how he wanted to be remembered as a poet—how this rock'n'roll thing had gotten far beyond his ability to control the public's perception of him. He was acutely uncomfortable, hiding behind unkempt hair, a thick beard, and an excess of avoirdupois. With a mischievous snicker he talked about the great joy in life of being "out there—on the very edge," and suggested that to spend that evening trading drinks with Jim one-on-one might be an appropriate way for me to do some edge testing. Knowing Jim was trying to suck me into something that was only going to lead to trouble, I replied, "Jim, being on the edge is terrific. The trick is not to bleed."

Jim was different with everyone, as if he was somehow matching his psyche to yours. I have seen him range from beatific to horrific—smashing a studio IBM electric typewriter with an emergency fire ax, bringing our office manager to the point of tears wondering what *she* had done to *him*—which was in fact nothing. Jim's anger seemed to come in fits, and once the explosion had occurred, a nervous calm took over. The great danger of Jim's anger was that you never knew whether it was real or whether he was putting it on. But you just didn't take those chances.

To get sucked into Jim's entourage, however, was to trade your turf for his, with both of you losers. Besides, I had seen an unsettling side of him. If you adored Jim, as did his lady, Pam, he could and would put you down with heartless cruelty and withering sarcasm, toying with you like a cat toys with a ball of yarn. The same if you wanted something from him. He made you jump through hoops. Jim's gifts were his to give, but only on his terms.

At the conclusion of the sixth and final album under our agreement, Jim and I talked about re-signing. To re-sign the Doors, you addressed each of the constituencies discreetly—the lawyer, manager, Jim, and the "boys." Jim listened to my well-reasoned argument, his face showing no emotion. And when I had finished, he said, "Jac, make your best offer and we'll compare it to CBS's." For someone who had been so close to the group, to think that they were even entertaining leaving the label, although perhaps unrealistic, was excruciatingly painful. Jim said it all with a straight face, walked away, looked at me over his shoulder, and smiled that smile. I still don't know whether he was teasing or serious. But we did re-sign the group for an extra album, which was to become *L.A. Woman.*

So many memories, escaping with Jim from the Long Island concert at which the Doors played with Simon and Garfunkel, crowds jostling the car and pounding on the windows, with Jim sitting in the back seat, unbelieving yet loving every minute.

Jim drunk and almost unable to come onstage at the Fillmore, getting into a fistfight with his manager and wildly swinging the heavy microphone stand—out of control and out of his world.

The famous "young lion" black-and-white photography session with Jim at his most feline, appearing to posture outrageously, and the camera capturing the essence and the depth of his sexuality. Two years later, when Jim was more bloated, someone looked at those pictures and asked, "Did he ever really look like that?" And the answer was "Yes, once, for twenty minutes."

When all the *Rashomon* aspects of the Doors are dissected ad nauseam, one powerful memory lingers and it is more in my heart than in my mind. On February 15, 1968, the doorbell rang in my Los Angeles home. It was the evening of my son Adam's tenth birthday. There was Jim, now a star, shifting uncertainly from foot to foot, clutching an erratically wrapped present for my musically inclined son. He came in, sat quietly with Adam, and showed him how to play the kalimba, an African thumb piano. They sat there for an hour, fully absorbed—two children alone in their own world.

FROM *MR. MOJO RISES: JIM MORRISON, THE LAST HOLY FOOL*
DAVID DALTON

Jim:

> The city is looking for a ritual to join its fragments. The Doors are look-
> ing for such a ritual, too—a sort of electric wedding.

January 1966. The Doors get a job at London Fog, a small club on Sunset Strip next to Whiskey à Go Go.

DOORS—BAND FROM VENICE reads the marquee. It might just as honestly have said:

THE DOORS

PERFORMING THE GOLDEN BOUGH

NIGHTLY! LIVE! ON STAGE!

See the Fisher King draw rain out of an industrial sky! Oedipus, Theseus and the Minotaur, Alexander the Great, the Unknown Soldier, the Ancient Snake, Endless Night, ladies and gentlemen, see them all right here. *Caballero existencialista,* Jeem!

In the hallucinated darkness of the club, Lord Jim of the American Night invokes the cave primeval, the psychosexual Cabinet of Dr. Sigismundus, an attic out of which, as in a Goya etching, bats fly. The bats are his thoughts. Bad thoughts. Reason is asleep. Reason is the reasonable, the silent majority that has fallen asleep during a commercial on the Johnny Carson show while a demonic Pied Piper steals their children's souls. "All the children are insane." (All that is sacred will be profaned.)

The Doors are conjurers of dark tableaux ("Weird scenes inside the gold mine") in the same way that during the French Revolution actors, at climactic points in the drama, would pose in *tableaux vivants* of Jean-Louis David's famous pictures. They would mimic the figures in the *Oath of the Horatii,* just as in the painting.

Doors' performances were like a series of (what else?) film clips. Slow fades, jump cuts. Freeze-frame stills. Noirish sequences. Jim's leather pants were his personal shadow, his cloud in trousers that followed him like that of the man who sewed his shadow to himself. The Doors' producer, Paul Rothchild:

> The Doors brought their theater from a film view of theater. It was broader, deeper, more psychologically oriented than the rat-tat-tat-tah of the English music hall. The Doors were one of the very first American groups to appreciate very personal entertainment. It was very deep, sometimes dark, just as Jim and the other Doors like the darker directors of film.

At the Fog, the theater of "The End" begins to evolve. John Densmore develops his "shamanistic drumming."

The club's clientele consists of deviates, pimps, whores, gangsters and tourists. (They don't make audiences like that anymore.) To two recent film school graduates this suggests a smoky, decadent, art deco cabaret in Weimar Berlin. So as part of their project of developing as an Art Rock quartet, the Doors include in their repertoire "Alabama Song," from the 1927 German expressionist opera *Mahagonny.* Almost no one in the audience is likely to recognize the source. Can you imagine the bizarreness, had you never heard a Bertolt Brecht/Kurt Weill song, as this strange chant comes lurching at you from some entirely alien plane of existence? Written by some extraterrestrial songwriting machine on the theme of an imaginary country called America. Jim pronounces "Alabama" as if he had never heard the word before.

"Alabama Song" is for the Doors a scene from a historical movie with a mad celeste player. Its framing of a song already in deep quotation marks makes you see the cocktail jazz element in other Doors' songs in a different light. The schmaltz becomes an artifact.

But Alabama is only the first stop in a time- and space-warped geography. There is "The End," which had begun innocently enough as the Doors' encore at the Whiskey and stretched into a molten fresco of travel-weary faces and images. A broken-off love affair, rejection, a bad trip—all seem to trigger off accumulating detonations that finally reach critical mass in the last section. "C'mon, baby, take a chance with us," Jim cajoles, summoning up terrors real and imagined, all pulsing with phosphorescence and decay. The music ebbs and swells flawlessly in sync with Shaman Jim's psychotic trance. (The organ at the climax exultantly chiming "The freaks are loose!")

Even in its early incarnations "The End" was weird enough ("take the snake to the lake," etc.) but then one night, recalls John:

> He was in his room and he wouldn't come out. So we kinda . . . come on, Jim. . . . And he finally let us in. And he was under the bed and had taken a lot of acid and encouraging us to take acid. And we're going, we got a gig, y'know, let's. . . . We got him over to the Whiskey and we're doing "The End" and he threw in the Oedipal section. Got very quiet. I think we were fired that night.

"The End" is an allegorical drama of numbing naiveté whose meaning the storyteller has neglected (some might say, mercifully) to elaborate. A Symbolist drama in which the actors portray abstract ideas, feelings, theories.

The nakedness of the symbolism is both emotionally dauntless and excruciatingly embarrassing.

Many have found "The End" a bit too verbatim. The sort of raw, unchewed Freudian theory that is meant to *underlie* our chaotic and tormented lives, not serve as its text. But this apparently underestimates Jim who, according to Paul Rothchild, never thought of this sequence as anything *but* symbolic. Rothchild:

> Jim kept saying over and over kill the father, fuck the mother, and essentially it boils down to this, kill all those things in yourself which are instilled in you and are not of yourself, they are alien concepts which are not yours, they must die. The psychedelic revolution. Fuck the mother is very basic, and it means get back to the essence, what is reality, what is, fuck the mother is very basically mother, mother-birth, real, you can touch it, it's nature, it can't lie to you. So what Jim says at the end of the Oedipus section, which is essentially the same thing as the classic says, kill the alien concepts, get back to reality, the end of alien concepts, the begin-

ning of personal concepts.

Still others have been uncomfortable with the temperamental explicitness of this piece. As with much of the Doors' material, there are no emotional stops. The distance felt to be essential to art has collapsed, the emotions are pumped up, unmediated, the sentiments portentous and overblown. The traumatic effect of the climax of "The End" depends on an almost too direct connection between infantile sexuality and mythical thinking.

As the emblematic Child Jim tiptoes stealthily along the hallway carpet, lightning flashes turn various familiar objects into fetishes of totemic dread. The looming door to the parents' bedroom opens and the veil of the temple is ripped revealing . . . the Primal Scene, directed by Alfred Hitchcock, with sets by Salvador Dali, and Admiral Morrison as the Minotaur.

Sex, humiliation, human sacrifice, mystery, horror, seduction. . . .

Later, one of the blessings/misfortunes visited upon this hothouse Freudian melodrama was to be its use as a soundtrack in Francis Ford Coppola's film *Apocalypse Now,* forever linking it with an unintentional video of indelible beauty and horror. It now seems to be all about Vietnam. Oedipus at Dien Bien Phu.

The Whiskey à Go Go was an ideal space for the Doors to practice their alchemical plays. A median between private and public space where they could experiment. It was intimate enough for the empathy required of the audience to be believable, and public enough to oblige the Doors to structure their performance. Still, it involved an almost excruciating intimacy. Robby:

> Jim would be on the edge of reality all the time and that's what came through in the music. . . . I think what Morrison was trying to do and what we were trying to do in those days was reality on stage and in music. It was more like what we were really feeling than like a show or a sort of an act. We were doing what we really felt on stage.

NEW HAVEN POLICE CLOSE 'THE DOORS'

THE NEW YORK TIMES, DECEMBER 11, 1967

The police stopped a rock 'n' roll concert at the New Haven Arena, forcibly removed the lead singer of "The Doors" group and arrested three journalists last night.

Those arrested were Jim Morrison, 24 years old, leader of "The Doors" one of the nation's leading rock groups; Michael Zwerin, music critic for The Village Voice; Tim Page, a freelance photographer on assignment for Life magazine, and Miss Yvonne V. Chabrier, researcher for Life.

According to the police, Mr. Morrison was giving an "indecent and immoral exhibition" when he was off the stage.

One witness, Fred Powledge, a writer working on a rock 'n' roll story, said Mr. Morrison started singing a song and then began a monologue concerning an earlier confrontation with a policeman in a dressing room.

"Morrison," Mr. Powledge said, "told the audience of about 2,000 persons that he was talking to a girl in the dressing room when a policeman came and told the couple to move. Morrison said he hesitated, and the officer sprayed Mace in his eyes."

Mace is a form of tear gas the police use in attempting to quell persons who become violent.

The police gave a different version of what had happened in the dressing room.

Lieut. James P. Kelly wrote in his arrest report that Mr. Morrison and an 18-year-old co-ed from nearby Southern Connecticut State College were "standing and kissing" in the dressing room.

The patrolman said he asked the performer to leave and a scuffle broke out. The officer said he used Mace on Mr. Morrison to subdue him.

At this point, Richard Loron of New York, Mr. Morrison's agent, pleaded with the police not to arrest the singer so he could appear with his act. The police agreed, and Mr. Morrison was allowed on stage with "The Doors"—the last act in the show being staged for a New Haven college scholarship fund.

Mr. Powledge said that when Mr. Morrison began his narrative of the dressing-room incident, "the lights came on and six officers dragged Morrison off stage."

Lieutenant Kelly told the audience the show was over.

The police contended they had received complaints from audience members who did not like foul language that the performer allegedly used.

The audience left the arena, and several scuffles broke out between the police and the crowd.

Mr. Page, the photographer, said he was arrested while taking a picture of a policeman "roughing up a kid."

The police said Mr. Page, Mr. Zwerin and Miss Chabrier were arrested for "breach of the peace, interfering with an officer and resisting arrest." They were released on $300 bond each.

Mr. Morrison, in addition to the indecent exhibition charge, was cited with breach of the peace and resisting a policeman. He was released on $1,500 bond.

"23 MARCH 1968" FROM *THE FILLMORE EAST: RECOLLECTIONS OF ROCK THEATER*
RICHARD KOSTELANETZ

By now, they have become the greatest rock performers I have ever seen, probably because they are as spectacular theatrically as they are musically. (One contrast on this last score is Procol Harum, who turn out to be on stage a bunch of rather uptight Englishmen.) Both Jim Morrison and Ray Manzarek are a pleasure to watch—Morrison for all his bisexual suggestiveness, his crotch stuffed to suggest a permanent erection (in the male version of "falsies"), and Manzarek for his evidently intimate relationship with his instrument. The organist also has an engaging throaty voice which complements Morrison's nicely. Manzarek's trick as an instrumentalist seems to be positing a riff and then doing rather academic variations on it. He knows how to exploit his two electric keyboards, placed one atop the other, for a variety of timbres. In a recent issue of *Cheetah,* one critic made a case for Robbie Krieger as the best musician, but I could hardly hear him from where I was sitting, even though every move of his that I could see looked like it sounded stunning. In performance, the group's renditions of their recorded songs are invariably more extravagant—this evening's "Light My Fire" made even more blatant the orgasms represented in the instrumental interludes. In these last sections, the Joshua Light Show was equally spectacular (and it is gratifying to see that Bill Graham, who turns out to be younger and more clean-shaven than I imagined, gives the light show bottom billing on the theater's marquee). The Doors also presented a film sequence in the background to accompany "The Unknown Solider."

The group was called back for two encores, both of which were extensive and slap-happy. For the first they brought out a bottle of New York

State (Morrison said) champagne, from which they sipped for the rest of the evening, occasionally pouring some on the floor or on one another, much like victorious athletes do. Then Manzarek did a talking blues, seemingly extemporaneous, about how every hippy was really a straight person and, if he accepted this, he would be a better human being (and, by extension, maybe as prosperous as Manzarek). Toward the end of this bit, Morrison proclaimed, away from the microphone but audibly enough to be heard, that this patter wasn't true for him. He then began his own talking blues, purportedly about a more direct truth, which of course turned out to be sexual intercourse. (His arrest in New Haven for making love backstage to an undergraduate was too appropriate to be anything but true, even if he did eventually forfeit bail.) This very last song was hairy as hell, in a tasteful and unobvious way, as it became ever more apparent to the audience staying past the customary closing time of 3:00 A.M. that these Los Angeles boys were about to give New York the greatest rock concert they had ever seen. It ended at 3:45 in the morning. Watching the apprehensive faces of spectators who wondered how they would get home at this late hour, I was grateful that I lived around the corner.

IT'S HARD TO LIGHT A FIRE IN MIAMI
STEPHANIE HARRINGTON

It must have been rather like the Titanic. Unless you were there you couldn't know exactly what happened, and the survivors were so dazed that all reports didn't fully jibe. So maybe Jim Morrison didn't really drop his pants in front of 8000 teenagers at a Doors concert at the municipally owned Miami Dinner Key Civic Auditorium on March 1.

But if, not knowing the revelation that was in store, you didn't happen to be on hand, all you can know is what you read in the local papers.

Of course hereabouts minor events and non-events tend to get writ rather large. Like the prominent headlines about the student strike at the ever-militant University of Miami, a strike organized (by the president of the student government no less) around such burning issues as increased campus parking privileges for undergraduates—a strike, however, that never came off because the president of the university recognized the validity of the student demands. And then there was the great police stakeout of Miami U. in anticipation of dangerous agitation by the campus SDS chapter, which numbers about 25. The police eventually had to end their occupation when no one showed up to be occupiers. But so as it shouldn't have been a total loss, they did arrest two SDS members, one of whom said he happened by only because he heard on the radio that there was to be a major disruption by SDS and had to rush over and see it to believe it.

At any rate, the Miami Herald's follow-up on the March 1 Doors concert rather succinctly summed up the general impression of Morrison's surprise solo: "'The King of the Orgasmic Rock,' whose records currently outsell any others in the U.S., screamed obscenities from the bandstand, appeared to masturbate in full view of the audience, exposed himself and assaulted officials of Thee Image, a local rock concert hall that sponsored the show."

But poor Morrison. Having thus gone about as far as he could toward sharing divine flesh with some 8000 disciples, the only morning-after response he got was a junior legion of decency movement that is threatening to pack 50,000 teenagers into the Orange Bowl to protest what Morrison offered them. If a certain Mr. Portnoy thinks he has rejection problems, one shudders to contemplate Morrison's mutilated ego. You can hardly blame him for having immediately retired, with his group, to a Caribbean island (Aruba, we hear).

The problem, however, will be coming back. For, in addition to having set loose a plague of adolescent Savonarolas, his revelation of the sacred relics has also resulted in the swearing out of warrants against him, one of which is for a felony, which means he can be extradited from any state in the union. Nonetheless, in that it indicated that at least someone regards his potency as fearsome, the felony warrant must be about his only consolation at the moment.

The general consensus is that what emboldened Morrison to give the performance that landed him on his island retreat was in fact that he was stoned—and not, children, on pot, acid, or speed, but that quaint stuff called booze that Janis Joplin so recently rescued from the far reaches of camp. (Ken Collier, one of the concert's sponsors, claims that Morrison's contract stipulated that the star's dressing room be supplied with two six-packs of beer.) It also seems that another quaint affliction thought to affect those over 30 was involved. To wit: the profit motive.

But like the gospel, the versions of what the Master actually did and why are various. For instance, Collier, a partner in Thee Image (Miami Beach's answer to the Fillmore), which staged the Doors' happening, says he did not see Morrison actually drop his pants. (Another eye witness says he did.) And while he does admit that there was a money hassle between Thee Image and the agents, managers, and other members of the Doors' palace guard, Collier disputes one published story. According to the story, the Doors were angry because they computed their $25,000 fee (a percentage of the house) for the hour-long concert on the understanding that the auditorium was "scaled" for a $42,000 maximum, and that Thee Image later upped the scale without upping the Doors' percentage. Collier insists that there was no percentage deal, that the Doors were simply offered and agreed to take a flat fee of $25,000. They let out the word, Collier explains, that they would play Miami and then sold themselves to the highest bidder, which was Thee Image. Then, Collier maintains, five weeks after the contract was signed and only eight days before the concert, the Doors' agents began demanding more money. The disagreements that ensued were of such magnitude that, says Collier, Thee Image plans to sue the Doors' agent for $1 million.

Hostilities raged right up to show time so Collier, as he tells it, took the precaution of introducing the Doors with an admonition to the audience to keep its cool, raising his hand in the standard peace gesture as he gave way to Morrison. ("The peace symbol really means something in Miami," one is earnestly assured by Collier, who is an ex-marine paratrooper, a former New York Daily News reporter, and a Democrat with political aspirations styled after a synthesis of Gene McCarthy and a peace-loving rewrite of "Wild in the Streets." Peace is very big with him.)

But Morrison came on stage saying he didn't want to talk about peace or war or love, but about having a good time. Which sounded okay to Collier, who did not then understand how much of a good time Morrison was contemplating. And it didn't exactly swing at the star. In fact the one point on which all versions of the gospel agree is that until its (so to speak) climax, the program was pretty dreary, consisting mainly of a not impressively coherent Morrison ("The Doors could barely find the microphone," complained one erstwhile teenage fan who was there) reciting bits of poetry (his own, presumably) and fooling around with snatches of songs like "The End," "The Snake," "Touch Me," and "Light My Fire." But evidently neither the Freudian symbolism nor the invitation produced sufficient response for Morrison who then proceeded to strike his own match.

"I saw him reach into his pants and fondle himself," says Collier, "so I rushed up and took the mike away from him and said 'This is Miami and it's not going to happen here,'" again warding off the evil eye with the peace symbol. The wave of children who at that moment had been surging forward in answer to Morrison's urging that they come up and dance (where, since every inch of space was occupied, is one of those puzzling questions of rock metaphysics) then receded, only to surge forward again when Morrison recaptured the mike. Like two moon men Collier and Morrison proceeded to hypnotize the sea of youth before them, the one drawing the waves up, the other causing them to fall back.

"And all the time," says Collier, "I'm wondering what the hell to do. Have the cops drag him away? No, that would cause a riot."

As Collier was thus lost in thought, Morrison, apparently having come to a conclusion of his own, pushed Collier's brother Jim (also a partner in Thee Image) off the stage. Collier, thinking fast, retaliated by unplugging the instruments and kicking in the drums, while his wife, somewhere in the balcony, managed to turn the house lights on as one Larry Pizzi, manager of Thee Image and a black belt in karate, came up from behind and flipped Morrison into the crowd, into which he sank, bobbed up again, and beat a retreat, apparently unnoticed, through the by then literally rocky sea of kids. Then at what Collier calls "the very Gotterdammerung end of it," like the phantom of the opera, the vision of the unscarred Morrison appeared briefly in the balcony.

The police, meanwhile, faked everybody out by behaving like very models of a progressive, humanitarian force. In fact they seemed to be the only ones who responded to Collier's invocation of the peace signs and symbols. (The kids, too, kept remarkably calm despite what Collier says were invitations by Morrison to get with each other, take off their clothes, have the revolution now, etc.) They, having sized up the overwhelming odds against them and the potential hysteria of the scene, wisely kept their cool. The police didn't even get around to drawing up the warrants against Morrison until he had already skipped town, thus bringing down the wrath not of the left for brutality, but of the forces of law and order for the lack of it. (There was no need for haste, however, since as soon as Morrison sets foot on U.S. soil again—which he will probably do sooner or later—he can be extradited to Miami on the strength of the felony warrant.)

And if and when he does return, Morrison will have to face not only arrest, but the spectacle of what he has wrought: a teenage anti-obscenity movement inspired by him, aided and abetted by a young local Catholic priest, and dedicated to keeping rock clean. And the youthful clean-up brigade, though its first meeting was at the office of a Catholic newspaper called, ironically, the Voice, is interdenominational. The kids are bent on serving notice that they are no longer open for exploitation by idols who charge them $6 or $7 a person to be subjected to the performers' whims. One girl wrote to the Miami Herald that she had been "grossed out" by the Doors. Her phrase was particularly apt, considering the price of admission.

It is just possible that the kids, provoked by Morrison, may succeed in their drive to keep clean with the Beach Boys. And if they can pack the Orange Bowl for the Beach Boys, can Pat Boone be far behind?

THE THEATER AND CRUELTY
ANTONIN ARTAUD

An idea of the theater has been lost. And as long as the theater limits itself to showing us intimate scenes from the lives of a few puppets, transforming the public into Peeping Toms, it is no wonder the elite abandon it and the great public looks to the movies, the music hall or the circus for violent satisfactions, whose intentions do not deceive them.

At the point of deterioration which our sensibility has reached, it is certain that we need above all a theater that wakes us up: nerves and heart.

The misdeeds of the psychological theater descended from Racine have unaccustomed us to that immediate and violent action which the theater should possess. Movies in their turn, murdering us with second-hand reproductions which, filtered through machines, cannot *unite with* our sensibility, have maintained us for ten years in an ineffectual torpor, in which all our faculties appear to be foundering.

In the anguished, catastrophic period we live in, we feel an urgent need for a theater which events do not exceed, whose resonance is deep within us, dominating the instability of the times.

Our long habit of seeking diversion has made us forget the idea of a serious theater, which, overturning all our preconceptions, inspires us with the fiery magnetism of its images and acts upon us like a spiritual therapeutics whose touch can never be forgotten.

Everything that acts is a cruelty. It is upon this idea of extreme action, pushed beyond all limits, that theater must be rebuilt.

Imbued with the idea that the public thinks first of all with its senses and that to address oneself first to its understanding as the ordinary psychological theater does is absurd, the Theater of Cruelty proposes to resort to a mass spectacle; to seek in the agitation of tremendous masses, convulsed and hurled against each other, a little of that poetry of festivals and crowds when, all too rarely nowadays, the people pour out into the streets.

The theater must give us everything that is in crime, love, war, or madness, if it wants to recover its necessity.

Everyday love, personal ambition, struggles for status, all have value only in proportion to their relation to the terrible lyricism of the Myths to which the great mass of men have assented.

This is why we shall try to concentrate, around famous personages, atrocious crimes, superhuman devotions, a drama which, without resorting to the defunct images of the old Myths, shows that it can extract the forces which struggle within them.

In a word, we believe that there are living forces in what is called poetry and that the image of a crime presented in the requisite theatrical conditions is something infinitely more terrible for the spirit than that same crime when actually committed.

We want to make out of the theater a believable reality which gives the heart and the senses that kind of concrete bite which all true sensation requires. In the same way that our dreams have an effect upon us and reality has an effect upon our dreams, so we believe that the images of thought can be identified with a dream which will be efficacious to the degree that it can be projected with the necessary violence. And the public will believe in the theater's dreams on condition that it take them for true dreams and not for a servile copy of reality; on condition that they allow the public to liberate within itself the magical liberties of dreams which it can only recognize when they are imprinted with terror and cruelty.

Hence this appeal to cruelty and terror, though on a vast scale, whose range probes our entire vitality, confronts us with all our possibilities.

It is in order to attack the spectator's sensibility on all sides that we advocate a revolving spectacle which, instead of making the stage and auditorium two closed worlds, without possible communication, spreads its visual and sonorous outbursts over the entire mass of the spectators.

Also, departing from the sphere of analyzable passions, we intend to make use of the actor's lyric qualities to manifest external forces, and by this means to cause the whole of nature to re-enter the theater in its restored form.

However vast this program may be, it does not exceed the theater itself, which appears to us, all in all, to identify itself with the forces of ancient magic.

Practically speaking, we want to resuscitate an idea of total spectacle by which the theater would recover from the cinema, the music hall, the circus, and from life itself what has always belonged to it. The separation between the analytic theater and the plastic world seems to us a stupidity. One does not separate the mind from the body nor the senses from the intelligence, especially in a domain where the endlessly renewed fatigue of the organs requires intense and sudden shocks to revive our understanding.

Thus, on the one hand, the mass and extent of a spectacle addressed to the entire organism; on the other, an intensive mobilization of objects, gestures, and signs, used in a new spirit. The reduced role given to the understanding leads to an energetic compression of the text; the active role given to obscure poetic emotion necessitates concrete signs. Words say little to the mind; extent and objects speak; new images speak, even new images made with words. But space thundering with images and crammed with sounds speaks too, if one knows how to intersperse from time to time a sufficient extent of space stocked with silence and immobility.

On this principle we envisage producing a spectacle where these means of direct action are used in their totality; a spectacle unafraid of going as far as necessary in the exploration of our nervous sensibility, of which the rhythms, sounds, words, resonances, and twitterings, and their united quality and surprising mixtures belong to a technique which must not be divulged.

The images in certain paintings by Grunewald or Hieronymus Bosch tell enough about what a spectacle can be in which, as in the brain of some saint, the objects of external nature will appear as temptations.

It is in this spectacle of a temptation from which life has everything to lose and the mind everything to gain that the theater must recover its true signification.

Elsewhere we have given a program which will allow the means of pure staging, found on the spot, to be organized around historic or cosmic themes, familiar to all.

And we insist on the fact that the first spectacle of the Theater of Cruelty will turn upon the preoccupations of the great mass of men, preoccupations much more pressing and disquieting than those of any individual whatsoever.

It is a matter of knowing whether now, in Paris, before the cataclysms which are at our door descend upon us, sufficient means of production, financial or otherwise, can be found to permit such a theater to be brought to life—it is bound to in any case, because it is the future. Or whether a little real blood will be needed, right away, in order to manifest this cruelty.

"SHAMANISM" FROM *BREAK ON THROUGH: THE LIFE AND DEATH OF JIM MORRISON*

JAMES RIORDAN AND JERRY PROCHNICKY

By now the forces of shamanism were shaping Jim Morrison more than he knew. He joined no cult, attended no services, and followed no spiritual leader, yet his belief in this occult religion provided the prism through which all his other influences were refracted. Shamanism crystallized the bits of Nietzsche, Blake, Artaud, Kafka, and Rimbaud. It focused the passion behind his rebellion and the power behind his persona. It was his magical side—it helped make him special and it no doubt helped destroy him.

Shamanism is the primitive religion of many American Indian tribes and some Ural-Altaic peoples of northern Asia and Europe in which the unseen world of gods, demons, and ancestral spirits can be interacted with through the shamans of high priests of the tribe. It can also occur independently as a psychological technique that employs religious notions. The shaman–medicine man, obtains power from the supernatural through trances brought on by hypnotic music, chanting, and dancing. A mystic, he has the power to leave his body at will through various "techniques of ecstasy" (dreams, visions, trances).

As Morrison said, "The shaman was a man who would intoxicate himself. He was probably already an unusual individual. And, he would put himself into a trance by dancing, whirling around, drinking, taking drugs—however. Then he would go on a mental travel and describe his journey to the rest of the tribe."

The shaman is medicine man, priest and psycho-pomp to the tribe. The key to his power comes from his being possessed by a spirit, and once the trance state is achieved, the supernatural being speaks through his mouth. At that point the "free soul" of the shaman can be guided on long journeys to the sky or the underworld. Through his power to leave his body he is believed to cure sicknesses and escort the souls of the dead to the other world. The tribe considers the shaman the lord of the three realms—the sky, earth, and underworld.

Jim Morrison said many times that he believed he was possessed by the spirit of a shaman and there are many startling similarities between his life and shamanistic rituals. Traditionally, shamans are poets and singers and much of their activity centers on creating works of art, but they are also considered "sacred politicians" who continually live out a symbolic ritual of mystical death. Morrison once described The Doors as "erotic politicians" and his performances often contained elements of symbolic death. Through his journey the shaman supposedly helps his patients transcend their normal ordinary definition of reality and realize that they are not emotionally and spiritually alone. In order to extract the evil spirits from a patient, the shaman is often obliged to enter the patient's body or take the spirits into his own body and in doing so he may struggle and suffer more than the patient himself. This self-sacrifice results in an emotional commitment from the patients to struggle alongside the shaman to save themselves.

"I see the role of the artist as shaman and scapegoat," Morrison told Lizze James in *Creem* Magazine: "People project their fantasies on to him and their fantasies come alive. People can destroy their fantasies by destroying him. I obey the impulses everyone else has but won't admit to. By attacking me, punishing me, they can feel relieved of those impulses."

Those who believe in shamanism believe that the shamanic vocation is obligatory and one cannot refuse it. The process can be accelerated, however, by a chance encounter with a semi-divine being, the soul of an ancestor, or as the result of some extraordinary event. Such an encounter usually begins a familiarity between the future shaman and the spirit that has determined his career, hence the term "familiar spirit." The souls of the shaman ancestors of a family choose a young man among their descendants.

There are three ways of becoming a shaman: first, by hereditary transmission of the powers; second, by personal quest; and third, by spontaneous vocation (the call). This "call" can sometimes occur following a traumatic shock or a highly unusual event and one such experience alone can be enough to bring about the metamorphosis. Jim Morrison's belief that he was a modern-day shaman extends back to the incident that happened to him when he was only four years old. Morrison often recounted the accident story and many of his friends believed it. Producer Paul Rothchild was one: "As a child he was driving with his parents, and there was a truck full of Indians that had crashed and overturned. There was a medicine man dying at the side of the road, and Jim, this four- or five-year-old child *vividly remembered* a mystical experience when, as the shaman died, his spirit entered Jim's body. That was the pivotal event of his entire life. He always viewed himself as the shaman, having mystical powers and the ability to see through many façades to the truth. It was this power that drove him. This was the great force that pushed his life and took him out of the rigid, military environment of his youth and turned him into a seer."

Morrison's story not only fits classic shamanistic tales of the "call" happening through a trauma and a chance encounter with a spirit, but it also conforms to several other rites of shamanism. The shamanic vocation is nearly always manifested by a crisis, a temporary derangement of the future shaman's spiritual equilibrium that sets him apart from others. And no matter what method by which a man becomes a shaman, it is a form of initiatory death and resurrection that consecrates him. This initiation must include the ordeal of entering the realm of death, which means the potential shaman must either nearly die through an accident or severe illness or have suffered a psychological or spiritual trauma through exposure to such an experience. This encounter with dying and death and the subsequent experience of rebirth and illumination is the only authentic initiation for a shaman.

As children, future shamans experience rapid transitions from irritability to normality and from melancholia to agitation. The deep-seated desire they possess to contact the spirit world is counteracted by the fear of surrendering their will. These kinds of rapid mood swings are certainly in line with Morrison's turbulent childhood. "Shamans could be any age," Morrison said in a 1969 NET special. "The tribe pushed him into his trip. The shaman was not interested in defining his role in society, but more interested in pursuing his own fantasies. If it becomes too self-conscious of a function, it tends to ruin his own inner trip."

A shaman must be instructed in two areas—the ecstatic (dreams, visions, trances) and the traditional (shamanic techniques, names and functions of spirits, mythology of the clan, and the secret language). The teaching must be done by the old master shamans or by the spirits themselves, but it may be accomplished entirely through dreams or ecstatic experiences. During his time at UCLA and in his early days with The Doors, Jim Morrison took vast quantities of LSD on a regular basis and many of his acid trips centered around primal symbols—the earth, moon, and sun. It is very possible that he felt he was receiving shamanistic instruction at this time.

A key element in shamanism is the songs of the shaman and this seems to be the next phase Morrison encountered in his development. The trancelike inspiration he experienced on the Venice rooftop when he "heard" most of the songs to the first two albums is typical of how a shaman receives his songs. The receiving of songs and chants reportedly marks the moment that a shaman's psyche has been transformed from the vulnerable and wounded soul of a man to one heavily influenced by a powerful spirit.

Shamans often use various forms of drugs in their quest for what they call "magical heat." They believe that smoke from certain herbs and the combustion of certain plants increase their power. The trance or ecstasy state is sometimes induced by mushrooms, narcotics, or tobacco, but since shamanism is primarily a state of mind, the drugs are an option and not a requirement. After the Sunset Strip days Morrison pretty much abandoned the use of LSD, believing he had exhausted the augury power of psychedelics. When The Doors were at their zenith he maintained that he could take the trip without the drug.

The art of the shaman is his most vital adaptation and Morrison's use of shamanic lore appears everywhere in his work. He used images from the history of man—broad, universal symbols such as the sun, the sea, the tide, the moon, the earth, running, falling, and climbing. "We appeal to the same human needs as classical tragedy and early Southern blues," he said, describing The Doors. "Think of it as a séance in an environment which has become hostile to life; cold, restrictive. People feel they're dying in a bad landscape. So they gather together in a séance in order to invoke, palliate, and drive away the dead through chanting, singing, dancing, and music. They try to cure an illness, to bring back harmony into the world."

Shamans awaken a particular kind of experience in their audience. The onlookers become participants, experiencing a catharsis during the trance state that results in a sort of psychological healing. Morrison believed his art could heal "sick" minds and that his mental revolution could lead the way to freedom. Traditionally, shamans use songs, rhythms, and dances in a tribal ritual that must always take place at night in a large enclosed space. Jim tried to translate shamanism into the modern-day rock concert. He attempted to lead the audience on a metaphysical trip in much the same way the shaman leads the tribe on such encounters, by subjecting his body to a trance brought on by rapid movement and chanting. And there are those who believe that he sometimes achieved it.

Ray Manzarek is one of them: "I've never seen a performer like Jim— it was as if it wasn't Jim performing, but a shaman. The shaman was a man of the tribe who would go on a voyage in his mind, who would let his astral body project out into space and, in a sense, heal the tribe and find things that were needed for the safety of the tribe, for the continuance of the species. So, in a modern sense, Jim was exactly the same thing. Like a snake coiling around your body. Morrison would work your mind . . . He would build up a tension to the point where he had total control. He was like a preacher leading the congregation to salvation or slaughter, depending on the mood he was in. In retrospect it may have been a bit premeditated and overly theatrical, but at the time the energy we felt was real."

Shamans often exhibit hysterical and schizoid behavior and bring order to their psyches through entering the trance state. Morrison went through a complete metamorphosis onstage—his voice changing from soft-spoken to a fierce rattle and his personality going from low-key to completely dominant. Offstage Jim was known for teasing and playing games with people's minds, but onstage that side became a sorcerer and all his games were magic spells. In his stage presence he was wild, inner-driven. Like a shaman he would close his eyes, spin, whirl, and dance, creating images set to music by the other Doors. In one form of shamanism the shaman pulls out the sickness of his audience with eerie, earth-shattering screams such as Morrison was known to do. In all forms, the entrance into the trance state is helped by singing. The shaman typically has special "power songs" which increase in tempo as he approaches the trance. There are many Doors songs that fit this scenario, but the most obvious is "The End."

Shamans communicate in a metaphorical style, a "secret language" that may appear as incomprehensible refrains repeated during the trance. The secret language is sometimes called an "animal language" because it originates in animal cries. In his book *An Hour for Magic,* Frank Lisciandro described one of Jim's stage performances: "He made strange animal sounds, screamed, and cried out as if in pain . . . his movements and gestures became fitful and spasmodic, like a person in seizure. He danced, not with graceful and fluid motions, but with short hopping steps and pistonlike motions, bent forward, head snapping up and down. He moved like an American Indian performing a ritual dance."

Shamans are held to be masters over fire, believing that a fire transforms man into spirit, but their séances take place in complete darkness. It is only in the darkness or with his eyes closed that the shaman can block out the world around him and perceive the nonordinary reality he seeks. But darkness alone is not enough for shamanic "seeing." Often the shaman must be assisted by drumming, rattling, singing, and dancing. The drum and the rattle are important shamanistic tools for establishing contact with the other world and there are significant parallels here with

Morrison's maracas and Densmore's drums. The shaman's rattle was considered a sacred instrument, enclosing stones in which spirits hide, summoning the helping spirits and frightening away the evil ones. The beginning of the steady, monotonous sound of the rattle and the drum is a signal to return to the shamanic state and the lightness of the shaman's trance is the reason that a drumbeat must often be maintained to sustain him. If the drumming stops at the wrong time, the shaman might come back too early and thus fail in his work. Laboratory research has demonstrated that drumming produces changes in the central nervous system. Electrical activity in many sensory and motor areas of the brain is affected because a single drumbeat contains many sound frequencies and transmits impulses along a variety of nerve pathways.

The common shaman dance and one that Morrison frequently did was the circle dance which is a form of ghost dance. Traditionally, the dance circled around a pole that was the phallic symbol of manliness and power. In like manner, Morrison danced around a mike stand. Going around and around in a circle was designed to resurrect the dead, but it meant much more than that. The great Indian chief Black Elk described the circle dance in this way: "You have noticed that everything an Indian does is in a circle and that is because the Power of the World always works in circles, and everything tries to be round. Everything the Power of the World does is done in a circle. The sky is round, and I have heard that the earth is round like a ball, and so are all the stars. The life of a man is a circle from childhood to childhood, and so it is in everything where power moves."

In traditional séances a shaman circles a birch tree several times in ecstasy and then kneels to pray. The dancer's spirit finds its dramatized expression in dance steps, tempo, facial expressions, and gestures. The movements range from a sort of sneaking pace to sudden flying leaps to an almost reptilian writhing. It was very common for the shaman to begin writhing and then leap into the air and try to emit inarticulate sounds which are supposed to be the voice and private language of the "spirits." Anyone who ever saw Morrison in concert remembers his moving in just this way as well as his often inarticulate chanting. (Paul Rothchild remembers a drunken Jim "involuntarily talking in tongues" sometimes in the studio.) The shaman's dance culminates in his exciting himself to the point where he falls to the ground inanimate, in ecstasy. "Sinks," as these sudden drops were called, referred not only to the physical act, but also to the belief that the shaman was able to visit the underground worlds during these periods of ecstasy. Onstage Jim Morrison was known for suddenly dropping to the ground, almost as though he had been struck down, but also he frequently ended emotionally charged numbers such as "The End" by sinking to the ground and remaining motionless for a time.

"In the séance, the shaman led," Morrison said. "A sensuous panic, deliberately evoked through drugs, chants, dancing, hurls the shaman into trance. Changed voice, convulsive movement. He acts like a madman. These professional hysterics, chosen precisely for their psychotic leaning, were once esteemed. They mediated between man and spirit world. Their mental travels form the crux of the religious life of the tribe."

It is during the trance state that the supernatural being enters the shaman's body and speaks through his mouth. His soul then can be guided on long journeys to the sky or the underworld in a magic flight. One type of shamanic séance required a horse sacrifice to ascend to the sky. Similarly, in "Horse Latitudes" Morrison wrote of a ship that had to sacrifice its cargo of horses to continue its journey. In his book *Shamanism: The Beginnings of Art* (McGraw-Hill, 1967), Dr. Andreas Lommel describes the journey of a shaman: "The soul of the shaman (journeys) into the deepest interior of the earth where the creative power of the world—pictured as a snake—dwells in the depths of the water . . . The aborigines say that various animals, especially snakes, assist the shaman on his journey and give him the strength, the 'medicine' for his office."

Often shamans were assisted by guardian spirits known as power animals. These include more commonly the horse, dog, bear, and eagle, but also the lizard. The power of the guardian spirit made one resistant to illness, providing a "power-full" body that resists the intrusion of external forces. A power animal or guardian spirit not only increases physical energy and the ability to resist contagious disease, but mental alertness and self-confidence as well. The power even makes it more difficult for one to lie. Morrison was known for having great physical energy and could function without sleep for exceptional periods of time. And he was also known among his friends as someone who always told the truth.

A shaman may discover that he already has an unusual connection with a particular animal. This may result from a deep childhood association, a recent peculiar encounter, or a longtime tendency to collect images and drawings of the particular creature. Morrison's central symbol, the Great Snake, with its slippery equation of freedom and violence, appears everywhere in his poetry including both "The End" and "The Celebration of the Lizard." According to Lommel, if a man has a vision of a snake "this means that all snakes assume the status of fathers for him." The idea that Morrison's frequent use of snakes and other shamanic symbols is coincidental seems unlikely in view of this passage from Lommel: ". . . the people demanded that, to prove he has been called, the new shaman shall dive down into the (lake) and bring back medicine . . . the young shaman dives down into the depths to (The Great Snake) and says to it, 'There are many people standing on the bank, they want to see you.' The old shaman follows him and the two come to the surface with the snake. The two shamans ride on the snake in the water . . . the snake scatters crystals around it. After a while it disappears into the depths again . . . but the two shamans distribute crystals to all those present."

Shamans obtain power by surrendering their will to the "spirit of the night" and in that sense they are possessed. The concept of possession has been distorted by popular films and literature to imply a perfectly normal person being violently and completely overtaken by a demonic spirit and undergoing a sudden and usually horrifying transformation. True possession simply means falling under the control of a spiritual entity. The process is usually gradual and not sudden and requires at least the implied consent of the person being possessed. In most cases, possession occurs only after the subject actively seeks to submit his or her will to an entity or demon. This may involve a conscious choice to come under the entity's control or a series of small choices to do the demon's bidding until, finally, the ability to choose otherwise has deteriorated to nothing. Most shamans are probably possessed, but possession is a universal phenomenon that affects more cults than shamanism. Jim Morrison believed he was possessed by the spirit of a shaman, but it's unlikely that this could have occurred when he first encountered the entity at age four. The fixation probably began there, but the actual possession is more likely to have taken place on the Venice rooftop when Morrison, by then well-educated in the ways of shamanism and similar philosophies, made a conscious choice in that direction.

Shamanistic lore maintains that once a man accepts the call to become a shaman, he must continue in the vocation or the spirits force him into madness and sickness until he either perishes under the coercion or frees himself by accepting his role. To those around Jim Morrison his "possession" was regarded more as imaginative and hip behavior than as an actual state of his mind. His personality changes, the voices he heard, and the lack of control he had over his life were chalked up to his unique creative talents instead of a force that frequently manipulated them. One of the press's favorite quotes describing Morrison in those days came from Elektra publicist Danny Fields, who said, quite simply and ironically, "Morrison's possessed."

While Jim Morrison may have sought guidance from a shamanistic spirit he gave little thought to the source of that spirit's power. Like many during the occult revival of the sixties, he simply assumed that all spirits were good spirits, thus opening himself to be used and abused by any spiritual entity that happened to come along. The result may have been some amazing inspirations, but also a tragically restless and misdirected life.

In the 1960s the youth movement in America was at its strongest and The Doors were among its chief representatives. In some ways they did serve as its shamans, its medicine men. As modern youths grow up and approach adulthood, the musicians they listen to often serve as their conscience. All America is one big tribe, according to some sociologists, and that's why it acts like a giant family that "loves everyone" yet can still hate so much at the same time. The young and the hip of the sixties strongly exhibited a form of tribal consciousness. And if they saw themselves as a sort of community, many of them also saw Jim Morrison as a leader, their super medicine man, their shaman. In Indian societies, the shaman ruled the tribe with awe and mystical power. In modern America, the rock superstar holds similar reign over his audiences.

PART TWO

Jim
Morrison:
Lizard
King/Poet/
Filmmaker

The spectacle is heir to all the weakness of the project of Western philosophy, which was an attempt to understand activity by means of the categories of vision. Indeed the spectacle reposes on an incessant deployment of the very technical rationality to which the philosophical tradition gave rise. So far from realizing philosophy, the spectacle philosophizes reality, and turns the material life of everyone into a universe of speculation.
—GUY DEBORD, *The Society of the Spectacle*
(trans. Donald Nicholson-Smith)

I think in art, but especially in films, people are trying to confirm their own existences. Somehow things seem more real if they can be photographed and you can create a semblance of life on the screen. But those little aphorisms that make up most of The Lords—*if I could have said it any other way I would have. . . . A lot of the passages in it, for example about shamanism, turned out to be very prophetic several years later because I had no idea when I was writing that I'd be doing just that.*
—JIM MORRISON in an interview with Bob Chorush

Naked Lunch *is a blueprint, a How-To Book. . . . Black insect lusts open into vast, other planet landscapes. . . . Abstract concepts, bare as algebra, narrow down to a black turd or a pair of aging cajones. . . . How-To extend levels of experience by opening the door at the end of a long hall. . . . Doors that only open in* Silence. . . . Naked Lunch *demands Silence from the Reader. Otherwise he is taking his own pulse. . . .*
—WILLIAM S. BURROUGHS, *Naked Lunch*

In song and dance the man expresses himself as a member of a higher commu-
nity; he has forgotten how to walk and speak and is on his way toward
flying through the air, dancing. His very gestures express enchantment. Just as
the animals now talk, and the earth yields milk and honey, supernatural sounds
emanate from him, too: he feels himself a god, he himself now
walks about enchanted, in ecstasy, like the gods he saw walking
in his dreams.
—*Friedrich Nietzsche,* The Birth of Tragedy *(trans. Walter Kaufmann)*

In a description of the importance of the poet Arthur Rimbaud (1854–91), Albert Camus pointed out that at the height of his poetic powers he was a powerful mixture of contradictions: "At the moment when he carries in his breast both illumination and the darkness of hell, when he hails and insults beauty, and creates, from an insoluble conflict, the intricate counterpoint of an exquisite song, he is the poet of rebellion—the greatest of all." This force was behind Rimbaud's poetry and the myths surrounding his life; and this was what attracted Morrison to his poetry and gave the rock star a wealth of dark imagery to inspire his songs. But Morrison, as the reminiscences in this book demonstrate, was also a protean artistic force: he was the Lizard King, but he also wrote poetry, sang songs, and made films. Rimbaud had visions and he put them into his poetry; Morrison sang about the dark images in his head and he wrote about and created visions for the screen.

This section begins with Morrison talking to himself and producing a provocative portrait of the artist as a young rock star. Collected here are three poems Morrison wrote on film aesthetics that were published in his first book, *The Lords*. Also in this section are two poems by Rimbaud translated by Wallace Fowlie, the man Morrison wrote to in 1968 to thank for translating the complete poetry of the French poet.

Morrison's interest in poetry and film began before he was singing and writing for the Doors and James Riordan and Jerry Prochnicky describe here Morrison's experience of studying film at UCLA. This is followed by a writer who may be called the most important commentator on Morrison and the Doors: Jerry Hopkins, who with the help of Danny Sugerman, began what we now call the Doors Industry of biographies and criticism with the 1980 *No One Here Gets Out Alive*. Hopkins's "Mr. Mojo Rises" describes the effort to bring the story of the Doors to the screen and it is prophetic about the outcome of Oliver Stone's film. Bruce Harris, the former director of advertising for Elektra, writes about talking film with Morrison and the essays by me, Tony Magistrale, and Yasue Kuwahara describe, in a somewhat academic vein, Morrison's poetics, his vision of America, and the importance the Doors have in American culture.

SELF-INTERVIEW
JIM MORRISON

I think the interview is the new art form. I think the self-interview is the essence of creativity. Asking yourself questions and trying to find answers. The writer is just answering a series of unuttered questions.

It's similar to answering questions on a witness stand. It's that strange area where you try and pin down something that happened in the past and try honestly to remember what you were trying to do. It's a crucial mental exercise. An interview will often give you a chance to confront your mind with questions, which to me is what art is all about. An interview also gives you the chance to try and eliminate all of those space fillers . . . you should try to be explicit, accurate, to the point . . . no bullshit. The interview form has antecedents in the confession box, debating and cross-examination. Once you say something, you can't really retract it. It's too late. It's a very existential moment.

I'm kind of hooked to the game of art and literature; my heroes are artists and writers.

I always wanted to write, but I always figured it'd be no good unless somehow the hand just took the pen and started moving without me really having anything to do with it. Like automatic writing. But it just never happened.

I wrote a few poems, of course. I think around the fifth or sixth grade I wrote a poem called "The Pony Express." That was the first I can remember. It was one of those ballad-type poems. I never could get it together though.

"Horse Latitudes" I wrote when I was in high school. I kept a lot of notebooks through high school and college, and then when I left school, for some dumb reason—maybe it was wise—I threw them all away. . . . I wrote in those books night after night. But maybe if I'd never thrown them away, I'd never have written anything original—because they were mainly accumulations of things that I'd read or heard, like quotes from books. I think if I'd never gotten rid of them I'd never been free.

Listen, real poetry doesn't say anything, it just ticks off the possibilities. Opens all doors. You can walk through any one that suits you.

. . . and that's why poetry appeals to me so much—because it's so eternal. As long as there are people, they can remember words and combinations of words. Nothing else can survive a holocaust but poetry and songs. No one can remember an entire novel. No one can describe a film, a piece of sculpture, a painting, but so long as there are human beings, songs and poetry can continue.

If my poetry aims to achieve anything, it's to deliver people from the limited ways in which they see and feel.

Jim Morrison

Los Angeles, 1969–71

"AT UCLA" FROM *BREAK ON THROUGH: THE LIFE AND DEATH OF JIM MORRISON*
JAMES RIORDAN AND JERRY PROCHNICKY

Carol Winters, a close friend of Morrison's in those days, remembers another of Felix and Jim's drug exploits when they came to her apartment after ripping off an entire case of doctor's samples from somewhere in Culver City. "They just sat down on the floor and went through everything in the bag taking one of each." It wasn't long before Morrison was out on the balcony screaming and having dry heaves. But, according to friends, this was not all that unusual and soon he was ready for more action.

It was an easy time to get drugs. LSD was not yet illegal and the general public and most authorities were not that hip to grass yet. It was a time of testing limits anyway and no one really thought you could get hurt by it. The feeling was that if you ingested a lot of various exotic drugs the worst that might happen is they would make you sick and throw up. To many that little bit of inconvenience was well worth the risk. That is, until a few years later, when people started dying left and right from drug overdoses or from doing insane things during bad LSD trips.

Drugs are a bet w/your mind

Even though Morrison was playing the same games as many of his friends, he was a lot more vulnerable, and a lot younger. He hung out with some bizarre, but intellectually heavy people and he really didn't yet have the intellect to compete with them. And those were the days when intellect was everything and if you didn't have it, you had better learn to fake it or compensate for it. Jim did both exceedingly well and consequently he was driven to prove himself through more physical acts like fast driving, drugs, and booze. Michael Ford remembers Jim's reading Rimbaud while balancing himself on the ledges of tall buildings at UCLA for a student film. Another time in the cinematography lab he just went wild, suddenly throwing cans of film and stuff all over the place. No one was quite sure why he did it, but it made a powerful impression.

Phillip O'leno, one of Morrison's best friends at UCLA, describes him in those days: "Jim was a very talented and very brilliant person who was a little too young to be wise." Part of Morrison's lack of wisdom at this time translated into proving himself with drugs. He may have been slow to join the drug revolution, but once he did, it became another obsession. And alcohol, the poet's classic weakness, was embraced with even more passion. Thus, over the years at UCLA, booze, the traditional sentimentalizer of the past, coupled with psychedelics, the reputed mind expander of the present, became Morrison's rather askew formula for growth. And why not? All of his peers were off-the-wall revolutionaries who might come to class stoned or drunk one day with little interest in what was going on, then work around the clock without sleep the next to complete a project they believed in. They had their own brand of academics. They all wanted to crack the barriers that held them back, each in his own way. And Morrison took it all in with his special gift for absorption. All the foolish brave talk. All the stoned, drunken days. All the wild, electric nights.

Michael Ford elaborates: "Jim didn't really start knocking back the booze until Felix was around, but it's not that Felix was some sort of demonic influence. We used to sit around the Gypsy Wagon and talk about reality and I think Felix thought he had to succumb to the nineteenth-century Romantic myth that you had to be a drunk and a womanizer in order to be a poet. I mean he might even have been joking but Jim had a tendency to take jokes very seriously."

As college continued Morrison became moodier and the show-off side of his nature more and more dominant. If he were visiting your apartment, you might be having a wonderful discussion about French poetry one moment and the next discover him throwing lighted matches onto your bed. If he crashed the night you might leave in the morning sure that he was your friend for life only to return later to discover he had smeared tuna fish all over your walls as some sort of vague gesture of protest toward you. Carol Winters remembers: "He was manipulative, but he was also very protective. We weren't lovers except for one weekend, but I really loved him and he looked out for me. He wouldn't let me do really dangerous stuff like drive a car when I was on acid. But he hurt me too. After he got famous he didn't want me in his new life. I guess he didn't want to remember that I'd been supporting him."

Many serious students accused Morrison of being a dilettante because he got drunk and goofed around so much. He seemed to be less interested in the "important issues of life" and more in the outrageous. He talked often of forming a band even though he was the first to admit he couldn't sing a note or play an instrument. But he wrote poetry regularly and it was obvious he wanted to join the burgeoning music scene that was at the center of the hippie culture. Morrison was intrigued with the idea of performing. Once, when he was visiting college friend Martin Bondell, he met a girl who had just returned from a Bob Dylan concert. "Jim sat down with the girl," Bondell recalled, "and quizzed her intently as to what Dylan sang, what clothes he wore, how he moved, and what the effect of his act was. He was totally fascinated by it."

But before these things took hold, Morrison did manage to complete one film of his own. It was his first and last, and predictably, it was very controversial. A few students called it a masterpiece of nonlinear filmmaking, but the faculty and most of the other students felt it was a waste of good celluloid. The film was essentially a work print with a sound track, and its one print appears to have been lost in the UCLA archives. The untitled original was first screened at a grading session, where it kept breaking in the projector because of poor splicing. When it was finally shown in projectionable form it came off as sort of a Freudian dream, a chain of startling surrealistic images. The film began with a black screen and strange sounds—erotic ones mixed with the chanting of a priest and children from a Catholic catechism hour radio show. It sounded primitive. The first image was of a group of men waiting for a stag movie to begin. When the movie breaks in the projector the men make shadow puppets of animals with their hands on the screen, but then become angry because the film hasn't come back on. Then the scene shifts to a blonde girl doing a striptease on top of a television set that is tuned into a Nazi storm trooper rally. After she takes off most of her clothes she straddles the TV, causing the marching German soldiers to look almost as if they are coming out of her. The film continues with images of a walking woman's rear and ends with a giant close-up of Morrison taking a hit off a huge joint and giving the audience the Big Wink!

Cinema, heir of alchemy, last of an erotic science

Morrison later called it "less a film than an essay on film" but it indicated that his fascination with blending violent and erotic images was present even then. Ray Manzarek gives his opinion of the film: "Jim just put a lot of things he liked into a film. It didn't have anything to do with anything. Everybody hated it at UCLA. It was really quite good."

It is certain that the lighting and camera techniques were not that good, but what about the effect of the images? The faculty unanimously agreed that it stunk and Morrison was given a "D" for his girlie/TV/ Nazi/pot movie. His friends said it was great. According to Richard Blackburn, "After the screening, Jim's film was attacked at length by a rather uptight faculty member who called it a product of a degenerate mind . . . A few minutes later, Jim was seen talking to someone in a phone booth, crying bitterly, tears streaming down his cheeks."

Morrison stated: "The good thing about film is that there aren't any experts. There's no authority on film. Any one person can assimilate and contain the whole history of film in himself, which you can't do in other arts. There are no experts, so theoretically, any student knows almost as much as any professor."

And that was the way Morrison had always wanted it. Even the most liberal department in one of the most liberal colleges in the country gave him a sense of being restricted or censored. Even those that supposedly championed individuality and eccentricity had left him with a sense of limitation. "I've always had this underlying sense that something's not quite right," he told *Eye* magazine's Digby Diehl. "I felt blinders were being put on me as I grew older. I and all my friends were being funneled down a long narrowing tunnel. When you're in school, you're taking a risk. You can get a lot out of it, but you can get a lot of harm, too."

Life continued to be an ongoing exciting experiment for Jim Morrison. Partly he was just out for a good time, and to hell with anyone that got in his way, but at the same time he was serious. His primary concern could best be said to be *vision*. He was always testing the bounds of reality and trying to find some meaning to it all. If that meant bending the reality or shaping it a bit, then he was all for it. And yet, still coexisting with it all at this time, just a hair's breadth beneath the surface, was the shy, repressed kid who used drugs not just for experimentation, but because they gave him confidence.

For Morrison at UCLA there was no fraternity rat-pack party scene happening. That classic college tradition had already faded into the deeper and more lasting freedom that would soon become the love generation. The music of this time in Los Angeles was that of Love, Buffalo Springfield, and The Byrds. And the partying was more along the lines of an occasional lunatic adventure or simply just bringing wine to a screening and passing it around. Often the film school students would go to see Ray Manzarek's band on the weekends. Rick & the Ravens was a somewhat uninspired little combo which featured "Screamin' Ray Daniels, the bearded blues-shouter." "Screamin' Ray" was Manzarek's alter ego and the band could usually be found playing (for five dollars each a night) at a bar on Second Street and Broadway in Santa Monica, improbably called The Turkey Joint West. It was the spring of 1965 and Rick & the Ravens had a nucleus of the three Manzarek brothers: Ray on vocals, Rick on guitar, and Jim on harmonica.

Since Manzarek had switched from studying for a law degree to being a film student and musician, his classmates used to say he changed from studying for the bar to playing in a bar. Manzarek remembers: "I was at UCLA and the money kept me paying the tuition. I would switch from film school grubby to a blue jacket with a velvet collar and a frilly shirt to be the bearded blues-shouter. Immediately afterward, I would put my sweatshirt and corduroy jacket back on and return to being a film student."

The brothers had played together in Chicago, and when the family moved to Redondo Beach, the blues band was formed for weekend gigs. The Turkey Joint West was frequented by a college crowd who came to hear Manzarek belt out "Money," "Louie, Louie," "Hoochie Coochie Man," and "I'm Your Doctor, I Know What You Need" in a somewhat forced Chicago blues style. Often the film school students joined in, participating in a sort of spontaneous live jam onstage. And one of these students was Jim Morrison. At Ray's beckoning Morrison would climb up on the stage, but once he was up there he was unable to do much more than clap along, shake an occasional tambourine, and shout, "Right on," every once in a while behind Manzarek's lead vocals. Ray remembers: "That was the first time Jim sang onstage. A whole lot of guys from the UCLA film department came down, and you know, there wouldn't be anyone in the club, so I'd say, 'Come up, Jim, come up Paul [Ferrara],' and there'd be about twenty of us screaming and jumping around." During one such gig Morrison sang an extremely rough version of "Louie, Louie" to a delighted film school audience.

Although he had been seeing her sporadically for some time, Jim and Mary Werbelow were coming to a parting of the ways. Her dreams of stardom now seemed like schoolgirl fantasies to him, and when she refused to appear in his student film because her agent advised her not to, Jim was furious. Mary also believed he was taking too many drugs, but the last straw came when she showed up unexpectedly at his apartment and caught him with another girl. Jim defended his position, claiming she had no business coming over uninvited.

As he drew nearer to graduation, Morrison became locked into the idea of never doing anything halfway. Thus, he drank not for enjoyment, but to get drunk, and he smoked grass not to get merely high, but to get stoned out of his mind. Both the creative and the destructive voices inside him were picking up steam and beginning to shape him into some sort of human bullet, one who would approach life as if he had been shot out of a gun. Very noticeable—very fast—and about to smash into something.

MR. MOJO RISES
JERRY HOPKINS

The maitre d' at the Ivy assured me that there was no reservation for anyone named Stone, and the impression I got was that the restaurant had more bookings per chair than a flight to Hawaii on United. I was early. I said I'd hang around for Oliver.

"Oliver?" the maitre d' asked, "Oliver Stone, the director?" I nodded.

"Ah, well, then, of course, if Mr. Stone comes, we can find a table, of course." Down the hall I saw Jim Morrison using the pay phone. I'd forgotten he was so tall. I laughed at myself. Morrison was dead, and this was Val Kilmer, the actor selected by Stone to play the '60s "Lizard King." It was eerie. The start of principal photography was two months off, and Kilmer was already into the part: the wardrobe, the hair, the manner, the grin.

I introduced myself and told him the maitre d' claimed there was no reservation. "Not to worry," said Kilmer, reaching for the phone again. He dialed Stone's office and said, "Jerry and I are at the Ivy, and they say there's no reservation for Oliver. You better have somebody call down here and say *Oliver Stone* in a real loud voice right away." No sooner had the phone been returned to the cradle than the maitre d' appeared and said, "I can take you to your table now."

At last. The Jim Morrison movie was really getting made. I had good reason to think it never would. I sold the movie rights to my Jim Morrison biography, *No One Here Gets Out Alive* (cowritten with Danny Sugerman), four times in seven years. That's probably no record, but in some circles in the 1980s, the Morrison story came to be regarded as one of those films that couldn't, or shouldn't, be made. Now that the project is finally under way—with Oliver Stone the writer-director for Carolco—I look back at the labyrinthine trail with some amazement. Over the years, dozens have been involved: Allan Carr, William Friedkin, Jerry Weintraub, Brian De Palma, Aaron Russo, Goland and Globus, Paul Schrader, Francis Coppola, Charlie Sheen, Irving Azoff and Martin Scorsese among the directors and producers, and to play Morrison, John Travolta, Jason Patric, Keanu Reeves, Michael O'Keefe, Gregory Harrison, Michael Ontkean, Steven Bauer, Christopher Lambert, the lead singers from INXS (Michael Hutchence) and U2 (Bono), Timothy Bottoms, Richard Gere and Tom Cruise.

The story of the Doors movie is one of pissing contests and soaring egos, of complicated fuck-you option deals and people changing partners and sides, of Indians dancing on a Malibu beach and an aging rock star dancing on Morrison's grave. It is the story of parents and siblings, along with the surviving Doors and who knows how many agents and lawyers and other movie-biz types, all sides talking about karma and curses and the forces of evil and light, bickering over the Morrison myth and who has the right to do what with it.

The final cast and crew includes, besides Stone and Kilmer, Meg Ryan (as Morrison's girlfriend, Pamela Courson), Kyle MacLachlan, Kevin Dillon, Imagine's Brian Grazer and rock promoter Bill Graham.

During the late '60s and early '70s, as the Los Angeles correspondent for *Rolling Stone,* I interviewed Morrison several times, and I drank with him. I spent a week with the Doors in Mexico, and he invited me to poetry readings and screenings. Even if he consciously behaved himself in my presence, even when he was drunk—I was, after all, the press—I think I came to know him pretty well.

When we were in Mexico City, he asked me to switch rooms with him so that when Pamela called in the middle of the night—as she did—she wouldn't interrupt Morrison and the girl he had picked up for the night. She got to talk to me instead. Naturally, I gave Pam his room number.

The next day, he smiled and said, "You really know how to hurt a guy."

If Morrison cheated on Pam, he showed an idiosyncratic honesty to his peers. He took the "generation gap" catchphrase of the time and made it his own, insisting that his parents were dead. When the truth came out, I asked why. He said they didn't ask to be a part of his rock life-style, so he left them out. The real truth was, he refused to talk to them; they *were* dead, for all he cared.

Maybe he was most honest with himself. When other rock musicians who proclaimed an allegiance to hippie frugality suddenly got rich, they immediately acquired big houses, fancy cars and expensive drug habits. Even when Morrison's band was the most successful in the U.S.—"the American Rolling Stones"—the lead singer continued to live in a $10-a-night motel room and owned only a couple of leather suits (which he never had cleaned), an American-made car (frequently destroyed as the consequence of his indulgences) and a couple of boxes of books.

Morrison had an IQ of 149 (a figure I got from his high-school files), read voraciously, remembered everything and put it together in a way that was fascinating, sprinkling his interviews with historical and philosophical references, spouting the poetry of Rimbaud and Baudelaire. Sitting with Jim Morrison in one of those tacky bars he favored was like slumming with a young college professor in leather pants and a Mexican wedding shirt who drank anything as long as it was cold and wet, and in enormous quantity. He was a classic literary character, the poet as obligatory hell-raiser drunk, thinly disguised as Lizard King or Indian shaman, two images he had created mainly for the publicity.

His favorite bar was the Phone Booth, a topless joint adjacent to the Doors' offices. Whenever I went there with him, "Love Me Two Times" magically fell onto the jukebox turntable and one of the dancers would come over and shake her Two Times in his face. I don't think Morrison was happier anywhere else, not even on a stage with tens of thousands of adoring fans.

Four gold albums in a row, two number-one singles, his face on magazine covers and writers calling him the sexiest new pop icon since Brando and Dean did not fit Morrison comfortably. He came to hate all the attention, and he went into "hiding." He grew a beard and got fat, began recording poetry instead of song, writing a screenplay with San Francisco poet Michael McClure. One day, McClure and Morrison and their agent, Sylva Romano, were at a restaurant in Los Angeles, and they played a game, revealing how old they *felt*. The agent said she always secretly thought of herself as 19. McClure said he never got past 11. Morrison said he felt not 27, but 47.

In 1971, after going back into the studio to record a final album, Morrison went to Paris with Pamela. He claimed that the Mr. Mojo Risin' in one of his songs, "L.A. Woman," was not just an anagram using the letters of his name but the code he would use when contacting the office after faking his death. So it was not surprising that four months later, after the Doors' manager announced that Jim had died of a heart attack in a Paris bathtub and had been buried several days before, there were many who doubted. Hadn't Morrison's poet-hero, Rimbaud, disappeared into North Africa to run guns? Wasn't it reasonable that Morrison would pull a similar stunt, seeking the freedom that anonymity brings? Today, dozens of fans visit his Paris grave every day, and on the anniversary of his so-called death, July 3, Père-Lachaise Cimetière is the site of a major pilgrimage. Many of those fans don't believe Morrison is buried there, they believe he is still alive. You can't do better than that for Hollywood myth-making. The big question is: What will Oliver Stone do with the myth?

Much of the early Morrison movie talk concerned making a documentary. In July 1981, on the 10th anniversary of Morrison's alleged death, a Boston filmmaker accompanied the surviving Doors to Paris, where they encountered a cluster of mournful fans gathered at the Morrison grave. Witnesses say keyboardist Ray Manzarek seized the moment as the cameras began to roll and climbed onto a nearby tombstone to make a fervent speech: "Do you think Jim Morrison is here? I never saw the body! Jim's too big for this little grave, man! Do you really think he's dead?"

The Bostonian's documentary was not completed and a second try by a Hollywood filmmaker almost failed as well, until the surviving Doors stepped in and assumed financial control. *A Tribute to Jim Morrison* runs an hour in length and blends new interviews with footage from concerts and the Doors' own early documentary, *Feast of Friends*.

Mr. Mojo Risin' had been dead or alive for nine years when my biography of him was published. In the summer of 1980, *No One Here Gets Out Alive* grabbed the number-one position on best-seller lists all over the world: It followed that Hollywood would show some interest. Rock and roll had been a key ingredient in several recent films, including *Saturday Night Fever* (1977), *Grease, The Buddy Holly Story* (both 1978), *The Rose* (1979) and *The Blues Brothers* (1980), all selling millions of albums as well as tickets.

In 1981, Sasha Harari, a recent immigrant from Israel, offered $50,000 for the rights to my book. Harari then got *Grease* producer Allan Carr to write the check, with a second payment of $275,000 promised if the film went into production.

About the same time, the star of *Grease* and *Saturday Night Fever*, John Travolta, told Manzarek that he wanted the film's lead role. Manzarek took Travolta on a crawl of Morrison's favorite bars and actually talked about reuniting the Doors, with Travolta taking Morrison's place as vocalist. "There was nothing around at the time that seemed as exciting to me," Travolta said. "The music was resurging, and I was really hot to do it." The actor began rehearsing to Morrison videotapes, and he was good.

However, the legal rights were tangled. When Morrison died, he left everything to Pamela Courson, described as his common-law wife. (She used to call herself "Mrs. Morrison," angering the other Doors, but the two had never officially married.) A lawsuit was filed against the estate by the three surviving Doors, who said the singer had taken more than his share of the communal checking account. This kept Pamela's legacy in the courts for more than two years, until 1974, when she finally was given more than $500,000, plus one-fourth of all future royalties and earnings of all the Doors' companies. However, less than two weeks before the court ruling, Pamela died of a heroin overdose.

This threw her interest in the estate into the laps of her parents, Columbus "Corky" Courson, a retired high-school principal, and his wife,

Penny. When Morrison's parents joined the fray, the estate went back into court for another five years, until 1979, when the singer's quarter-share of the Doors' earnings was divided between the Coursons and Morrison's parents, the recently retired Admiral George "Steve" Morrison and his wife, Clara.

In 1981, with Allan Carr's $275,000 dollar offer fresh in my fantasy, I was flown to California and put up in the chicest new hotel in Beverly Hills. A long, white limousine took me to Warner Bros., where the director of *The Exorcist* and *The French Connection,* William Friedkin, said he wanted Manzarek and me to do the script. But the deal fell apart, and in spring 1982, Allan Carr said I had dragged him into a fraudulent contract and demanded that I return the $50,000.

Three months later, when *Rolling Stone* put Jim Morrison on the cover, the headline read, "He's hot, he's sexy, and he's dead," and the issue became one of the magazine's all-time best-sellers. Soon after that, Allan Carr offered a new contract and made another token payment, but it was a lost cause. The Doors had decided Carr didn't understand Morrison, and as for Travolta, he was a nice guy, but Morrison wasn't nice; said drummer John Densmore, "Jim was scary."

Working with Travolta, Brian De Palma began writing a script titled *Fire,* about a rock star who faked his death. Largely because *Eddie and the Cruisers,* a film that took a similar plot line, was in development, De Palma couldn't get a studio interested. Meanwhile, others approached Harari and the Doors, including Jerry Weintraub, Aaron Russo, Irving Azoff, Francis Coppola and Martin Scorsese, while Morrison's sister and her husband announced they were making a documentary *and* a feature film.

In 1985, Sasha Harari convinced the three Doors to renew their support, and the man who had promoted Doors concerts in San Francisco and New York in the '60s, Bill Graham, was brought in to assist in negotiations with the Coursons and Morrisons. By the time those talks were complete, the Coursons were promised that their daughter would not be shown having anything to do with the singer's death. In the agreement with the Morrisons, a clause specified that no mention of them would be made in the film.

Harari called Oliver Stone's agent to ask if he'd be interested in directing the film. Harari was told he missed Stone by a day; he had just gone to the Philippines to make *Platoon.*

From 1985 to 1987, the project languished at Columbia under chairman Guy McElwaine. When David Puttnam succeeded McElwaine, the project went into turnaround. However, when *La Bamba* hit big in 1987, it proved once again that rock-and-roll biography could work in film. More important, 1987 marked the 20th anniversary of the Summer of Love, a media event that suggested a new psychedelic era might be standing in the wings. United Artists and Warner Bros. showed interest in the Doors' story, but Imagine Films Entertainment acquired it, and Ron Howard was first in line to direct. The efforts of the initial screenwriter, Randy Johnson (*Dudes*), were rejected, however, and a second writer, Ralph Thomas (*Ticket to Heaven*), was given the assignment. That was when the Writers Guild went on strike in 1988.

In the movie biz there is something called *force majeure*, French for an "act of God." As it is applied to Hollywood business practices, it can mean that if there is a writers' or directors' or actors' strike, all contracts in force at the time of the strike's beginning are extended for the length of the strike. When the strike lasted six months, Imagine assumed its option on the Doors' life story and rights to the Doors' music were extended for a like period.

No way. It was a legally unsupportable tradition, said the Doors' representatives: It wasn't in writing and if Imagine didn't come up with $750,000 on August 1, when the contract expired, all rights would revert to the Doors. That may not seem a large figure by Hollywood standards, but Imagine had taken a terrible beating in the stock-market crash the previous year and, according to some, the production company's cupboard was bare.

Producers and agents began circling. I started getting calls from Charlie Sheen, who said he wanted the movie rights and intended to produce the film and cowrite a script on spec with a friend, Scott Goldman. He said he had a production deal with Orion and U2's lead singer, Bono, was ready to jump in as Morrison. At that time, Bono included a Doors medley in his band's performances.

"I've seen U2 in concert four times," Sheen told me, "and Bono does Morrison so fucking great, it's chilling. This is how it'll happen. We write the script in three weeks. Normally, I take 10 days, but this is special. We send the script to you first, you tell me what you want. Sound good to you?" He told me to have my agent call his friend Goldman.

My agent did that and then called me and said, "Goldman is 23, and everything I say, he says, 'Oh, wow, that's really radical, what do we do now?'" I never heard from Sheen again.

The August deadline loomed and, at the final moment, who should come riding to Imagine's rescue but Carolco. The Doors were paid $750,000, thus keeping the rights to the band's likenesses, story and songs from reverting to the three surviving band members, the Coursons and the Morrisons. Once again, Morrison belonged to Hollywood.

Still another writer, Bob Dolman (*Willow*), was hired. That script was rejected, too. Oliver Stone first became involved in discussions of a Doors movie in 1986 with Imagine's Brian Grazer, and it was then that Stone suggested Val Kilmer for the role. Now, with his own two-picture deal in place at Carolco, Stone became firmly attached to the project. Once committed, Stone devoured Morrison's poetry and my book; he watched the Doors' video and film collection over and over again; he visited the scenes of the singer's life; he listened to the music constantly; then he wrote a screenplay.

As we ordered the first glasses of wine, waiting for Stone to join us, I couldn't get over how much Kilmer looked like Morrison. From watching him as the renegade swordsman in *Willow,* I knew he had the right coloring, cheekbones and muscled jaw. Now he was in character. Cowboy boots, hair the right length. He even blinked in precisely the same sleepy way that Morrison blinked and tilted his head shyly yet confidently.

"I feel very lucky. Everybody wanted the part. Timothy Bottoms, Tom Cruise. . . ," Kilmer said. "Actors do the best they've ever done when they work with Oliver."

We ordered more wine—of course we did, wasn't I drinking with Morrison again?—and I asked Kilmer how old he was. He told me he was 30. I said, "You were a kid in the '60s."

He agreed, "Yeah, I was, but I had an older brother who took me to a Jimi Hendrix concert and I've read a lot." He asked if I had the original tapes of my interviews with Jim, because he wanted to copy Jim's voice.

If Kilmer bore surface similarities to Morrison, Stone's resemblances to the musician ran even deeper. They were only couple of years apart in age, and they came from similar Establishment backgrounds. Stone's father was a Wall Street stockbroker, Morrison's a Navy officer. Both were college graduates. There was a common interest in writing and film; they experienced the world within literary and visual contexts.

More important, I sense a shared, anarchic intensity. There was a brash daring to experiment, coupled with a fierce determination to find emotional buttons and to push them hard. They liked to give people the finger, to test them. Getting a reaction was important.

Professionally, they looked for an audience's soft spots and attacked with guns and concepts blazing, or with such calculated control it was maddening. Stone used great, looping, 360-degree pans that increased the pressure on the viewer in the same way that Morrison inserted long silences into his songs. Stone, as a writer, pulled a bloody head from a shoulder bag (*Year of the Dragon*), impaled a prison guard on a wall peg (*Midnight Express*), had the star throw his face into a heap of cocaine (*Scarface*) and, as the director of *Platoon,* had the good guy die with his arms outthrust like the crucified Christ's. Morrison posed for publicity pictures with an erection, frequently threw himself into the concert audience, vomited blood in one of rock's earliest videos and, in a notorious performance in Miami, allegedly dropped his pants.

In Stone, I sensed a volcano at rest. After he joined us at the table, I told him, "When I first heard your name associated with the project, I thought: Stone's not particularly subtle, but neither was Jim. You're perfect for each other." Stone showed his trademark gap-toothed grin.

Stone said he had a copy of a diary: a groupie's affair with the Shaman/Lizard King. He looked at Val and said, "Everything's in there! This is a woman who was naked with Morrison many times! He's so gentle and loving. And then he turns into a complete shit. A complete Jekyll and Hyde."

I returned to Los Angeles in May to watch a day's shooting as Stone's guest. The first thing I did was read the script, but Stone said I couldn't take it with me—I had to read it in an office at Carolco. I thought that odd, but the script was odd. Chronology and character were shuffled like cards in a deck, moved around for dramatic effect. And while it's true that Morrison was a sexual figure in practice as well as image, the amount of sex seemed disproportionate; more women dropped to their knees in the script than you saw during an old-style Catholic Mass. Plus, Morrison's sense of humor was, to use a phrase Stone should recognize, missing in action.

There also was the case of Patricia Kennealy. In the '60s, she was editor of a magazine called *Jazz & Pop* and a practicing witch who later married Jim in a handfasting ceremony that blended souls on a karmic and cosmic plane that has an effect on future incarnations of the two involved. Kennealy happily agreed to play the part of the priestess who, in real life, performed the handfasting. But when she arrived on the set, she was given only the pages of her scene. When Stone warned her, "I have you doing things in the script you didn't do," she replied, "That's OK, so long as they aren't things I wouldn't do."

At one point Morrison freaks out when he hears his band's biggest song, "Light My Fire," used for a car commercial, when, in reality, Jim stopped Buick from using the song and the commercial never happened. As Morrison is going onstage for the Miami concert, the Doors' manager tells him that there's a "fuck clause" in the contract—say the magic word and police with warrants already made out will come on the stage and arrest you—when that clause started appearing in Doors' contracts after and because of the Miami concert, where Morrison allegedly revealed himself.

And yet, all of these changes were made while attention was being paid to re-creating the smallest environmental detail. When I told Doors guitarist Robby Krieger that Stone's office called me repeatedly to determine precisely when certain pictures in my book were taken, to establish accurate wardrobe chronology, he admitted that the wardrobe was flawless. When Patricia Kennealy was flown to Hollywood to perform the handfasting, her New York apartment had been duplicated so perfectly that she saw bills bearing her Lower East Side address on the desk.

And the truth is, most of the script *is* accurate, most of the events depicted did occur as written. And while Stone has made a much bigger deal of it than Morrison ever did, Stone's theme of Rock Star as Indian Shaman is legitimate.

There is a story that Morrison told: He was four, in a car on a highway in New Mexico with his parents, when they encountered an overturned truck. Indians were lying all over the road. As they passed, Morrison's eyes opened wide at the chaotic scene, and the soul of one or two of the Indians leaped into the young boy's soul.

The shaman, or medicine man, was a part of Morrison's carefully crafted performance image. In college, he wrote a paper stating that crowds had sexual neuroses much like those of individuals, and that these derangements could be diagnosed and treated from the speaker's stage. In his early interviews, he quoted his own poetry in answer to questions, saying it was a time to "invoke, palliate, drive away the Dead. Nightly." In performance, he used the tambourine the way a medicine man would use a rattle.

Stone and his star were becoming obsessed with reincarnating Jim Morrison. When they talked about him, it was not only with respect, but with awe. They seemed to believe in him as shaman, in the concert as seance, in the performance as "sensuous panic, deliberately evoked through drugs, chants, dancing," in the audience as a tribe.

I asked, "Was this always the way you felt about Jim?" Stone said yes it was, even when he was in the jungle in Vietnam.

At sunrise on the first day of principal photography, approximately 150 members of the cast and crew gathered at Trancas Beach in Malibu for what Bobby Klein called the "rites of protection." Klein was a neighbor of Morrison's when the Doors were starting out. Soon after that, he was one of the first Doors photographers. Today he is an acupuncturist, psychotherapist, martial artist and student of American Indian thought.

"They're doing a ghost dance in the film, and that's the dance in the film, and that's the dance with the greatest power," Klein said. "That kind of magic can hurt people if you're not careful. I didn't want to see any lightning strike the equipment, or heart attacks. I did a ritual so that when they called the Great Spirit down, they were protected. A pipe was made for Oliver by one of the Indians, and Oliver became the chief for the duration of the picture."

Later on in filming at the Shrine Civic Auditorium in downtown Los Angeles, Stone led his actors and crew in a couple of scenes re-creating the Doors' live 1967 appearance on the *The Ed Sullivan Show*. Downstairs was the makeup and dressing room. The Doors were spread along the makeup table, attired in hippie finery. Kilmer had his booted feet on the table and Meg Ryan, in a strawberry-blonde wig, was hanging on his shoulder like a trinket. Stone, looking like an unmade bed—rumpled shirt and jeans, white running shoes, exhausted—approached Kilmer. They whispered for a few minutes, then Stone called for action, and an Ed Sullivan look-alike came to welcome the members of the band. He said there was a word in the song that he wanted them to change. This scene took all morning. In the afternoon, Stone led his troops upstairs and onto a stage that had been meticulously duplicated from specifications provided by CBS. The organ intro to "Light My Fire" began and, when the vocal started, Kilmer leaped precisely as Morrison once leaped, tossing his mane of dark hair, lurching and grabbing the mike as if starting a shaman's dance. And, of course, he didn't change a thing when he sang, "Girl, we couldn't get much *higher!*"

Keyboardist Ray Manzarek hated Stone's script, and he was the only one of the Doors to say so. "He left out the whole Maharishi thing," Manzarek said, "which is how the Doors came together. Oliver said it was a cliché. I told him it wasn't a cliché in the '60s, it was important. Oliver has no sense of the Light, in a cosmic, spiritual or evolutionary sense. He got the idea of the shaman, man, but he doesn't know what the word means. He's fucking with some heavy juju, some fucking heavy shit. He's not only calling down Jim's karma, he's calling down the Indians' karma. We're dealing with serious darkness, man.

"This isn't the story of the Doors you're going to see," Manzarek warned. "It'd be a great movie if it was about the New York Dolls or Aerosmith. It's the evil side of sex and drugs. You want to know what I think, Man? Oliver Stone was over there in Vietnam and the hippies were back here smoking dope and practicing free love, and he was jealous. Oliver Stone is using the Doors to get revenge.

"Sasha Harari went to a psychic in Santa Barbara, and she told him he was involved in a project with a death. Sasha said he was producing a movie about a man who died. The psychic said, No, not him, someone involved with the project will die. We call it the Curse. At one point, a boom on Venice Beach collapsed and injured a guy. Dorothy [Ray's wife] and I looked at each other and nodded: Of course, it was the Curse."

Stone said he made "repeated overtures to Ray to bring him into the project," but all Manzarek did was "rave and shout." Production office sources speculated that some of the Manzarek scenes would be cut, even if Kyle MacLachlan, of *Twin Peaks* and *Blue Velvet,* is playing the part.

The other two Doors, guitarist Robby Krieger (played by Frank Whaley) and drummer John Densmore (Kevin Dillon), seem quite happy with the production. The day I visited the set, the only reservation Krieger expressed was that Oliver had picked "the dopiest wardrobe." It wasn't inaccurate, he said, "they just aren't my favorite clothes." When Vince Trenor, who had been the Doors' equipment manager, said, "They left out Jim's mellow side," Krieger merely shrugged and said, "Yeah, well. . . ."

It seemed more important to him that he and Densmore and Paul Rothchild, who produced the Doors' records and is serving as musical consultant for the film, all agreed that Kilmer's voice was, quoting Rothchild, "as good as Jim's. You really can't tell them apart." Stone, who says he hates lip-synching because it "removes the actor from the action," asked Rothchild to strip Morrison's voice off the original Doors tracks, on top of which he now has recorded Kilmer's voice.

On the outside with Manzarek are the Lisciandros and the Coursons. Kathy Lisciandro was the Doors' secretary and her husband, Frank, was Morrison's in-house cinematographer. They have been collaborating with the Coursons on the posthumous publication of Morrison's poetry. Frank said he first met Stone when Stone was writing the first draft of his screenplay.

"I told him, yes, Jim was a drunken fool at times, but he was kind and intelligent and a poet, and we wanted to see that in the script, too," Lisciandro said. "A few months later, Oliver's staff asked us to come in for more talk. They wanted to look at my pictures. We said we wanted to see a script and when they said no, so did we. We're trying to rehabilitate Jim's image after 19 years of trashing. The first book of Jim's poetry is now in its 23rd printing. The third volume will be published this fall. When the movie comes out and the wave hits the beach and then washes out to sea, we can walk along the beach and pick up the debris. Depending upon the degree of bullshit, we'll do what we can do."

Unlike the Lisciandros, the Coursons signed a release giving Carolco the rights to their daughter's character. But Frank Lisciandro said they didn't see the script until after the film had been in production for a month. My requests to speak to the Coursons were referred to an attorney. Sources in the film production office said they may be gearing up for a lawsuit.

"The Coursons don't see this as a love story, but it is," said one of the producers. "Now that they've seen the script, they're unhappy. I told Penny last night, 'The train's left the station.'"

I hadn't seen Paul Rothchild in years. His hair, like mine, is thinning and his waist, like mine, is going the other direction. "You know," he said, "when you first interviewed me for the book in 1973, I didn't know why you cared. I didn't think anyone would care. Now look!" He waved his arm to take in the set with Meg Ryan hanging on Val Kilmer's arm, Oliver Stone whispering into their ears, a $20 million film in midshoot. It was as if Stone's recognition validated a 20-year-old dream.

"I think it all now makes sense," said Rothchild.

"Paul understood the poetic nature of who Jim was and molded it," reflected Klein. "Jim was fortunate in life to have somebody as sensitive to the poetry and the classics as Rothchild [producing him] and now somebody as sensitive as Oliver Stone posthumously directing him."

From many who were at the center of Morrison's personal storm in the '60s, I got the same sense of *déjà vu*—as if this aging cast of mellowed but still anarchic characters had signed up for a final ride on the roller coaster to paradise or hell, getting a chance to put the words and music out there one more time, and maybe make another million bucks. I came away from the film set feeling that Morrison himself would be amused or appalled, but either way, happily along for the ride.

When Morrison did interviews, he often incorporated his poetry into his answers. "Is there some other area you'd like to get into?" I asked him once, in closing.

"How about . . . feel like discussing alcohol? Just a short dialogue. No long rap. Alcohol as opposed to drugs?"

I said, "OK. Part of the mythology has you playing the role of a heavy juicer."

"On a very basic level, I love drinking. Getting drunk . . . you're in complete control up to a point. It's your choice, every time you take a sip. You have a lot of small choices. It's like . . . I guess it's the difference between suicide and slow capitulation."

Did Morrison really believe he was slowly drinking himself to death and not care because it fulfilled the poetic tradition of which he was so enamored? Was this part of his shaman thing, the "sensuous panic deliberately evoked through drugs"? Or did he simply, for dramatic effect, choose to suggest that this was his fate?

Finally, I said, "What do you mean by that?"

He said, "I don't know, man. Let's go next door and get a drink."

I think most of his interviews ended enigmatically because that was the way he regarded himself. The word webs he spun dazzled all of us who listened and made him a favorite to quote. Like Oliver Stone, we were entranced, enamored, emboldened. Morrison beckoned us with his intelligence and sucked us into his fantasy. "Break on through to the other side," he sang. And we went along for the ride, believing him.

Due to a press blackout on the set of The Doors, *former* Rolling Stone *writer Jerry Hopkins pursued this story independently in true gonzo fash-*

ion. Oliver Stone was not aware he was being interviewed at the time when they spoke.

CINEMA IS MOST TOTALITARIAN OF THE ARTS
JIM MORRISON

Cinema is most totalitarian of the arts. All
energy and sensation is sucked up into the skull,
a cerebral erection, skull bloated with blood.
Caligula wished a single neck for all his subjects
that he could behead a kingdom with one blow.
Cinema is this transforming agent. The body
exists for the sake of the eyes; it becomes a
dry stalk to support these two soft insatiable
jewels.

FILM SENSIBILITY SET THE DOORS APART
BRUCE HARRIS

As a joke, I once asked Jim Morrison to name the group he most liked to listen to—besides the Doors, of course. He pondered this question thoughtfully for a few moments, as though it were the toughest question in the world, and then replied, "You know the soundtrack from Fellini's '8 1/2'? I really like that."

Morrison's world was the world of film.

In sharp contrast to the rest of the Doors, Jim had no pick-hit top 10 favorites. He was certainly not a "music fan" in the common manner of the '60s: each new Beatles album was not a revelation for him; the Jefferson Airplane did not carry the message of his day; the stylistic experiments of the Byrds did not move him. He listened a bit to Dylan (but only "John Wesley Harding"), and he occasionally mentioned Elvis. But he much preferred *watching* Alfred Hitchcock's "The 39 Steps" to *hearing* anything.

Appropriately enough, one of the Doors' only "cover" songs was "Alabama Song (Whisky Bar)," a Kurt Weill–Bertolt Brecht musical-theater piece. Originally performed by Lotte Lenya and later recorded by David Bowie (who else?) in the '80s, "Alabama Song" was most recently sung by Sting in the Broadway production of "The Threepenny Opera."

The influence of theater and film on the Doors set them apart from their contemporaries. While the Beatles drew upon Carl Perkins and Buddy Holly, and the Rolling Stones drew upon Chuck Berry and the R&B music of the '50s, the Doors forged a completely different lyrical and musical path—and their apartness is reflected in their lack of descendants.

Countless groups have tried to imitate the Beatles, but there is no Bee Gees or Badfinger or Jellyfish to compare with the Doors. This is because, for all of their tremendous impact and success, the Doors have always been more of a monument than an influence.

Morrison's image was a cinematic mystique made up of the masculine/feminine mystery of Marlene Dietrich, the tragic (vaguely psychotic) fragility of Greta Garbo, and the tough yet sensitive soul of James Dean.

Jim was rock's first true *actor.* He made recitative a major part of every Doors recording and performance. He spoke his lines and created theater, but the true drama of the Doors lay in the suspense created by his self-destructive tendencies, evolving at last into a sort of living theater for the dying. There was a sense at a lot of Doors concerts that maybe tonight no one here would get out alive.

It is of note that all this visual communication took place in an era before the explosion of music video, before MTV, and before the broad media coverage of rock artists. In their heyday, more people *heard* the Doors via their albums and hit records on the radio than ever got to *see* them past an LP cover.

Hence it is fascinating to consider what might have happened if the Doors, instead of being a '60s group, had been a new act contending in today's marketplace. Would they be the masters of the video vehicle of exposure or victims of it? "The End" would seem like quite a different entity in heavy rotation on MTV. Every skin pore, every drop of sweat, every hemidemisemiquaver of a gesture would be under the video microscope. And repetition in the TV eye can breed, if not contempt, then certainly boredom.

Nevertheless, there is no question that, had the Doors come along later, they would have been master manipulators of the video image. Like David Bowie, Michael Jackson, and Madonna—who are among today's leading video performers—Morrison was a pioneer. Everything from his film-school background to his outrageous stage antics suggests that, were he breaking on through in the '90s, he would be a leader in the video field.

Even back in the '60s, Morrison's film (read video) for the Doors' single "The Unknown Soldier" was utterly revolutionary. It told a story, with

Jim starring as a Christ-like figure executed by the other Doors members, no less. And it intercut surreal blood-and-roses religious imagery with harsh TV news realities, creating a visual Greek chorus to the action. (R.E.M.'s current video of "Losing My Religion," for all its brilliance, is no more arcane.)

Oliver Stone's new bio-pic "The Doors"—really a two-hour-long rock video—shows what the Doors might be doing visually if they were still intact: Their videos might well look like Stone's movie.

Largely due to their intrinsic cinematic qualities, the Doors' image and music are still as vital now as they were the day "Light My Fire" went to No. 1.

"My eyes have seen you," Jim sang, "Free from disguise, gazing on a city under television skies." He subtitles his first published book of poetry, "Notes On Vision." He had the vision to *become* the vision. Unfortunately, Jim Morrison's life was his first and only video.

It is of little consolation that the flame that burns twice as bright burns half as long.

CAMERAS INSIDE THE COFFIN: JIM MORRISON'S CHALLENGE TO THE HEGEMONY OF VISION
JOHN ROCCO

He sought exposure and lived the horror of trying to assemble a myth before a
billion dull dry ruthless eyes.
—JIM MORRISON[1]

The spectator feels at home nowhere, for the spectacle is everywhere.
—GUY DEBORD, The Society of the Spectacle

After taking off most of her clothes, the dancer sits down on top of the TV she has been gyrating on; the marching Nazi storm troopers on the screen appear to be emerging from between her legs: the birth of the fascist eye. The film then cuts to the backside of a woman and then to Jim Morrison taking a hit from a huge joint (a California joint, not a New York one that "you can pick your teeth with"). Morrison winks at the camera and then one of the great unseen films ends.[2] The film is *Triumph of the Will* spliced into *Deep Throat* with Nietzsche as editor and Rimbaud as screenwriter ("the poet makes himself a *visionary* through a long, a prodigious and rational disordering of *all* the senses" [xxx]). Casting by Artaud. Costumes by Baudelaire. Choreography by Norman O. Brown. Visions by Blake. Produced by the Mad Ones from Kerouac. It is a famous film and it does not exist. Like the elaborate Elizabethan masques, this is a one night show: after the performance the scenes are torn down and the drunk spectators join in the dancing while everyone tries to forget about the problems with keeping Ireland under control. It was Jim Morrison's student film at UCLA. He got a "D" for it. It was lost somewhere in the UCLA film archives. Morrison called it "less a film than an essay on film" (Riordan 65) and "a film that was questioning the film process itself" (Hopkins 51–52). The big wink at the end of this film/essay was the beginning of a long involvement in film throughout Morrison's career as rock star and poet. The wink, the closing of the eye, is emblematic of Morrison's interest in challenging what he called in a poem "injurious vision" (17). It was a challenge he would make throughout his work, throughout his words.

At UCLA Morrison was drawn to the more experimental theories about film and to avant-garde film makers like Andy Warhol and Jean-Luc Godard. (Francis Ford Coppola was a student in the film department at the same time; years later he would inject "The End" into Conrad's vision of the horrors of colonialism: the Unknown Soldier sent to Vietnam to assassinate Kurtz.) Morrison took a very unacademic approach to studying film: "The good thing about film is that there are no experts. There's no authority on film. Any one person can assimilate and contain the whole history of film in himself" (Hopkins 66). And he displayed his assimilation in the notes he kept throughout film school that would later be published as *The Lords: Notes on Vision*. He described the book as "a thesis on film esthetics" (Hopkins 57). The book is made up of poem/ aphorisms—a style he probably picked up from Nietzsche—which describe vision and film in terms ranging from the camera being an "all-seeing God" (17) to the voyeur as "masturbator" with the "mirror his badge" (41). (Shades of Jacques Lacan: "The *mirror stage* is a drama whose internal thrust is precipitated from insufficiency to anticipation . . . and . . . to the assumption of the armour of an alienating identity" [4].) The poems run through the history of cinema by examining its origins, its apparatus—"Muybridge derived his animal subjects from the/ Philadelphia Zoological Garden" (49)—and its contemporary significance—"[Oswald] escaped into a movie house" (19). Throughout the short book and pervading the concentrated poems is a sense of an overwhelming power controlling our perception, thoughts, and actions: "From the air we trapped gods" (33). The Lords are the rulers of vision and thought and, strangely enough, they often turn out to be ourselves sitting before a screen as "quiet vampires" (51) viewing the "spurious eternity" (53) of film. It was the dark side of film—"Cameras/inside the coffin" (15)—which fascinated Morrison: he called it a "religion of possession" (27). He gave himself over to the dark possession of film in order to use it to challenge the rule of the Western Eye.

In a certain sense, Morrison took a big chunk of his film school experience with him when he joined the Doors: the keyboardist for the group was fellow film student Ray Manzarek, and the band hired two men who went to school with Morrison and Manzarek—Paul Ferrara and Frank Lisciandro—to follow the band with movie cameras. The first product of this peripatetic film crew was the award-winning *Feast of Friends,* a forty-minute compilation of concert footage and backstage scenes. Ferrara and Lisciandro were also instrumental figures in two films which encapsulate Morrison's film making career: the short film featuring the other members of the Doors for the song "The Unknown Soldier" and the later film *HWY.*

The film for "The Unknown Soldier" was premiered at the Fillmore East in March of 1968; it depicts the sacrificial death of Morrison: he is tied to a stake and shot. Blood pours from his mouth onto the flowers at his feet. The film was unofficially banned because of its inflammatory nature. *HWY* was made after the infamous Miami show so Morrison had plenty of time to write, direct, and star in it. *HWY* can be said to be a dark version of *On the Road:* a hitchhiker is picked up on a desolate road and he ends up killing the driver who stopped for him. The killer on the road takes up a later incarnation in "Riders on the Storm" and in *HWY* Morrison plays the killer he will sing about on the Doors' last album. The soundtrack from the scene in which the killer makes a phone call to confess his crime is included on *An American Prayer;* its eerie inclusion on this album of Morrison's poetry is an indication of the importance of film to Morrison's aesthetics. The remaining Doors constructed *An American Prayer* like a film, a film that plays off of Morrison's life and interests.

When Bruce Harris, the director of advertising for Elektra, once asked Morrison what music he liked to listen to, he replied: "You know the soundtrack to Fellini's '8 1/2'? I really like that" (11). As with many of Morrison's remarks, this answer sounds like a joke, but it actually points to an important part of his artistic interests. The Doors were a band that challenged modern popular music through a variety of experiments: experiments in musical structure, experiments in lyrics and ideas, experiments in stage performance. An acknowledged but little examined experiment was their challenge to accepted ways of seeing. Challenging how we see was one of Morrison's artistic obsessions and this shows up in his writing (the poem that opens *The Lords* is one sentence: "Look where we worship" [11]), his performances, and his work in film. In a formulation typical of Morrison's inflammatory descriptions—a formulation made early on for the first album release—he described his aims:

> I've always been attracted to ideas that were about revolt against authority—when you make your peace with authority you become an authority. I like ideas about breaking away or overthrowing established order—I am interested in anything about revolt, disorder, chaos, especially activity that seems to have no meaning. (Hopkins 107)

One of the "established" orders he focused upon "overthrowing" was the Western reliance upon vision, a reliance that equated seeing with truth and clarity with the just. This kind of hegemony of seeing resulted in some of the most entrenched Western ideals and goals: colonialism (Vietnam), racism, sexism, and militarism. When Morrison told us to "Look where we worship" he was asking us to examine how we see the world around us. This challenge to the eye has deep roots, strange influences, and links to artistic rebellion from Rimbaud to the Beats. This is the best part of the trip: from Nietzsche's horse to the May 1968 riots in Paris.

Those who have never had the experience of having to see at the same time that they also longed to transcend all seeing will scarcely be able to imagine how definitely and clearly these two processes coexist and are felt at the same time. . . . With the Apollinian art sphere [the Dionysian] shares the complete pleasure in mere appearances and in seeing, yet at the same time he negates his pleasure and finds a still higher satisfaction in the destruction of the visible world of mere appearance.
—*FRIEDRICH NIETZSCHE*, The Birth of Tragedy

Morrison planned a film at UCLA that he never made. It was to show the famous scene of Nietzsche coming upon a man beating a horse in the street. As the story goes, the philosopher threw his arms around the horse's neck and collapsed into the insanity that only ended with his death.

Morrison did retell this story in *Feast of Friends:* he bangs upon a piano and recites a poem he seems to make up on the spot called "An Improvised Ode to Friedrich Nietzsche." Nietzsche sees the whipped horse, falls into madness, and whoops like Daffy Duck. The image of the whipped horse comes from Nietzsche's favorite novelist, Dostoyevsky, and it pushed him over the edge; Morrison brought up the image to describe the edge in his proposed student film, in *Feasts of Friends,* in the death of the horses in "Horse Latitudes," in "The Soft Parade's" injunction to whip the horses' eyes, and his writing against the dominating power of the Western Eye.

Nietzsche was Morrison's favorite philosopher and he quoted from his works regularly in interviews. Morrison's favorite of the German philosopher's works was the first book he wrote, *The Birth of Tragedy* (1872). In this book on the origins of Greek theater, Nietzsche first described the struggle between the form-creating Apollonian artistic force versus the form-destroying Dionysian power. The emblematic art of the Apollonian is frozen sculpture, while the Dionysian revels in chaotic, protean music. (Nietzsche in *Beyond Good and Evil:* "In music the passions enjoy themselves" [84].) Morrison identified with the Dionysian and he made it an aim to attack the frozen forms of the Apollonian imagination. Morrison took the Dionysian as a personal and artistic credo; Morrison on a plane to Robby Krieger: "[T]here are these Apollonian people . . . like, very formal, rational dreamers. And there's the Dionysian thing . . . the insanity trip way inside. . . . You're an Apollonian up there with your guitar . . . all neat and thought out . . . you should get into the Dionysian thing" (Riordan 185). Morrison followed the thing all the way to the final days in Paris.

As the above quote on seeing from *The Birth of Tragedy* indicates, the Dionysian can appreciate the world of solid appearances, but the other side of vision calls. Music cannot be seen, it can only be felt. The complete reliance on vision of the Apollonian is the classic force behind Western ideas about truth since the ancient Greeks. It was the Dionysian force that challenged it and it was Nietzsche who in the nineteenth century brought it to the surface. This is the reason why Nietzsche is such a formidable influence on poststructuralist thinkers like Jacques Derrida and Michel Foucault.[3] Nietzsche—along with the French philosopher Henri Bergson—can be said to be the first modern thinker to challenge what philosophers concerned with the power of sight call ocularcentrism. Ocularcentrism is structured around a powerful metaphor that has held sway over thinking about vision since Plato: seeing equals truth. (Deleuze on Nietzsche's critique of truth: "But there is no truth that, before being a truth, is not the bringing into effect of a sense or the realisation of a value" [104].) It was this metaphor that Morrison challenged in his poetry and music.

The whole life of those societies in which modern conditions of production prevail presents itself as an immense accumulation of spectacles. All that once was directly lived has become mere representation.
—GUY DEBORD, The Society of the Spectacle

1968: the world was on fire. Robert Kennedy and Martin Luther King Jr. are assassinated. The Democratic convention in Chicago is the scene of the largest police riot in American history. Soviet tanks roll into Prague and roll over the experiment of "Marxism with a human face." In Vietnam the year begins with the Tet offensive and ends with 540,000 American troops stationed there. In November, Richard Nixon is elected president. Two days after Nixon wins office, Morrison is reported to scream at a concert in Phoenix: "We are not going to stand for four more years of shit" (Riordan 274). Throughout the show Morrison is called "unbelievably provocative and obscene" and criminal charges are filed against him (Riordan 274). The charges are later dropped.

In Paris students and workers decide that they do not want to face any more years of shit. Led by a charismatic student named Daniel Cohn-Bendit—"Red Dany" was later expelled from France—a handful of students at the University of Nanterre begin a revolt against their society that spreads throughout the university system of the entire country. Their rebellion against everything they have ever known is so intense and so provocative that it quickly spreads to the working people of France. The students seize all of the schools and spend ten days fighting with police in the streets. Barricades, the likes of which have not been seen since the Paris Commune of 1871, rise in the streets. The revolt spreads throughout the work places of France and soon ten million French workers are on strike. France is paralyzed: no mail, no electricity, no banks, no stores. Government is dead and the people are alive. Words are born: all over Paris graffiti is written:

POWER TO THE IMAGINATION.

CONSUMER SOCIETY MUST DIE A VIOLENT DEATH. ALIENATED SOCIETY MUST DIE A VIOLENT DEATH. WE WANT A NEW AND ORIGINAL WORLD. WE REJECT A

WORLD WHERE SECURITY AGAINST STARVATION IS BOUGHT FOR THE RISK OF
DEATH BY BOREDOM.

I TAKE MY DESIRES FOR REALITIES BECAUSE I BELIEVE IN THE REALITY OF MY
DESIRES.

IT IS FORBIDDEN TO FORBID.

DON'T CHANGE EMPLOYERS; CHANGE THE EMPLOYMENT OF LIFE.

NEVER WORK![4]

Back to the past: this new world did not last. But it did have a pro-
found influence on French thought; Sartre's reaction to the world on fire
is an important example:

> Then May, 1968, happened, and I understood that what the young were
> putting into question was not just capitalism, imperialism, the system,
> etc., but those of us who pretended to be against all that as well. We can
> say that from 1940 to 1968 I was a left-wing intellectual and from 1968
> on I became an intellectual leftist. The difference is one of action. (qtd. in
> Poster 397)

A part of this "action" was a group of artists and thinkers who called
themselves the Situationalist International. The aim of the SI was, in the
words of Greil Marcus, to declare "culture . . . a walking corpse, politics a sideshow, philosophy a list of shibboleths, economics a hoax,
[and] art worthy only of pillage" (354). Guy Debord was their leader
and his 1967 *The Society of the Spectacle* defined their aim: the overthrow of a world controlled, motivated, and perpetuated through the
power of the spectacle. The modern world is seen as an endless parade
of visual constructions defining, channeling, and limiting our experience: advertisements, TV, politics, sports, window displays, museums.
The arcades that fascinated Walter Benjamin turned into electric mau-
soleums. The spectacle is everywhere and always open; Debord: "The
spectacle is a permanent opium war waged to make it impossible to dis-
tinguish goods from commodities, or true satisfaction from a survival
that increases according to its own logic" (30). May '68 was a reaction
against the "permanent opium war" and the spectacle was put to sleep
with the wine of rebellion.

But before May '68, and before the culture went on a drunk, Guy Debord made a film that challenged the smaller opium battle of movies. In 1952, *Hurlements en faveur de Sade* (*Howls for de Sade*) was premiered; it created a great deal of controversy because it lacked the essential quality of all film: images. The film just features two colors, white and black, and voices speaking as the colors alternate. The voices read passages from different texts: Joyce, the French Civil Code, dialogue from *Rio Grande.*[5] *Hurlements* is an attack upon the conventions of film based upon what Debord called *détournement,* or the overturning of cultural forms: "*Détournement* . . . is the fluid language of anti-ideology. It occurs with a type of communication aware of its inability to enshrine any inherent and definitive certainty" (146). Debord questioned the "certainty" of film and attempted to turn it on itself. In 1969 an American rock star attempted to turn the spectacle of himself on himself.

> *Our society is one not of spectacle, but of surveillance. . . . We are neither in the amphitheater, nor on the stage, but in the panoptic machine, invested by its effects of power, which we bring to ourselves since we are part of its mechanism.*
> —MICHEL FOUCAULT, Discipline and Punish: The Birth of the Prison

In Miami in 1969 Jim Morrison was on stage and he was drunk. The other Doors behind him tried to get him to sing by playing the music that usually moved him, usually provoked the words into life. The band tried to get him to sing the songs the crowd came to hear, but Jim Morrison did not want to hear the songs. He wanted to hear something else and he let the crowd know it:

> Hey, listen. . . . I used to think the whole thing was a big joke. I thought it was somethin' to laugh about, and then the last couple of nights I met some people who were doin' somethin'. They're trying to change the world and I wanna get on the trip. I wanna change the world. (Riordan 297)

The "people" Morrison referred to were the Living Theatre, the experimental theater troupe who traveled the world performing plays aimed at ending the world. The Living Theatre took Antonin Artaud's vision of a new theater as one of their starting points; they aimed at, in Artaud's words, theater "which . . . recounts the extraordinary, stages natural conflicts, natural and subtle forces, and presents itself first of all as an exceptional power of redirection. A theater that induces trance" (83).

In the days before the Miami show, Morrison attended every show the Living Theatre performed at USC. The shows included an original version of *Frankenstein,* Brecht's version of *Antigone* (Brecht on his *Antigone:* "And it is high time for a theatre for inquisitive people" [209]), and the now famous *Paradise Now.* If Milton's *Paradise Lost* is an explanation of the ways of God to man, then *Paradise Now* is an explanation of how the world controls and imprisons man. A large section of the "play" consists of the actors mingling with the audience and shouting their complaints about a world of chains: "I am not allowed to travel without a passport." "I don't know how to stop wars!" "You can't live if you don't have money!" "I'm not allowed to smoke marijuana!" "We cannot act naturally toward one another!" "*I am not allowed to take my clothes off!*" (Hopkins 222–223). The last complaint signaled the last action of the play: the actors began to strip.

Whether or not Morrison whipped it out that night in Miami will never be known for sure. Morrison's critique of vision takes on a literal form: no one seemed to have seen if he exposed himself or not; Ray Manzarek: "I don't know *what* he did. I was right there and I didn't see a thing" (Riordan 299). But what is for certain is that Miami was the beginning of the end for the band because in one show (or no-show) Morrison succeeded in completely obliterating his rock God image. All the crowd wanted was rock God stage antics and he gave it to them; he gave them the spectacle they wanted. He turned his image on its head; Debord: "The device of *Détourment* restores all . . . subversive qualities to past critical judgments that have congealed into respectable truths" (145).

But this shattering of the spectacle of his stardom had its price. In the above epigraph, Michel Foucault seems to directly reply to Debord's analysis of the ocular power behind modern culture: "Our society is one not of spectacle, but of surveillance" (217). The "panoptic machine" Foucault refers to comes from Jeremy Bentham's nineteenth-century conception of an all-seeing machine that would be used in prisons to "induce in the inmate a state of conscious and permanent visibility that assures the automatic functioning of power" (201). Foucault believed that modern society was controlled by this force, this power of the always visible. Morrison felt this kind of omnipresent surveillance ever since he became the first rock musician to be arrested *on stage* (New Haven, Dec. 9, 1967: the spectacle meets the panopticon). The FBI kept a file on him and they watched.

Morrison knew that the power of the eye could not be as cleanly defined as Debord (the spectacle) and Foucault (the panopticon) define it. Throughout his work Morrison attempted to describe the ambiguous, pervasive, and protean power of vision over cultural forms and practices. In one poem in *The Lords* he points to the two forms of power vision takes in film that is reminiscent of the ocular worlds of Debord and Foucault:

Cinema has evolved in two paths.

One is spectacle. Like the Phantasmagoria, its
goal is the creation of a total substitute
sensory world.

The other is peep show, which claims for its
realm both the erotic and the untampered obser-
vance of real life, and imitates the keyhole or
voyeur's window without need of color, noise,
grandeur. (65)

In a strange haunting, these words would come to describe the world Morrison found himself in in 1969: he was the spectacle inside the panoptic machine. He tried to break through it with a Nietzschean insight describing the hegemony of sight: "Ask anyone what sense he would preserve above all others. Most would say sight, forfeiting a million eyes in a body for two in the skull. Blind, we could live and possibly discover wisdom. Without touch, we would turn into hunks of wood" (Riordan 273–274). He attempted what Nietzsche described as "the destruction of the visible world of mere appearance," but the United States of the Panopticon had him in its sights. The Furies of vision chased him all the way to Paris.

Like Joyce, Morrison sought wisdom in exile (Stephen Dedalus in the diary entries which end *A Portrait of the Artist as a Young Man*: "I desire to press in my arms the loveliness which has not yet come into the world" [251]). But the rock star got to the City of Light a year too late: the ghost of Baudelaire was no longer erecting barricades. The night before he died, Morrison saw his last movie: the noir western *The Pursued* starring Robert Mitchum. A strange sign: the poet pursued by the Furies of the visual world sitting in a movie theater the night before the end. This is the end. All we have left of him are the poems, the music, and the movies. The rest is silence.

1. Quoted in James Riordan and Jerry Prochnicky, *Break On Through: The Life and Death of Jim Morrison*, p. 273. Morrison's quotes from biographies will be parenthetically cited throughout the text: (Riordan + page) for James Riordan and Jerry Prochnicky, *Break On Through*; and (Hopkins + page) for Jerry Hopkins and Danny Sugerman, *No One Here Gets Out Alive*.

2. But this is only one description of the lost movie: it comes from James Riordan and Jerry Prochnicky's *Break On Through* (p. 65). Jerry Hopkins and Danny Sugerman give a slightly different version in *No One Here Gets Out Alive* (pp. 51–52). Oliver Stone gives yet another version of the student film near the beginning of *The Doors* (1991).

3. See Martin Jay, *Downcast Eyes: The Denigration of Vision in Modern French Thought* (Berkeley and London: University of California Press, 1993), pp. 188–192, for a description of Nietzsche's challenge to ocularcentrism and its concomitant influence on French poststructuralist thought.

4. All graffiti translated by Mark Poster in *Existential Marxism in Postwar France*, pp. 382–383.

5. This description of *Hurlements en faveur de Sade* comes from Greil Marcus's *Lipstick Traces*, pp. 331–334. In a gesture of *détournment*, Debord removed all of his films from circulation after the murder of a friend was not adequately covered by the press. Like Morrison's student film, *Hurlements* is one of the great unseen films.

Works Cited

Brecht, Bertolt, "Masterful Treatment of a Model" in *Brecht On Theatre*. Trans. John Willett. New York: Hill and Wang, 1964.

Artaud, Antonin. "No More Masterpieces" in *The Theater and Its Double*. Trans. Mary Caroline Richards. New York: Grove Weidenfeld, 1958.

Debord, Guy. *The Society of the Spectacle*. Trans. Donald Nicholson-Smith. New York: Zone Books, 1994.

Deleuze, Gilles. *Nietzsche and Philosophy*. Trans. Hugh Tomlinson. New York: Columbia University Press, 1983.

Foucault, Michel. *Discipline and Punish: The Birth of the Prison*. Trans. Alan Sheridan. New York: Vintage Books, 1979.

Harris, Bruce. "Film Sensibility Set the Doors Apart." *Billboard,* Vol. 103, No. 16 (April 20, 1991): 11.

Hopkins, Jerry and Danny Sugarman. *No One Here Gets Out Alive.* New York: Warner Books, 1980.

Joyce, James. *A Portrait of the Artist as a Young Man.* New York and London: Penguin Books, 1985.

Lacan, Jacques. *Écrits: A Selection.* Trans. Alan Sheridan. New York: W. W. Norton and Co., 1977.

Marcus, Greil. *Lipstick Traces: A Secret History of the Twentieth Century.* Cambridge, Mass.: Harvard University Press, 1989.

Morrison, Jim. *The Lords and The New Creatures.* New York: Simon and Schuster, 1987.

Nietzsche, Friedrich. *Beyond Good and Evil.* Trans. Walter Kaufmann. New York: Vintage Books, 1966.

———. *The Birth of Tragedy and The Case of Wagner.* Trans. Walter Kaufmann. New York: Vintage Books, 1967.

Poster, Mark. *Existential Marxism in Postwar France: From Sartre to Althusser.* Princeton: Princeton University Press, 1975.

Rimbaud, Arthur. "Letter to Paul Demeny" in *Illuminations and Other Prose Poems.* Trans. Louise Varèse. New York: New Directions, 1957.

Riordan, James and Jerry Prochnicky. *Break On Through: The Life and Death of Jim Morrison.* New York: William Morrow, 1991.

EVENING PRAYER
ARTHUR RIMBAUD

I live seated, like an angel in the hands of a barber,
In my fist a strongly fluted mug,
My stomach and neck curved, a Gambier pipe
In my teeth, under the air swollen with impalpable veils of smoke.

Like the warm excrement of an old pigeonhouse,
A thousand dreams gently burn inside me:
And at moments my sad heart is like sap-wood
Which the young dark gold of its sweating covers with blood.

Then, when I have carefully swallowed my dreams,
I turn, having drunk thirty or forty mugs,
And collect myself, to relieve the bitter need:

Sweetly as the Lord of the cedar and of hyssops,
I piss toward the dark skies, very high and very far,
With the consent of the large heliotropes.

WILD CHILD: JIM MORRISON'S POETIC JOURNEYS
TONY MAGISTRALE

Two decades after his death by heart attack in 1971, Jim Morrison and the Doors are at the height of their popularity. Several biographies have been published with Morrison as their subject, there is a book collection of contemporary reviews all written during the band's tours in the late 1960s and early 1970s, at least two pictorial histories of the group, and many of America's finest newspapers and popular journals—from *The Village Voice* and *The New York Times* to *Rolling Stone*—have recently published long essays analyzing the band's continued prominence. These books and articles, along with the release of Oliver Stone's film, *The Doors,* can be seen as barometers to the nation's, and the world's, lingering fascination with the 1960's reputed Prince of Darkness.

In spite of the recent proliferation of critical attention allotted to the Doors and even the success of Oliver Stone's film, the lyrical verse of Jim Morrison—the Doors' real contribution to rock history—remains as cryptic and unappreciated as when it first appeared over twenty years ago. What was Morrison trying to convey in lyrics which were at once death-haunted and celebratory, apocalyptic and transcendent? In their 1980 biography of Morrison, *No One Here Gets Out Alive,* which certainly helped to launch the current Doors' revival, Hopkins and Sugerman refer to their subject's attraction to the symbolist poetry of Arthur Rimbaud and frequently cite the lyrics to many of Morrison's songs. But his biographers, and their glaring omission typifies the vast body of criticism written about the Doors in the past two decades, fail to analyze Morrison's contribution as a poet; the larger-than-life details of his meteoric career appear to overwhelm any attempt at reading his language as art. And this is particularly unfortunate in Morrison's case, as the need to separate commercial myth from poetic legacy is most acute. As his surviving colleague and friend Ray Manzarek remarked in 1981, "Jim was hounded by a lot of yellow journalism. . . . He was tired of being The Lizard King. Jim Morrison was a poet, an artist—he didn't want to be the King of Orgasmic Rock, The King of Acid Rock, The

Lizard King. He felt all those titles were demeaning to what the Doors were trying to do" (Doe and Tobler 65).

Manzarek thus raises one more reason, and it remains the most persuasive of all, to keep open the critical debate on Mr. Morrison and the Doors. Their artistry—the poetry and song lyrics, for the two should be viewed as inseparable—transcends the simple and reductive categories often applied to popular music, particularly rock. Most of the songs recorded by the Doors were originally conceived as poems; as the rock band's music grew in popularity and the demand increased for more material, Morrison's poetry notebooks became the wellspring for many lyrics. These notebooks supplied the Doors with complete compositions as well as poetic fragments from longer works which were then adapted into songs such as "Not to Touch the Earth."

Morrison is as much a product of the Romantic poetic vein as William Blake, Walt Whitman, Edgar Allan Poe, Emily Dickinson and the French Symbolists were a century before him. Indeed, Morrison shares much in common with his poetic predecessors—most similarly, he remained obsessed with "breaking through to the other side," to discover what possible realms existed beyond the immediate and the material. For all of them, poetry is a form of, or a means to, illumination, and the poet is a seer or visionary first of all. His best work reveals Morrison as a poet of revelation, providing insights to the kind of truth only the imagination can glimpse. The act of writing, like life itself, is an exploration of unknown limits, of Immortality and the Possible, of challenging finite barriers against the realm of the infinite.

The Scream of the Butterfly: Morrison's Poetics

Morrison's life was never orchestrated in half measures: he was capable of producing startlingly brilliant poetic images one moment only to lapse into complete obscurity the next. His talents were, like his personality, protean and spontaneous—but also undisciplined. Critic Nick Tosches believes that "The Doors' most ambitious work was often their worst. Trying to make of rock 'n' roll something it could never, should never, be, Morrison often seemed a pompous fool rather than the intrepid seer he fancied himself. With dark messianic urgency, in both his songs and his verse, he delivered images and ideas that sometimes were trite unto embarrassment" (Tosches 10).

These limitations notwithstanding, Morrison's most provocative lyrics and poems manage to defy quick dismissal. Although not always successful in their adaptations, he possessed wide-ranging poetic skills: producing ballads, lyric love songs, surreal juxtapositions of striking images, philosophical verse, aggressive political commentary and traditional rhythm and blues. There is also a subtlety to Morrison's best lyrical verse that undercuts our easy identification with his public persona as obnoxious rock star and decadent hedonist.

Above all poetic considerations, however, Morrison was interested in creating a new mythology appropriate to an age no longer heroic and out of touch with the natural world. "Our society places a supreme value on control, on hiding what you feel," Morrison stated in 1969. "It mocks primitive culture and prides itself on the suppression of natural instincts and impulses" (Doe and Tobler 80). Much has already been written regarding Morrison's Dionysian inclinations, his dark fascination with chaos and apocalypse. While these tendencies must never be undervalued in Morrison's psyche, the search for a new order, for some system of personal faith, more pagan than it ever was Christian, is also present in his writing: "Let's reinvent the gods, all the myths/of the ages/Celebrate symbols from deep elder forests" (Morrison 3). Morrison's interest in, and celebration of, the desert and its reptilian life—from his omnipresent leather pants to the nickname "Lizard King"—is further echoed in those poems with pronounced American Indian themes. Various examinations of death are often affiliated with these themes; it remains a mysterious perimeter in Morrison's poems and songs, but never a final one. Death is merely a door separating states of being, ultimately leading to something else, to another form of creation. His personality and psychic obsessions joined forces with his reading of Nietzsche and existentialism to make the experience of living a constant awareness of the coming of death and the imaginative realization of dying as the climactic experience of living. Morrison clearly embodies the Romantic infatuation with death as a means for escaping the earth. Perhaps this is one reason why so much of his poetry remains vague and elusive; the concrete realities of life bored him, which in turn led to his increasing preoccupation with worlds beyond the grave. . . .

As a lizard is forever undergoing change in shedding its skins and altering its protective coloration, Morrison used poetry (and drugs) to explore the shape his new life would take; he yearned to break the wall that separated our empirical world from the transformative energies of others. This helps to explain the many journeys which occur throughout his lyrics and poems. As in the writings of Carlos Castaneda, Morrison's voyages are always less geographical than psychological; his Spanish caravans, crystal ships, moonlight drives and recollected ghosts of "Indian scattered on dawn's highway bleeding" are analogs for the soul's journey inward—to landscapes of dream and imagination.

One of Morrison's most evocative lyrical poems, "Moonlight Drive," the first song recorded by the Doors, serves as a case in point. On the surface, the poem appears to be a simple invitation to share a romantic moonlight rendezvous. But a more careful reading enlarges its scope to suggest implications beyond the immediate sexual and sensory realm. In the initial stanza, the poet encourages his lover to swim with him "to the moon/Let's climb thru the tide" in an effort to "penetrate" a visionary world "That the city sleeps to hide." As he argues in many of his other poems, the "sleeping city" is a general metaphor for passive acceptance of the status quo, an indictment of the masses who lack both the interest and inclination to explore "the waiting worlds/That lap against our side."

No mere sentimental love song, the romantic and sexual connotations inherent in the call to "Park beside the ocean/On our moonlight drive," while never abandoned, are at least complicated by the invitation to swim out through layers of ocean, which comes to symbolize the poet's quest for visionary experience: "Let's swim out tonight, love/It's our turn to try." As the poem unfolds, its meaning expands to embrace other themes as well: intellectual and spiritual development; the superiority of the unknown over the known; the indulgence of imagination as the key to growth; and the significance of risk-taking over passive resignation, since only through action conceived in faith and spirited by the imagination can truth be apprehended and the soul made to expand. These ideas are found throughout Morrison's poetic canon, and they revolved around the poet's incessant call for self-transcendence. Like the voice of the poet in Walt Whitman's "Out of the Cradle, Endlessly Rocking," Morrison comes to realize that universal messages of life and death are encoded within the "wet forests" of the ocean. In "Penetrating the evening," Morrison and his anonymous lover share Whitman's understanding that sex and death are inextricably related to the rhythms of the sea—as the final lines of "Moonlight Drive" suggest: "Baby gonna drown tonight. . . ." Thus, what began as a sweet incantation to innocent romance, concludes with the intimation that while the symbolic truths of the ocean—and life itself—may be shrouded in mystery, they are still worth pursuing. Indeed, the poem further underscores the ultimate quest toward spiritual transcendence in Morrison's subtle undercutting of sexual oneness, cautioning his intended audience that the visionary journey is occasioned by the individual alone;

the experience can not be mediated even by a supportive lover: "You reach your hand to hold me/but I can't be your guide."

Morrison's lyric verse centers primarily upon transformation of spirit, his passionate acceptance of the superiority of new truths to old. In a 1967 interview, he outlined this process in mythic terms reminiscent of Joseph Campbell:

> Our work, our performing, is a striving for metamorphosis. It's like a purification ritual in the alchemical sense. First you have to have the period of disorder, chaos, returning to a primeval disaster region. Out of that you purify the elements and find a new seed of life, which transforms all life and all matter and the personality until finally, hopefully, you emerge and marry all those dualisms and opposites. Then you're not talking about evil and good anymore but something unified and pure. (Hopkins and Sugerman 143)

In this symbolic context, "The End," perhaps his most controversial achievement, becomes more than the "Oedipal lament" it has long been characterized. Better than three-fourths of the poem is *not* concerned with the violation of the incest taboo, but, rather, with something more analogous to Morrison's "striving for metamorphosis." Although Morrison implies that "a Roman wilderness of pain" bordering on insanity or perhaps even death itself is associated with an unresolved Oedipal urge, he also insists that all transgressions against patriarchal decrees ("The west is the best/Get here and we'll do the rest.") are essentially acts of personal rebellion. As he remarked in 1969, employing language that is especially relevant when applied to "The End" and its assault upon repressive states of being, "The most loving parents and relatives commit murder with smiles on their faces. They force us to destroy the person we really are: a subtle kind of murder" (Doe and Tobler 10). Consequently, the song is not only about "The end,/of everything that stands," but also about the beginning of a new consciousness born out of existential defiance: "Can you picture what will be,/so limitless and free." Morrison's invitations to "Ride the snake" and "meet me at the back of the blue bus" are suggestive once more of the visionary exploration cited in "Moonlight Drive": the willingness to "take a chance" and journey beyond the delusive safety of accepted dogma. In Morrison's poetry and song, this is only possible once the individual has repudiated all traditional limits—rejecting societal as well as personal constraints.

The value of using language in an exciting, imaginative manner is found throughout Jim Morrison's best work; even his love songs, long a staple element of rock music, reflect the urge to complicate and deepen the genre's overworked themes of sexual conquest and romantic separation. An early (1966) version of "The End," for example, was "no more than a nicely written song about faded love" (Hopkins and Sugerman 81). In subsequent drafts, however, the song evolved to the point where its initial premise was forced to accommodate more serious and disturbing speculations—pushing its subject matter beyond the merely personal and toward the archetypal.

"L.A. Woman," written late in Morrison's career, seeks to describe Los Angeles through feminine imagery, encouraging the listener to think of the city in a context that is uniquely human. The annual fall fires of vegetation growing on the sides of the hills surrounding the city remind the poet of a woman's auburn hair. And since the speaker is presumably a heterosexual man, the city as woman intensifies his own mixed feelings of excitement and hesitancy which remain consistent throughout the song. Indeed, Morrison makes explicit connections between the sexual aspects of urban life and women; and he feels a simultaneous attraction to, and a repulsion from, the feminine qualities of the city he describes: "Drivin' down your freeways. . . ." While Morrison remains intrigued with the glitter and urban pulse that characterizes Los Angeles, symbolized by the "little girls in their Hollywood bungalows," he also senses that under the surface of the city's open sexuality and opulence is a desolation that is revealed to anyone who comes into close enough contact with it—the poet included: "Motel money murder madness. . . ."

Morrison's ambivalence toward Los Angeles is, as "L.A. Woman" implies, really a symbolic indication of his ambivalence toward women in general. He wrote about women often and immortalized several in songs such as "Twentieth Century Fox," "Love Street," "Touch Me," "Hello, I Love You," "Wintertime Love" and "My Wild Love." But Morrison's attitude toward women, both poetically and personally, was often less than laudable. Hopkins and Sugerman detail the abuse Morrison directed at his many female groupies, frequently extending his mistreatment to include his "cosmic mate," Pamela Courson. As is often the case in the poems of Poe and Baudelaire, as well as many other Romantic writers, in Morrison's lyrics and verse women are less flesh and blood human beings than sexual and poetic inspirations—necessary diversions who provide release from the frustrations and restrictions of "The screaming maggot/group-grope called life" (Morrison 142). Although he is usually aligned with the "Bad Boy" school of sexist rockers, Morrison's lyrics never approximate the level of blatant misogyny so readily apparent in, for example, the Rolling Stones or many of the male rock groups who are heirs to the Doors. His romantic scenarios most often feature a male who offers or invites—with the option to be accepted or rebuffed—rather than commands, a woman to participate in some kind of sexual exploration. As one of Morrison's tenderest love lyrics, "The Crystal Ship," illustrates . . . Morrison needed women, just as he required a constant supply of alcohol and illegal drugs, primarily as another means for helping him enter into an idealized realm. Against the threatening chaos of the world, the women in Morrison's lyrics and poems are both inspiration and salvation; as evinced in "Moonlight Drive," the sexual bond is analogous to the visionary quest itself—one more avenue to transport the poet beyond this world and toward idyllic perfection.

Morrison would often turn to the love of a woman as a means for the soul's survival. Nowhere is this tendency better articulated than in the haunting poetry of "Riders on the Storm." Punctuated by the background sound of steady falling rain in the recorded version of the song, Morrison describes a world on the edge of an abyss. In sparse language which is uncharacteristic of Morrison's canon, the poem strikes a lonely existential lament over the human condition; we are all "riders on the storm," isolated and helpless from the moment of birth: "Into this world we're thrown. . . ."

The first stanza gives rise to the second, where a lone psychopath hitchhiking along a highway threatens the welfare of an unsuspecting family. Juxtaposed to the first stanza, the "killer on the road" continues to represent the stark absurdity of life—the Dionysian undercurrent that might at any point destroy everything we most cherish and nurture to survive. Capturing the true spirit of a Greek tragedy, even "long holidays" and children at play become potential victims to the sudden violence of a capricious fate: "Take a long holiday. . . ."

The third and final stanza is meant to counterpoint the inhospitable terrors raised in the first two. As the line "Riders on the storm" is repeated twice in the opening, the repetition of "Girl, you gotta love your man" now serves as a balancing refrain. For the poem concludes with the call for love as kind of light amidst encroaching darkness: "Take him by the hand. . . ." Reminiscent of Matthew Arnold's "Dover Beach," Morrison's poem clings to the stability of human affection in a volatile universe. The love of a woman remains the sole source of permanency and sustenance: "The world on you depends. . . ." Furthermore, in contrast to the killer's unsettled brain "squirmin' like a toad," woman's sweet reason and gentle touch will "make [men] understand" the importance of resisting panic or desolation; the constancy of love between a man and a woman, concludes Morrison, is a last sanctuary against the storm of madness raging in the world.

"Riders on the Storm" is emblematic of the Romantic dualism at the heart of Morrison's nature. The poet was pulled by the two opposing principles embodied in the lyrics: the enduring capacity for love's survival and the dark void represented by acts of random destruction. In the end, Morrison's personal demons drew him to the edge of the abyss and pushed him over into it. But until that point, a persistent faith in the transcendent powers of poetry and music helped to insulate him from despair.

We Want the World: Morrison's Politics

In a recent essay tracing Morrison's ascension to rock legend, Mikal Gilmore wonders why the musician continues to interest the modern rock audience, especially since today's youth is more conservative than Morrison's first followers in the 1960s. Gilmore concludes that Morrison's defiant hedonism strikes a sympathetic cord with contemporary listeners:

> The truth is, Jim Morrison is the ideal radical hero for a conservative era. Though he may have lived a life of defiance and rebellion, it was not defiance rooted in any clear ideology or political vision, unlike, for example, the brand of rebellion that John Lennon would come to aspire to. Morrison's defiance had deep personal sources—it derived from a childhood spent in a family with a militaristic and authoritarian disposition. (Gilmore 34)

Jim Morrison may be perceived as a radical hero for our times because his complete rejection of limits—personal as well as social—and his apocalyptic vision of the future correspond precisely to the psychological orientation Christopher Lasch and other social scientists have identified with contemporary narcissism. Morrison's poetics may not be fully comprehended by the vast number of Americans who listen to his songs. But his focus on the self combined with the naked, apolitical rejection of all authority and institutions that characterize his verse and lyrics certainly help to explain why Morrison's popularity has endured and his legend has transformed into myth.

At the same time, however, there is much in Morrison's work that gives rise to his role as a hero for a progressive age. While Gilmore may be right in his assertion that the poet's spirit of defiance and rebellion had its initial roots in "deep personal sources," Morrison's "political vision" was at least as acute as John Lennon's—in fact, more so. Embodying the rebellious social discontent of the 1960s, several of Morrison's poems and song lyrics allude to his generation's dissatisfaction with the values of American middle class life. Morrison never wavered in his condemnation of American capitalism and its steady insistence on conformity. The uninspired materialism he found in southern California, his own familial background as the first-born son of a U.S. admiral, coupled with the rich legacy of social activism Morrison discovered in the Romantic poets with whom he identified, created a tension that produced some of his most memorable work. In poetic diction as poignant as T.S. Eliot's in "The Love Song of J. Alfred Prufrock" or "The Hollow Men," Morrison's most compelling images are of a contemporary American waste land where, as he insists in "The Soft Parade," most of us lead lives devoid of meaning and authentic communication: "All our lives we sweat & save . . ." (Morrison 50).

In the late 1960s, as America's tragic involvement in Vietnam became impossible to ignore, Morrison produced his most political writing. His critical interpretation of the futility of that conflict is apparent in songs such as "The Unknown Soldier" and "Peace Frog" (a.k.a. "There's Blood in the Streets") and the long poem *An American Prayer:* "Do you know we are being led to/slaughters by placid admirals/& that fat slow generals are getting/obscene on young blood" (Morrison 3). But unlike Lennon, whose overtly political songs frequently descended into personal despair or political cynicism (e.g. "A Day in the Life" and "The Dream Is Over"), even Morrison's most politically confrontational work contained an element of resurrection; his lyrics reflect his belief that a new social order was not only possible, but imminent.

A popular stereotype of the Doors is that their music typifies the darkest, nihilistic impulses of the 1960s. David Dalton, for example, finds "the use of the Door's eerily crooned 'The End' on the soundtrack of *Apocalpyse Now,* so right, so timely, it seemed as if it had been written for the film" (Dalton 157). It is certainly true that Morrison is critical of the wasted energies he saw expended in Vietnam and in the maintenance of a rigid middle-class mentality at home. But the thrust of his invective is against our superficial selves, our social and conventional and conforming selves, which he fears will prevent our being true to the deeper self. In "Ship of Fools," the poet applies the medieval metaphor to contemporary America, mocking this country's complacent attitude toward its space "progress" by reminding us of some lingering business neglected at home: "People walkin' on the moon/Smog will get you pretty soon. . . ." Morrison's elusive ambiguities are fodder for our conflicts and doubts, for the constant complexities of feelings which constitute daily life in the modern world. But his social critique, while often searing in its approach to American institutions and their demand for conformity, did not conclude in pessimism or desperation. In the song "Five to One," Morrison acknowledges that while the "old" guard possesses "the guns," a new order—composed of "young and stronger" challengers with whom the speaker identifies—has "the numbers. . . ." Morrison believed in the powers of transformation, that change—personal as well as social—was always within our grasp if only we would awaken sufficiently to recognize and pursue it. "I offer images—I conjure memories of freedom," Morrison proclaimed in 1967. "But we can only open doors—we can't drag people through" (Dalton 28).

The lyrics to "When the Music's Over" suggest that Morrison was not only conscious of the need for collective political action—his emphasis on the violation which has occurred to "*our* fair sister"—but that he was likewise one of the first American musicians to elicit a radical response to environmental degradation: "What have they done to the earth? . . ." This is not the language of "self-regard that has become so identified with the Reagan-Bush era" (Gilmore 34). Instead, it is an angry protest against those very forces—militaristic and capitalistic—which continue to rape the earth and threaten its survival. Indeed, the next stanza in the song summons those who share the poet's concern over the endangered status of the planet. Morrison issues a general alarm: reject apathy ("We're gettin' tired of hangin' around") and repossess an environment that has been stolen and polluted by monied interests. Few songwriters or poets, John Lennon included, have ever posited a more emphatic or persuasive call for revolutionary action. . . .

Morrison was committed to the value of change in all of its manifestations; he viewed the Doors as a rock version of revolutionary theatre, a kind of incendiary device for igniting radical momentum. As Ray Manzarek summarized: "We [the Doors] wanted to change the world, make the world a better place to live in, and we were trying to do it. The fact that it wasn't happening—OK, a temporary setback, it was still going to happen" (Doe and Tobler 79). But Morrison clearly believed that the basis for any *lasting* political action had first to emerge from within the individual. Without first undergoing the journey to heightened consciousness, the very concept of a revolution would remain superficial, and true social change would not be sustained. The individual is at the center of Morrison's politics and poetics; the enlightened self carries the guidance of the godhead. Thus, like Emerson and Thoreau, two other famous American poets who also developed the interrelationship between spiritual expansion and political activism, Morrison's poetry and lyrics emphasize the importance of transcendence: from the progressive nucleus of the self, expansion outward toward other transformative states of being is infinite and natural. If people would only break out of the "jail/within a white free protestant/Maelstrom," we might then "invent Kingdoms of our own/grand purple thrones" (Morrison 7–8). While Morrison was never interested in providing a specific course of action for achieving this higher status of selfhood, or in defining the exact shape the Kingdom would take, he trusted implicitly in their existence and accessibility.

Dance on Fire . . . Until the End: Morrison's Legacy

The inability of critics to explain adequately the full range of Morrison's contributions to rock music is related to the elusive nature of his art. At his best, Morrison produced superb examples of Symbolist poetry; his song lyrics and poems juxtapose incongruous themes and present us with events and objects which bear little or no apparent relationship to one another. We appreciate "The End" or "The Soft Parade" element by element, symbol by symbol, and finally we complete these long song-poems for ourselves, through the inclusion of some component discovered within ourselves. This suggestive ambiguity represents the essence of the Symbolist movement, and in Morrison's case it is what most distinguishes his lyrics from the banality of rock music in general.

The Doors took their name from a line in William Blake's poem *The Marriage of Heaven and Hell*: "If the doors of perception were cleansed,/everything would appear to man as it is, infinite." The wellspring of their baptism could not have been more appropriate; more than any other group of musicians before or since, the Doors created a marriage of polarities: metaphysical and physical, historical and universal, secular and profane. They were both children of the 1960s in their lusts and hopes and precursors to the 1970s in reminding us continually of the tragic gap separating this world from a transcendent one. The Doors were the Beatles' hedonistic alter-egos; where the English band preached love's harmony and selflessness, the Doors shared an explicit interest in singing about a nation not at ease with itself, and individuals not at ease with one another. Morrison wished to unfetter his imagination, to test and validate its very boundaries and transmute all his personal experiences and emotions into art. If in doing so, he believed himself to be excused from obedience to accepted rules of behavior, Morrison was simply reaffirming the Romantic doctrine of the primacy of imagination: the myth of the divinely inspired shaman who, finally, refuses to submit to all authority lest he fail in the pursuit of fulfilling himself.

Works Cited

Dalton, David. *Mr. Mojo Risin': Jim Morrison, The Last Holy Fool*. New York: St. Martin's, 1991.

Doe, Andrew and John Tobler. *The Doors In Their Own Words*. New York: Putnam, 1991.

Gilmore, Mikal. "The Legacy of Jim Morrison and the Doors." *Rolling Stone* 4 April 1991:31–4.

Hopkins, Jerry and Danny Sugarman. *No One Here Gets Out Alive*. New York: Warner, 1980.

Morrison, James Douglas. *The American Night: The Writings of Jim Morrison, Volume 2*. New York: Villard, 1990.

Tosches, Nick. Foreword. *Mr. Mojo Risin': Jim Morrison, The Last Holy Fool*. By David Dalton. New York: St. Martin's, 1991.

CINEMA HAS EVOLVED IN TWO PATHS

JIM MORRISON

Cinema has evolved in two paths.

One is spectacle. Like the Phantasmagoria, its
goal is the creation of a total substitute
sensory world.

The other is peep show, which claims for its
realm both the erotic and the untampered observ-
ance of real life, and imitates the keyhole or
voyeur's window without need of color, noise,
grandeur.

APOCALYPSE NOW!: JIM MORRISON'S VISION OF AMERICA

YASUE KUWAHARA

After twenty years since his mysterious death in Paris, Jim Morrison remains a popular culture hero not only among those who have lived the late 1960s, listening to his songs, but among younger generations who know the legendary rock'n'roll star only as images in books, on records and on videos. Morrison's continuous popularity can be explained by youthful rebellion which he epitomized and which, regardless of time periods, appeal to teenagers who rebel against authorities, e.g., the parents and schools that try to control their lives. Morrison formed a rock'n'roll group, the Doors, with Ray Manzarek in 1965, released the first album in 1967, and remained a regular on the hit chart, producing eight consecutive gold records before his death in 1971. Throughout his career, Morrison, who sang about the Oedipus complex and the devil without reservation, was rebellious, dramatic, controversial and demonic in his songs as well as on stage. Reflecting the time, his songs explicitly criticized the war, lamented the ongoing battle between protesters and the government, and offered rebellion as an alternative. When the group's popularity was reaching its peak, Fred Powledge said, "The Doors' music . . . is satanic, sensual, demented and full of acid when you first hear it, and it becomes even more so when you play it over and over again" (86). Powledge's remark was visually verified when Morrison, led by his interest in film and drama, enacted on stage the images of his songs rather than merely singing them (Kennealy 32–3). Often drunk on stage, Morrison feared nothing and thus left his name in the history of rock'n'roll as the first performer arrested on stage once and charged several times for inciting a rebellion. In short, Morrison lived the violent time as violently as few other rock'n'rollers would have dared.

While his emergence and subsequent rise to stardom are often considered with regards to American society of the late 1960s, the close association of Morrison's songs and American cultural traditions has been seldom discussed. Examination of his songs, poems and career reveals Morrison's frequent reference to Christianity as well as an important theme in American culture, i.e., the myth of the Promised Land, which suggests that Morrison rebelled not only against American society of the mid-twentieth century but against the fundamental cultural belief. The brief career of Jim Morrison with the Doors coincided with the period when America was swept by violence. Escalation of protest movements and the increased involvement in the Vietnam War through the late 1960s and the early 1970s threatened many Americans domestically as well as overseas and compelled them to reconsider their society and culture. A well-read, talented man, Morrison found in such a time a good opportunity to project his apocalyptic vision of America through rock'n'roll. This paper will first discuss Morrison's view of America in the late 1960s and then consider its relationship to American cultural traditions, especially the myth of the Promised Land.

The Myth of the Promised Land

The myth of the Promised Land—the idea that America is a special place which promises unlimited opportunities for anyone who wants to make his or her dream come true—is the oldest and most powerful cultural belief in America. As such, the myth of the Promised Land has been a primary force shaping the national character, has largely determined the course of American history and also has generated or influenced other myths, such as the myth of the West and the myth of rags-to-riches.

The origin of the myth of the Promised Land is found in Medieval Europe. Ever since Columbus' discovery of the new continent, many Europeans had believed that God had finally revealed a new heaven as He had prophesied in the Bible. This idea gave hope to a group of religiously persecuted people who, viewing themselves as the "chosen people" and thus following the example set in the Exodus, were to cross the Atlantic.

In America, the idea of a new heaven gave the Puritans a sense of mission; their errand into the wilderness was to establish the City upon a Hill. This idea also began to be used by other groups in the New World. Whatever the reasons for their emigration, the idea of America as a new heaven was appealing and convenient for those who severed their ties with the Old World. At first strictly interpreted in religious terms, the mission idea was gradually secularized and consequently survived the decline of the Puritans. It was the revolutionary Whigs who elevated the idea to the national myth of the Promised Land. Their justification of their act against the mother country was based on the promise of liberty, equality and democracy in the New World, which was later declared in the Constitution.

After independence was attained, the myth became the basis of Manifest Destiny and of the myth of the West, which kept inspiring the westward movement of pioneers. Meanwhile, in the already developed eastern states, the myth, through its emphasis on progress and the future, contributed to the development of capitalism. Furthermore, the myth was working overseas as well, attracting those who suffered economic and political hardships to the New World. To these people, the promise of the myth was not limited to freedom, equality and democracy; independence, mobility, property, a higher standard of living, wealth, education and whatever they desired were waiting for them in America. Nineteenth-century immigrants added the image of the land of opportunities to the myth of the Promised Land, and this image was later most eloquently expressed by the rags-to-riches myth of industrial America (Bercovitch 20).

The myth, while promising unlimited opportunities, has also kept informing Americans of their mission as the defenders of democracy. In order to keep the promised land alive, they have to be willing to fight against hostile forces. Thus, the Civil War was fought to give slaves an equal share of the promise of America. The myth of the Promised Land provided theoretical and spiritual justification for the bloody fight within the country (Bercovitch 32). The myth also provided justification for the later wars: WWI and WWII, the Korean War, the Cold War and, finally, the Vietnam War. It was America's mission to save the oppressed and, if necessary, to bring them to the land of the free. Except for a few decades after 1924 when immigration was officially banned, America has kept open its door to immigrants in spite of the increase of domestic problems such as race relations and poverty which were the focus of protest movements during the 1960s.

My Eyes Have Seen You . . . Show Me Some More

Reflecting his interest in film, Morrison shows a great concern with sight in his songs as well as poems. He writes in his book of poetry, *The Lords and The New Creatures*, that "[t]he body exists for the sake of the eyes; it becomes a dry stalk to support these two soft insatiable jewels" (52). His eyes are the reason for his existence as well as the power which enables him to understand and to express things. For example, the characters of Morrison's songs often look at others' eyes which reflect their minds. In "Easy Ride," the character sees his girl's eyes, which reflect her beauty "like polished stone." The "wild child," a "savior of the human race," has "freedom in her eyes" and dances with the "Pirate Princes," "staring into the hollow idol's eyes." The importance of sight is also expressed in the following song in which Morrison expresses the fear of losing sight: "Can't see your face in my mind. . . ." Unable to see, Morrison feels the approach of the end of his relationship with the girl and of his life. This song also shows Morrison's idea that "seeing" is the function of the mind as well as of the eyes and, more importantly, that the mind creates an image of what is seen through the eyes. Morrison says that "I can't see you in my mind" because, when his (or her) love weakens, the girl standing in front of him looks different from his image. In short, the view he acquires through the eyes becomes in his mind a vision which reflects his own idea.

Morrison, moreover, tries with his penetrating eyes and mind to see what is not visible. In "Shaman's Blues," observing the brokenhearted character, Morrison says, "Look at him/Optical promise," because he thinks he can see the pain the character is feeling inside and enjoys seeing it. In "My Eyes Have Seen You," Morrison similarly says to the character, "Beaten inside/Show me some more." With his eyes, Morrison can make happen even what is forbidden; he writes in *The Lords and The New Creatures*: "You may enjoy life from afar. You may look at things but not taste them. You may caress the mother only with the eyes" (45). The eyes permit him to do whatever he wishes.

Future's Uncertain And The End Is Always Near . . . Let It Roll

Morrison's songs, which presented a vision of America based on what he saw, indicate that he wished to see America moving toward destruction and, at the same time, anticipated the coming of a new society. It is apocalyptic in a traditional sense because, although the word "apocalypse" tends to be used as a synonym for "disaster" today, its original meaning is "a revelation of spiritual realities in the future" (Zamora 2), which is supposed to come after the destruction of the present world. Describing the present and the future of America in his songs, Morrison, a self-appointed present-day apocalyptist, not only prophesies the destruction of current society but also replaces it with his own kingdom, thus reflecting a question about the myth of the Promised Land among Americans in the late 1960s.

Morrison's apocalyptic vision of America, as it is symbolically expressed by the dark image of Southern California, challenges the fundamental belief in the myth of the Promised Land. Throughout history, Southern California, situated at the southwestern edge of the country, has been viewed as an ultimate promised land where unlimited opportunities to make their dreams come true were waiting for people. The region acquired the promised land image as early as the seventeenth century when it was named after the imaginary utopia in a popular romantic novel and established it in the popular consciousness during the eighteenth and nineteenth centuries when pioneers continued to move westward until they reached the southwestern shore of the country (Aquila 420). A warm climate which blessed the region all year round, if nothing else, reassured farmers of the promised land image. In the following century, while continuously attracting people, especially from the dust bowl region which John Steinbeck wrote about in *The Grapes of Wrath,* the image was reinforced by the concentration of entertainment industries begun by the move of film companies to Hollywood. Rich and beautiful people who built their lives around the silver screen and the stage reassured Americans that everything but worries and pains was possible in Southern California. The make-believe world of the Disneyland built in 1955 also symbolized the fantastical image of the region.

Morrison came to Los Angeles when he was twenty in order to study at the UCLA film school. Los Angeles remained the source of his identity as well as his home for the rest of his life because no other city would have been more appropriate for fulfilling Morrison's desire to project the apocalyptic vision. Thomas Pynchon writes about Los Angeles:

> For Los Angeles, more than any other city, belongs to the mass media. What is known around the nation as the L.A. Scene exists chiefly as images on a screen or TV tube, as four-color magazine photos, as old radio jokes, as new songs that survive only a matter of weeks. It is basically a white Scene, and illusion is everywhere in it. (254)

Whether or not he was one of many who were lured to Los Angeles by the promised land image, Morrison was well aware of that image as he sarcastically wrote in "The End": "The West is the best/Get here and we'll do the rest." The West he saw, however, was not exactly the promised land the popular image informed him of. The above phrase in "The End" is followed by the much-discussed Oedipus section which implies the murder of father and the rape of mother by the son and thus symbolizes Morrison's view that Southern California, supposedly the best region of the country, is chaotic. His poem on Venice Beach creates the similar image of Southern California and its influence on the residents, including himself: "Running, I saw a Satan. . . ." Morrison sees two sides in Southern California, as expressed in "L.A. Woman": "Are you a lucky little lady/in the City of Light? . . ." In this song, Morrison renounces the popular image of Los Angeles and Hollywood, describing what is actually taking place—a fight over motel money and the cops outside the topless bar—in the heart of a promised land. The L.A. woman who drives in the suburbs on a Sunday afternoon is more alienated than anybody else Morrison has ever seen. The reality of Southern California, in short, hardly resembles the popular image. The discrepancy between reality and the image is also implied in "Twentieth Century Fox," a song about a perfect woman. Morrison says at the end of the song that she is "locked up inside a plastic box," implying that an impeccable woman can exist only as an image on the silver screen, and, therefore, "she's a twentieth century fox."

The dark image of Southern California is merely a segment of Morrison's apocalyptic vision, for Los Angeles is a microcosm of an America moving toward destruction, and people are alienated, deceived and full of despair everywhere. In a poem collected in *Wilderness: The Lost Writings of Jim Morrison,* Morrison writes his vision of America which creates a stark contrast to the promised land image by depicting scenes from an industrial America: "I have a vision of America. . . ." Similar images are expressed in his songs. In "The Soft Parade," Morrison says that people rationalize their lives, which they know will end up in nothing but a "shallow grave," by thinking "everything must be this way." It is implied in "Queen Of The Highway," that Americans still believe in the power of the frontier, which made them the "most beautiful people in the world," in order to avoid the destructive present situation. Morrison sings that such people look "ugly," "wicked" and "strange" in their strange places in "People Are Strange" and, moreover, he sees the beginning of the end among these people, for the "soft parade" of animals has begun the destruction of the Earth. Although men fight against the animals with their guns, it is a losing battle because there is no place left to hide and no hope in God who has left them. While, in "The End," Morrison draws upon the historical analogy between the Roman Empire and America and thus predicts the end of the prosperous state, the prediction is more explicit in "Strange Days," which contains phrases on destruction, confused dreams, and Morrison's declaration of the end, "And you know this is it."

While predicting the end, Morrison tries to escape from the painful present society and to survive in the new one. As in "The Soft Parade," Morrison predicts the final battle in "Five to One. . . ." Whereas Morrison is still hopeful of winning the battle even if the odds are one to five in this song, he merely tries to run away from the present society in other songs, such as "Been Down So Long," "The Crystal Ship," and "Break On Through." The desperate escape from disaster is most vividly expressed in "Not To Touch The Earth." Morrison and his girlfriend continue to run day and night, along the rivers and highways, passing a mysterious mansion and the dead president until they get to the "Kingdom" because, as Morrison says, there is nothing left for them to do but to run.

It is interesting to note that Morrison draws upon the analogy between life and driving. In *The Lords and The New Creatures,* he writes, "Modern life is a journey by car. The passengers change terribly in their reeking seats, or roam from car to car, subject to unceasing transformation" (32). Viewed from this perspective, some of his songs about driving also prophesy the end or describe an escape from the disaster. For example, the following phrase in "End Of The Night" seem to indicate the end of the life: "Take the highways to the end of the night. . . ." Through [the song's] phrases, Morrison implies that his life will be over with summer—the time of pleasure and gaiety. The same theme is repeated in "Summer's Almost Gone," in which he expresses anxiety about the uncertain future by saying, "Where will we be/When the summer is gone." "Roadhouse Blues" is a death cry of those who seek the final pleasure before an inevitable end. They drive to the roadhouse to "have a real good time" because it is for the "people who would like to go down slow." At the end of the song, Morrison writes, "Future's uncertain/And the end is always near" and thus implies that nobody can stop society moving toward its end and, therefore, escape his inevitable death. On the other hand, "The Rider On The Storm" [sic] is about an attempt to escape by the character who, alone amid the storm, continues to ride on the road where a "killer" is waiting. This song shares the same image of dangerous escape with "Not To Touch The Earth." Thus, these songs also create the image of disaster which is supposed to come prior to the revelation of a spiritual future.

The anticipation of the revelation which constitutes the other half of Morrison's apocalyptic vision is most clearly expressed in "Waiting For The Sun." The character who has escaped from the "strangest life" in "Eden" reaches "freedom's shore" and there waits for the sun, which will allow him to live again. Anticipation of the future is also expressed in the songs about Morrison's desire for a flight to foreign countries which, importantly, indicates that Morrison thinks that the revelation of God's promised land takes place not in America but in foreign countries. He longs to go to Spain where treasure is waiting for him in "Spanish Caravan," takes a trip to "L'America" to change his luck and to find himself, and remembers the days he and the wild child, a "savior of the human race," spent in Africa.

Emphasizing the end of the present society and, at the same time, pointing toward the future, Morrison presents the apocalyptic vision in his songs. Importantly, Morrison, a self-appointed apocalyptist, consciously models his vision after "The Book Of Revelation," as observed in his use of symbols, such as a horse and other animals, reptiles, numbers, the river and blood. Various animals and reptiles appear as often as people in Morrison's songs, such as "Love Street," which mentions the hangout of "creatures," and "The Soft Parade," in which he watches the parade of animals with a cobra on his left and a leopard on his right. These are the images drawn from the fifth chapter of "The Revelation," where it is said that prior to the destruction of the Earth, four beasts surrounded the throne on which was the sacrificial lamb (*Good News Bible* 310). Similarly, Morrison refers to the mounted troops which appeared to kill a third of mankind when the sixth angel blew his trumpet during the destruction of the Earth when he writes at the end of "The Soft Parade" that "When all else fails/We can whip the horses' eyes" to make them sleep (*Good News Bible* 313). Whipping the horses' eyes is the final strategy used by people to fight against the wrath of God. "Seven horses" which appear in "Love Her Madly" also connote the Bible, for seven is the most frequently used number in "The Revelation." The most explicit use of the biblical image appears in "Peace Frog" which refers to the battle between protesters and the combined force of the National Guardsmen and police in Chicago in August, 1968. Morrison writes, "Blood in the street runs a river of sadness . . . The river runs down the legs of the city." In "The Revelation," the rivers and the springs of water on the Earth turn into blood when the angel pours out the third of the seven bowls of God's anger (317). Moreover, following the above-cited phrase, Morrison says, "Blood will be born in the birth of a nation," thus suggesting the last scene in the final destruction of the Earth in "The Revelation." In addition, the title of the song must have come from the same scene in the Bible, for it is said that the "three unclean spirits that looked like frogs" appeared after the sixth bowl of God's anger was poured out (317). Thus, consciously modeling the scene of Chicago after that of "The Revelation," Morrison predicts the apocalypse in twentieth-century America in this song.

Mr. Mojo Risin'

In spite of the frequent use of biblical symbols, Morrison continues to sing about the powerlessness of God and thus to deny Christianity throughout his career. Not only does he write, "Cancel my subscription to the Resurrection" ("When The Music's Over") and "you cannot petition the

Lord with prayer" ("The Soft Parade") but, in "The Soft Parade," Morrison mocks the monk, groups the dog and God together and implies homosexuality by saying that "one is to love your neighbor till his wife gets home." "Ship of Fools," the song about the man who, having heard that his race was dying out, tries to flee with his "Grandma," seems to refer to Noah's escape from the flood, but Morrison sings that the character's attempt is meaningless because there will be "no one left to scream and shout." The second Noah cannot exist when God has lost his power. The new savior of the human race, "wild child," is a "terrible child, not your mother's or father's child"; against the Christian tradition, she is an illegitimate child.

While continuously denouncing God, Morrison gradually changes his self-image from a refugee from disaster to the leader and the king. The character who tries to "break on through to the other side" or who seeks shelter in the "soul kitchen" in the Doors' first album becomes the deliverer who leads people to freedom in the fourth album and ultimately names himself as the "crawling king snake" in the last album. The progression of Morrison's self-image can be observed visually as well as musically. Wrapping himself in black leather suits, designing his hair after the statue of Alexander the Great and hanging a cross around his neck, Morrison looked like the reincarnation of an ancient demigod in the early days of his career. When he sang on the darkened stage, with his eyes closed, "Send my credentials to the house of detention. I got some friends inside," he was apparently an antagonist, if not a satan. Later in his career, however, he stopped wearing the black suits, grew hair and a beard, and, using a lighting device, projected a cross on the back wall of the stage. Morrison thus began to assume the image of Christ, as the picture taken during a concert in Miami clearly shows. Holding a lamb, Morrison made clear in this picture his identification with Christ, while his black glasses indicated the sharp line Morrison drew between them. The change in his appearance also shows that Morrison had begun to see himself as a king who was to replace God in a new society.

Morrison's challenge to God culminates in the Doors' last album, *L.A. Woman,* in which he identifies himself as a king and asserts that his power is equivalent to that of God. In the first tune, "The Changeling," Morrison shows his immortality ("But I've never been so broke/That I couldn't live"), reveals the prevalence of his power among people by saying that he is the air, foods, friends and the sun, and predicts his rise to the top ("I'm a changeling/See me change"). The title song, "L.A. Woman," is the most ominous challenge to God, for Morrison raises himself to the equal of

God with one phrase, "Mr. Mojo rising," which refers to his resurrection. According to his biography, *No One Gets Out Alive,* Morrison often told the band members and friends that "Mojo" was not a mere anagram but the name he would use after his "split to Africa," presumably his death (Hopkins and Sugerman 343). By singing about his own resurrection, Morrison identifies himself with Christ and thus assumes God's power. In "Hyacinth House," a song about his desire for a new life, Morrison again implies his resurrection since Hyacinth is a young male deity in Greek mythology who was slain and resurrected as a flower. Morrison's challenge to God is further reinforced when he declares himself as the "crawling king snake." He is the king who has been exiled from the Eden. Morrison's idea expressed in *L.A. Woman* can be observed in his poem entitled "Power" as well: "I can make the earth stop in its tracks. . . ."

Break On Through to the Other Side

Peculiar as it may seem, Morrison's apocalyptic vision was deeply rooted in the tradition of American culture as well as rock'n'roll. Discussing Robert Johnson, the most legendary Mississippi Delta blues singer of the 1930s, whom he regards as an ancestor of rock'n'roll, Greil Marcus writes that Johnson, through his music, represented the terror of the devil which had lingered in American culture as a counter image to the myth of the Promised Land throughout history. Since the day when the Puritans tried to build "a city upon the hill," the fear of failing to realize their dreams has been expressed as the image of the devil by Americans, and thus the image of a promised land and that of the devil have coexisted in American culture:

> . . . the legacy of the men who began the American experience as a struggle between God and the devil, the legacy of Puritan weirdness, something that those who came after have been left to live out.
>
> The dreams and fears of the Puritans . . . are at the source of our attempts to make sense out of the contradictions between the American idea of paradise and the doomed facts of our history. . . . (Marcus 33)

Johnson who, it has been said, offered his soul to the devil in exchange for skill to play the guitar and who sang about his communication with the devil symbolized the contradiction in American life and thus the tension surrounding the myth of the Promised Land. So did Morrison, who denied the myth of the Promised Land head-on and who challenged God in his songs. Both Johnson and Morrison were aware that America was not a promised land because unlimited opportunities, which the myth promised, were seldom given to a black and a youth in twentieth-century America, and thus they posed a question about the belief in the myth of the Promised Land among Americans through their music.

While Johnson's blues were his attempt to make sense out of the world which, in spite of a promise of equality, discriminated against blacks, Morrison's apocalyptic vision expressed in his songs showed the feeling toward the myth of the Promised Land among Americans during the late 1960s. The myth, which promised unlimited opportunities to everyone, led minority groups to protest movements. America intervened in the Vietnam War partly because the myth had it that America's mission was to defend democracy and to save the oppressed from communist force. Thus, the myth exercised a powerful influence over Americans, although the immediate tragedies, such as the war, the recurring street riots and the death of family members or friends, made it hard to feel the function of the myth. Morrison manipulated such a situation in his songs by renouncing the popular image of Southern California as a promised land as well as God's power, at the same time prophesying the coming of a new society. His songs, which expressed his desire to break on through to the other side, from the present society to a new one, appealed to Americans because they represented the feeling many people shared. Morrison named his rock group after Aldous Huxley's *The Doors of Perception* because he wished to be the door to a new society.

Works Cited

Aquila, Richard. "Images of the American West in Rock Music." *The Western Historical Quarterly* 11 (Oct. 1980).

Bercovitch, Scavan. "The Rites of Assent: Rhetoric, Ritual and the Ideology of American Consensus." *The American Self: Myth, Ideology, and Popular Culture.* Albuquerque, NM: U of New Mexico P, 1981.

Good News Bible: Today's English Version. New York: United Bible Societies, 1976.

Hopkins, Jerry and Danny Sugerman. *No One Here Gets Out Alive.* New York: Warner, 1980.

Kennealy, Patricia. "When the Music's Over: An Audience with The Doors." *Jazz & Pop* 8 (March 1968).

Marcus, Greil. *Mystery Train: Images of America in Rock'n'Roll Music*. New York: Dutton, 1982.

Morrison, Jim. *The Lords and The New Creatures: Poems*. New York: Simon and Schuster, 1969.

————. *Wilderness: The Lost Writings of Jim Morrison*. New York: Villard, 1988.

Powledge, Fred. "Wicked Go The Doors." *Life* 64 (12 April 1968).

Pynchon, Thomas. "A Journey into the Mind of Watts." *The California Dream*. Dennis Hale and Jonathan Eisen, eds. New York: Macmillan, 1968.

Zamora, Lois Parkinson, ed. *The Apocalyptic Vision in America: Interdisciplinary Essays on Myth and Culture*. Bowling Green, OH: Bowling Green State University Popular Press, 1982.

CIRCUS FROM *ILLUMINATIONS*
ARTHUR RIMBAUD

Husky fellows. Some of them have exploited your worlds. Without cares and in no hurry to use their brilliant faculties and their knowledge of your consciences. What virile men! Eyes deadened, like a summer's night, red and black, tricolored, of steel spotted with golden stars; faces deformed, ashen, pale, ruddy; wild hoarseness! The cruel demeanor of decorations!— There are some young fellows—what would they think of Cherubino?— with dangerous voices and terrifying resources. They are sent to the city for trade, decked out in disgusting *finery.*

Oh! the most violent Paradise of the enraged smile! No comparison with your Fakirs and other stage antics. In improvised costumes and in the style of a bad dream, they recite sad poems and perform tragedies of brigands and spiritual demigods such as history or religion never had. Popular and maternal scenes are mixed with bestial poses and love by Chinese, Hottentots, gipsies, fools, hyenas, Molochs, old fits of madness and wily demons. They would interpret new plays and sentimental songs. As master jugglers they transform the place and the characters and use magnetic comedy. Their eyes catch fire, their blood sings, their bones grow big, tears and red rivulets stream. Their farce or their terror lasts a minute or for months on end.

I alone have the key of this wild circus.

CAMERA, AS ALL-SEEING GOD

JIM MORRISON

Camera, as all-seeing god, satisfies our longing
for omniscience. To spy on others from this
height and angle: pedestrians pass in and out of
our lens like rare aquatic insects.

* * *

Yoga powers. To make oneself invisible or small.
To become gigantic and reach to the farthest things.
To change the course of nature. To place oneself
anywhere in space or time. To summon the dead.
To exalt senses and perceive inaccessible images,
of events on other worlds, in one's deepest inner
mind, or in the minds of others.

* * *

The sniper's rifle is an extension of his eye. He
kills with injurious vision.

Jim Morrison: Lizard King/Poet/Filmmaker

PART THREE

Looking
Back at
The End

The One remains, the many change and pass;
Heaven's light forever shines, Earth's shadows fly;
Life, like a dome of many-coloured glass,
Stains the white radiance of Eternity,
Until Death tramples it to fragments. —Die
If thou wouldst be with that which thou seek!
Follow where all is fled! —Rome's azure sky,
Flowers, ruins, statues, music, words, are weak
The glory they transfuse with fitting truth to speak.
—PERCY BYSSHE SHELLEY, "Adonais"

I think of myself as an intelligent, sensitive human being with the soul
of a clown, which always forces me to blow it at the most important
moments.
—JIM MORRISON in an interview with Salli Stevenson

Twenty years didn't seem to make much difference in how I felt about
Jim, though it did give me a bit more insight into why he had behaved
as he did. But as long as I did not face what I still so deeply felt, I could
only heal so far. . . . It had become so huge and difficult and charged a
burden that it took something as big as this film, someone as forceful as
Oliver Stone ("This is a job for Superman!"), to get me past it.
—PATRICIA KENNEALY MORRISON, *Strange Days: My Life With and*
Without Jim Morrison

Artists are not men of great passion, whatever they may like to tell us
and themselves. And this for two reasons: they lack any sense of shame
before themselves (they observe themselves, they are too inquisitive) and
they also lack any sense of shame before great passion (they exploit it as
artists). Secondly, however, their vampire, their talent, grudges them as a
rule that squandering of force which one calls passion.—If one has a tal-
ent, one is also its victim: one lives under the vampirism of one's talent.
—FRIEDRICH NIETZSCHE, *The Will to Power*
(trans. Walter Kaufmann and R. J. Hollingdale)

What is a ghost? Stephen said with tingling energy. One who has faded into impalpability through death, through absence, through the change of manners.
—JAMES JOYCE, *Ulysses*

This entire book is a look back at a band and a man who will never come back. They won't come back, but they are everywhere. Morrison is gone, but he is here in these pages, in your albums, in that juke box in Rudy's, the Pull Box, the Dart Inn, Jack Dempsey's, Molly Bloom's, Finnian's Rainbow, The Red Lion, AKA, the Roadhouse of your choice.

In one of the more important pieces in this book, Lester Bangs looks back at Morrison with the cranky brilliance that made his writing the most explosive and provocative and *honest* to be produced on rock in our time. (Remember, this is the man who wrote: "I would suck Lou Reed's cock, because I would also kiss the feet of them that drafted the Magna Carta. I leave you to judge that statement as you will, because it is not to Lou Reed but to you that I surrender myself, you who read this.") Bangs catches forever Morrison's contradictions and embraces Whitman's line that to contradict oneself is fascinating and human.

Richard Witts looks back at the life of Nico and describes how Morrison blew her mind and showed her how to write songs. Richard Goldstein looks back at his first look at Morrison. Bernard Wolfe looks at Morrison's end a year after he was found in the bathtub in Paris and describes how Morrison himself provided the background for all the contradictions and myths that still color our understanding of his final days.

Before Albert Goldman died, he had planned a controversial project (nothing new for the man whom Bono cursed in the name of Lennon): a biography of Jim Morrison. What this book would have looked like can be judged from his essay on Morrison's death, "The End." Following this essay are two interviews Goldman had with two people who were there when Morrison's body was found. Next is a letter from Dr. John Morgan to whom Goldman had written for advice on the cause of Morrison's death. This letter is a piece of detective work and a look back at a body that was never fully scrutinized under a medical eye. The obituary reprinted here first appeared in the *New York Times* and is indicative of how Morrison's death was treated by the press: they get his age wrong and focus on his legal troubles and the nation's response to his "indecency."

The last essay in this book is a review of Morrison's poetry by Patricia Kennealy Morrison, the woman who married Morrison in a Celtic hand-fasting ceremony. In a reflection printed after the review, she looks back on her writing and back on the man. This book ends with a Morrison poem describing the futility of looking back because, as we know, looking back often means to look into mirrors.

JIM MORRISON, 25, LEAD SINGR WITH DOORS ROCK GROUP, DIES
THE NEW YORK TIMES, JULY 9, 1971

LOS ANGELES, July 8 (UPI).—Jim Morrison, the 25-year-old lead singer of "The Doors" rock group, died last Saturday in Paris, his public relations firm said today. His death was attributed to natural causes, but details were withheld pending the return of Mr. Morrison's agent from France.

Funeral services were held in Paris today.

In his black leather jacket and skin-tight vinyl pants, Jim Morrison personified rock music's image of the superstar as sullen, mystical sexual poet.

"The Doors," a quartet founded in 1964 in and near the film school at the University of California at Los Angeles, became by 1967 one of the most popular groups in the country, attracting the attention of serious critics who discussed their music's origins and meanings, as well as screaming, hysterical teen-agers who sometimes had to be peeled off the performers by stage-hands at the group's frenzied concerts.

Their performances were invariably treated by reviewers as events of theater, for the Doors helped to take the electronically amplified rock music that bloomed on the West Coast out of the sound studio and into the concert hall.

Their music was loud and distinctive, but perhaps the most attention was paid to the lyrics, written by Mr. Morrison, which were filled with suggestive and frequently perverse meanings abetted by Mr. Morrison's grunts, sneers and moans on stage.

"Think of us," Mr. Morrison once said, "as erotic politicians."

One critic echoed others when he called Mr. Morrison's presentations "lewd, lascivious, indecent and profane." Indeed, in one of his most famous episodes, he was arrested and later found guilty of indecent exposure at a rock concert in Miami in March of 1969.

It was this concert, which shocked even some of his teen-age fans, that led to a giant "Rally for Decency" in the Orange Bowl later that month, attended by 30,000 persons. Mr. Morrison was also forcibly removed from a New Haven stage in 1967 after he allegedly exposed himself.

Mr. Morrison's first two hits were "Light My Fire" and "People Are Strange." One of his important works was "The End," an 11 1/2-minute "extended popsong" that ended with a vision of violent death.

THE REAL-LIFE DEATH OF JIM MORRISON
BERNARD WOLFE

Minutes before dawn, July 3, in the bathroom of his Paris hotel suite, at age twenty-seven, James Douglas Morrison, most flamboyantly swinging but least known of The Doors, a Los Angeles rock group, stopped breathing. The causes, reported six days later and with judicious press management, were described as "natural."

There is no nagging, no tattling. Only agreeable items are being circulated, in close to wholesale lots. The spirit of the mourning hour is exquisitely civilized, almost tight-lipped. Yet many who knew Morrison are disconcerted: the paragon now being ceremoniously evoked, family man, dedicated poet, inspired film maker, crowd shunner, bears no resemblance to the man they observed in the amok flesh.

Whatever the motive, the news of the death was overhandled. Los Angeles *Times* pop-music columnist Robert Hilburn felt the wonderment about this had to be faced: he called his obituary note: "Why Morrison Death News Delay?" The answer, after talks with Bill Siddons, The Doors' personal and press manager, was a letdown—no particular reason, except "to avoid all the notoriety and circus-like atmosphere that so surrounded the deaths of Janis Joplin and Jimi Hendrix." The question on many minds was posed in order to dismiss it: "Official Paris police reports . . . confirmed the original information—Jim Morrison died of a heart attack while taking a bath. Just that. Natural causes. Nothing more."

No facts have emerged to contradict the managed account. All the same there are people who consider it less than complete. When someone in the earliest prime of life, practically a millionaire at an age when his peers are worriedly getting out of law and medical schools, when such a smiled-upon young man dies in his bathtub of a heart attack, there's nothing "natural" about it unless Nature, as Rimbaud exerted himself to think, is a maniac.

Sherry, a Pasadena girl who knew Morrison well:

"I couldn't make sense out of the stories in the papers. Suppose he had that heart attack exactly as they reported, is that what he died *of*? My God, might as well say Ernest Hemingway died of extensive brain damage. If you want to know the *cause* of Jim's death, not just the physiology of it, ask what triggered his heart to stop and whose finger was on the trigger."

Morrison's associates are not asking Sherry's questions, at least not in public, but the paradox remains. On the one hand they consider their friend's death totally "natural," as those of Joplin and Hendrix, O.D. cases, were transparently not. On the other, it is a senseless, grotesque event, a *violation* of Natures' usual way. Morrison, they insist, was "finding himself," "unwinding," "shaking L.A. out of his system," "getting to lead his own life instead of the life the public wanted him to lead," "cutting down on his drinking," "making a go of a new marriage," "writing the poetry he'd been aching to write," "turning to film projects that excited him"—how, at a moment like this, when the man is geared for living as never before, does an errant blood clot form in his infected lung (Siddons' speculation), make its way into his bloodstream, cause a cardiac arrest?

Some of his friends see blanks in the causational picture. Dan Knapp writes, "He was beginning to be happy, to find himself. But he had punished himself too severely too often." Elmer Valentine: "He wasn't a doper. He drank himself to death." Even Siddons looks briefly into the shadows: "Jim was very strong but he pushed himself to the limits." Michael McClure: "I'll be very interested in finding out what the contributing factors of his death were. Pam . . . is probably the only person who knows. I know from talking to him that he never expected to live very long." Kathy Lisciandro: "He'd have no regard of his physical body. He'd just abuse it. He's fallen out of windows—just in February he fell out two stories at the Château Marmont hotel—just playing." Sherry: "They give all facts but the relevant ones. I don't know all the details of Jim's weeks in Paris but I knew him too well to believe there'd been a sudden surge of life-affirming in him. Maybe statistically he'd cut down on the drinking but with him that could mean going from three-quarter lethal doses to three-fifth ones. During the last two years in L.A. he was alarmingly lazy, passive, sodden, lumpish, inert, and getting more so all the time, and, well, I don't think a process like that is easily reversible, not without help, anyhow. Maybe he did finally marry the girl they all kept saying he couldn't live with or without—I wish the people in his circle would stop quoting themselves instead of the facts—maybe he did marry Pam but I know from a phone conversation with him in May that he kept up his old on-again-off-again style of living, one apartment with her, one without. Maybe he was finally doing something close to reasonable amount of writing. Maybe. The Jim I knew had a king-size block as a writer. For him to get off even a few lines a week might look like a burst of productivity from up close. I suppose he'd have been pleased to find himself but my impression was he didn't know where to look and had long ago given up trying, except maybe in the bottle. You know what people find in vodka bottles, vodka. Of course he didn't O.D. No chance. Still and all you can't say a driven alcoholic and a blowtop has a heart attack at age twenty-seven for no reason, just because Nature turned quirky that day. I feel he died by his own hand, the one all those thousands of martinis with all those thousands of beer chasers got lifted by. He died for the simplest of reasons, that he couldn't stand living. I can't help it if that's a medically unsatisfactory postmortem. It sums up all I know about the dude."

I met Sherry three years ago when I undertook to interview Morrison for *The New York Times Magazine.* We were turning up at a series of stage doors at the same time for the same reason, though with different ends in mind.

The *Times* editors had taken note that Morrison was beginning to be talked about as "the most potent sex symbol to come along in our popular culture since Jimmy Dean and Elvis Presley"; his song, *Light My Fire,* had sold two million records in a very short time, and others like *Break on Through, Back Door Man* and *The End* became anthems for a generation turning inward, away from politics; the editors had asked me to look into the source of the commotion. Sherry, opposite of a groupie, was hanging around in the swarm of Morrison-besotted teeners hoping for some sort of access to the "sex symbol," ready to break on through to whatever other side he'd consent to be tour-guide to.

She was uneasy with the role of camp follower, particularly an unrecruited one. She carefully explained that she was a writer, the she was writing a movie script around a rock hero patterned after Morrison, that to get her portrait authentic, she needed to be close to her model. Pressed, she said frankly that she had no idea why she was hovering about on the edges of Morrison's world—all she knew was that she couldn't stay away.

The more I thought about sex-symbolization as a function ascribed to certain order of human beings the less I understood the words. I was after Morrison's thoughts on this, but it was hard to pin him down to appointments and when he made them there were long waits. Sherry was usually somewhere in the neighborhood. Her conversation did not go soggy at key points in the groupie's schizoid style; her head seemed to contain no dripping wet wash. I needed some answers, if not thoughtful at least audible. Morrison tended to mumble as he got along in his drinking.

Was Morrison in her eyes a sex symbol? "Oh, yes. Oh, you bet. Eyes are the least of it." How could a man symbolize one aspect of men? Didn't you have to have a part standing for a whole or a concretion suggesting an abstraction before you had what is generally known as a symbol? "Any part of that boy wants to stand for the whole in my presence I'll be only too happy. If it doesn't want to stand it can lie down or do backbends, I'm permissive. Whenever he's in sight one thing does suggest another, for example, his lying down on stage and making those movements suggests I ought to lie down and do them too, with him right away."

Sharp takeoff on groupie responses. Now could we try again? In symbolism a portion of a thing is said to represent, suggest, evoke its entirety. Here they were saying the whole, a man, represented sex, one part of a man—wasn't this then a sloppy wording?

"Listen, any man who cuts himself down to just that one part of the whole and nothing but, the way Jim does, becomes a lot *bigger* than the whole, he's finally *made* himself whole where the rest of us who pretend that there's a lot more to us than just *that*, we stay split up and down and sideways."

Witty, but wasn't this dodging the question? Phallic symbols are *not* phalluses, they just *remind* us of the male organ. A man can't *remind* us of himself through some slight overlapping of traits, he *is* himself, with all the ingredients that make him up, sexual and otherwise. "Look, Jim no doubt started out a full man with penis just one organ among *many*. But what he does that other men don't, he makes the whole of him *into* penis, his entire *being* is turned into sex, so that means he symbolizes sex, doesn't it—the whole *man's* a phallic symbol?"

Debatable interpretation, though neat. In his performances he repeatedly clutched at his crotch; by her theory this was trunk penis reaching for branch penis, which seemed redundant, at least unfunctional. Seriously, how could a man symbolize a man? Any of the qualities or functions associated with the human condition?

"Who's talking about the human condition of human anything? Jim's *stopped* being human, gotten himself up and out of all the crap, that's why he's fascinating. The human condition is to be all chopped up, and what Jim does, he chops *off* all the unneeded pieces, the chunks they tied on you that weigh you down and slow you down."

We could take that for our working hypothesis if she wanted. This still didn't make the man a concrete sign suggesting the intangible or divine, flag reminding us of country, halo turning our thoughts to divinity.

"Oh, he's a flag. That tells of a country where they've sloughed off all restraints and nicenesses and do anything with body and mind they feel like, the never-never land of the polymorphous-perversers. He's Norman O. Brown in black leather pants and set to acid freakout music."

Ingenious formula: Morrison came on as the negation of the humdrum and lackluster state of affairs you expected to find down the block or along the freeway, everywhere on the human landscape. He did then resurrect something in the paved-over human potential, something at least assumed to be there, fantasy freedom, fantasy sex, fantasy departure, through the trick of *escaping* from the human or going through the *motions* of escape. Clever reasoning. Did she then imagine that something special might emerge from an involvement with Morrison, something to put it in her language, *beyond*?

"For sure. *This* side of the door's no good."

She counted on a breaking on through with Morrison?

"*That's* what he symbolizes, what's available on the far side of all the closed doors. Everything missing here. I sure hope I get to meet him."

Then she did know what she was looking for in the alleys around these recording studios and auditoriums—to get out of the human?

"Well, to get *somewhere*. We're all so *stalled*. This dude's in *motion*."

Morrison finally stayed put long enough to talk about this. It was in his favorite bar on Santa Monica Boulevard. It was not his favorite subject.

"Everybody has to stand for something, that's what we're here for. If Spiro Agnew stands for law and order, all right, say I stand for sex. Chaos. Movement without meaning. Cop baiting. Fifty-two week paid vacations with double overtime every year."

But wasn't he using words inexactly? Agnew certainly stands for law and order but in the sense of program, not symbol. Did *encouraging* free sexuality, *advocating* it, mean to be a *symbol* of it?

"Every entity in the world's a symbol, it can't be helped. I mean, everything parades as itself, but really stands for something else, everything you see and smell is a small deposit of the intangible, the everywhere mystery. Know what I think? If there were real things in the world instead of just a panorama of symbols all the poets would have been accountants and census takers."

Could he expand on that? As he condensed the thought it was a little hard to follow, confusing too, since there *are* accountants and census takers in the world and they even count poets.

"It's summed up in a poem I just finished: 'They are filming something in the street in front of our house.'"

Promising beginning: how did the next lines develop.

"That's the whole poem. Haiku compression compressed some more. When I get out a volume of my things I'll print it on a page by itself." (A year later he did just that.)

Would it have diluted the poem's intention to have added a few words hinting at the content of the film, the director, the actors? As it stood now didn't it have a slight cliff-hanger quality?

"You don't get my point. People have the feeling that what's going on outside isn't real, just a bunch of staged events, all I did was record this feeling. I can't give any plot line because it's what all the people experience all the days, all the meandering happenings. I don't say this just because I studied film at U.C.L.A. and it's the thing I plan to get into. It's my view of things."

He meant, in short, that it was not inaccurate, not a violation of reason, to call him a sex symbol?

"Better than being called a chime lesser."

Would he mind repeating that?

"A chile—mlesser."

Child molester. Right. Was there a point to his drinking this many stingers with beer chasers?

"Yes, there is a point to my drinking this many, it's as much as I can drink."

Did he have a reason for drinking his capacity every time he drank?

"I believe I have, to get drunk."

Would he comment on a recent article referring to his "performing prodigious feats of marathon sexuality"?

"I'm a performer. I'm called upon to perform."

Feats?

"Acts. Performers are actors. What actors perform are acts."

Of an order to be taken for feats?

"Well. They tag you for a prodigy. I don't know how that happens, maybe they see you as a child because you don't behave like their definition of an adult, then they remember you're past childhood so if you still look like a child you must be a special kind, a child prodigy, say, that's better than child mlesser. So if they've got you pegged for child prodigy, then each and every thing you do has to be prodigious so you put on the act and they see a feat, you know? I believe I will perform a prodigious feat of marathon something. I believe that although I have reached my prodigious capacity I will have another drink."

I went to the lyrics for clues. Words as assembled by Morrison for purpose of song don't have the function they do in ordinary human discourse; they are a painter's rationed brushstrokes, one given for every ten needed to make a picture, they tease rather than steer. The strategy in them, as in the straight poetry, is to inch briefly and somewhat spastically up and down the thin edge of meaning without ever breaking through—this is the sense of a breakthrough art. The listener fills in the empty spaces; according to the kind of filler he uses he will find the lines a feast of significations or short change. This order of writing makes everybody within earshot a writer, composition goes communal.

I was looking for the sex Morrison was said to symbolize. I thought I found traces of it here and there, though alternate readings might take the reference points to childhood, swimming, running, arson, amputation, ordering a beer, catching a bus. Wherever sex appeared to be the subject under oblique discussion it was not dealt with in and for itself. Invariably it was traveling with a nonsexual—by ordinary standards even antisexual—thematic companion: drowning, abandoning, being abandoned, running away, breaking and entering, seeking asylum, using somebody, blood, annoyance with the other party's need for and dependence on you, deception, killing with a patricidal flavor, rape with a matricidal focus, suicide in pact and solo. Its steadiest escort was death.

Those who saw Morrison as a "sex symbol" took his renditions of "bacchic frenzy," "unholy praise of forbidden fruit," "a flagitious assault on the libido," "radiating sexuality," a roar against "the agony of the armored man," a drive "not simply to catharsis but beyond to orgasm," "Dionysian," "polymorphism at the end of the tunnel of perversity," "like something burning." Textual analysis, though, established that his constant subject was Sex-Death or Death-Sex, how you get to one by means of the other.

Over and over, as he performed these songs in concert, Morrison at the dramatic high points cupped his hands over his genitals. The gesture was as ambiguous as the words: was he featuring these organs in carnalizing revelry or protecting them for one last moment from the imminent and urgently solicited smashup?

Sherry: "Don't ask me to put it in words because he can't and that's the whole point to the lyrics, they bring us up against the wordless. His message is, you can finally say true things only in animal sounds plus long silences. Why does he grab himself? What else is a man going to hold on to in this mess, with politics making everything slippery?"

Was that what you came to after all the hard work of publicizing yourself from head to toe, taking hold of yourself for support? The end product of liberation is masturbation?

"Maybe he's not scared, just tired after the work. Maybe he reaches for himself in the spirit of relying on yourself, you know, falling back on your own resources, the really freed man has after all only himself to hold on to."

And sing over and over about the many ways in which sex can be deadly and death sexy?

"You can get too damn analytic about these things. Who knows what death he's talking about, anyway, maybe he's referring to the death of the deadening, sex-squelching sides of him, the sides he's killing and peeling off."

The singer's father and mother seemed to occupy prominent places on the casualty list.

"Only natural, man. How're you going to live without killing your parents stone dead? It's you or them, little buddy."

Sherry, going on twenty-four, was living at home. There wasn't a chance of getting her own place unless she realized some money from her movie script about Morrison.

Parent-killing and parent-mauling were stated themes of his celebrated number, *The End*. Twice I watched him do it in concert.

Explaining to his "beautiful friend," his "only friend," that this is "the end of our elaborate plans," he encourages her to "ride the snake, to the lake, the ancient lake," the reptile being defined as "seven miles long," "old," "cold." His growly baritone is almost sweet, almost down to a love whisper, as he laments (or crows?) that "I'll never look into your eyes again": but there's the rasping edge even when pitched low, the suggestion of a snarl held back, the mixture of Arctic distance and muted parody. At the mother's bedroom door, music having left him altogether (by this time he's visited pop's room and unceremoniously, with some melody still lingering, wiped him out), he falls into a toneless, grinding, dirge-slack recitative. On the verge of the ghastly ellipsis, the point at which words as well as music cave in, his eyes clamp shut, his lips form the unspeakable syllables, "I wa-a-a-ant"—he screams.

Just what has happened to this troubled fellow? Has he, after wiping his father out, gone on to ravish his mother? Sherry: "It's certainly a possibility." But the final lines could be taken to mean that the restless young man has given up his impossible appetites and accepted restrictive reality, couldn't they? Sherry: "The thing is to be free. Whether he gets rid of the old bag by balling her or by throwing her out of his head is his business, don't you see. Let him get there any way that works. Christ, man, who cares about the technicalities?" She didn't want her lyrics to be a bit more informative? "I happen to think good writing doesn't clutter up the place with details."

Morrison: "*The End* is about three things, sex, death, travel."

With a suggestion that sex is a means of travel to death?

"You can take it that way, you can also take it the opposite way. The theme is the same as in *Light My Fire,* liberation from the cycle of birth-orgasm-death."

How? By dying? That route wouldn't eliminate the cycle so much as speed it up, some might argue.

"Then take the resolution as a coming to terms, a bowing to the inevitable. Of course, it could be a *not* coming to terms. Any way you want. I'm just saying there's one cure for the plague, run away fast and come back slow."

That sounded like a reasonable therapy wherever the bubonic might be a threat. Was there perhaps some political burden to his message? Since he had been quoted as calling himself an "erotic politician"?

"If the erotics I work with make the Agnews tear their hair, I guess they're political. I guess patricide and incest are political, once you start killing and balling your parents no telling how far you'll go, you might go on to governments. I don't make programs, the way I see myself I primarily open doors."

Any and all doors? Some led straight into the nineteenth century, that was when the themes of patricide and incest were heavy on people's minds.

"If you want to take *The End* as being about patricide and incest. Read the last note to mean accommodation, not extermination, if that suits you more, that's as twentieth century as you can get. I only aim to please."

Didn't his heavy drinking open a wide door to times past and, some argued, surpassed? His peers appeared to be energetically down on alcohol as an old-hat ease-giver.

"I have several answers to that. Old hats often fit best. Ease isn't what I get out of booze, just the energy to raise my voice and cop-out unconsciousness to keep the cops out when my voice gets loud enough to attract the fuzz. My peers are all dopers. Dope's all the go now. Well, I always have to buck the stream. I don't feel right in the majority. The most revolutionary thing you can pump into your system these days in the midst of all these dopers is good old rotgut firewater. Booze is mother's milk to me and better than any milk ever came from any mother."

Can we talk for a moment about snakes and lakes? Why was his lake ancient, his snake so old and cold? Why did his snake have to the be the one means of transportation to his lake, why not a Greyhound express bus or a nonstop 747? Why was it so important to establish his snake's length as being in the area of seven miles, surely a herpetological hyperbole? Was the intention in these details to scare somebody?

"You don't seem to realize that when you're going on two everything looks old and big as hell and fells pretty chilly, *you're* the one scared. Listen, I'll make a deal with you, don't mess with my lakes and snakes and I won't mess with yours."

Why did he reach for his genitals at climactic moments in his performances?

"Because they're there. Because to have is to hold. Because the audience wouldn't be stirred if I reached for my nose or my elbow. Because I'm a politician and politicians have a long reach. Because there's no drink to reach for. Because these vinyl pants are too f——-king tight. Because."

He rambled. Some of his more reverberant phrasings came in these marginal spatters, without connective tissue:

"Nietzsche was right. In *Rebirth of Tragedy out of the Spirit of Music*. About lyrics and music being incompatible. At some point as rock develops the poets and the musicians will walk away from each other. . . . We have this new ghetto, a ghetto of the young. . . . I'm shy except when I'm on stage. . . . Snakes are fine animals with no ecological function. I don't care about their use value. . . . I bring chaos in lyrics, the others in the group bring back order in music. . . . Rimbaud, Apollinaire, Breton, Cendrars, Max Ernst, Céline, Burroughs. From religion as the road to knowledge to chaos as the road. Though chaos with a road isn't so chaotic. Unless the road curves back on itself. Peters out. Gets lost. I like the idea of a road getting lost. You could write a song about the San Bernardino Freeway winding up in San Luis Obispo. . . . You can stun people so easily today, they're blasted enough by the headlines. They look for something else from us, something that's not like the news and maybe counteracts it. If you could give them some quiet, some sag in the nerves, that might be the biggest thing. The kids think they come to us for incitement but maybe all they really want is to relax for an hour. . . . Kids and cops, cops and kids. Two-handed game between them that neither player understands. The mob scenes at our concerts. These kids are so used to taking orders and accepting authority, they're scared to go all the way in baiting the cops. They want a wrestling match, sure, but on the other hand they're kind of glad the cops are there and as strong as they are. They *want* the cops to hold them back, they wouldn't know what to do if they took over the place and could really run wild. To run wild you've got to *be* wild, that takes vocation and practice."

Perhaps we should focus on the recent articles about him. Wasn't there a contradiction running through them? How could "an angel in a Renaissance painting" be a "gaunt Ariel from Hell," a "warlock of pop-culture," a "demonic vision out of a medieval Hellmouth," a "black priest of the Great Society," an "exterminating angel"?

"You know how it is with writers. I'm lucky, I just have to put the skeleton on paper, thirty or forty words, say, and flesh them out with voice and gestures. I write the bare structure and perform the content. These poor magazine hacking sons of bitches, they don't have a stage to deliver their words from so they've got to get all their vocalizing and gesturing on the printed page, so naturally their prose gets a little pumped up."

Kurt von Meier had discovered in him rich "suggestions of sex, death, transcendence." What transcendence did he have in mind, death through sex or sex through death?

"The first on Mondays, Wednesdays, and Fridays, the second on Tuesdays, Thursdays, and Saturdays."

If he was actually producing a "music of outrage," just what was the object of his rage, the world (a political stance) or the body (a Manichaean one)?

"Depends on what's within reach. Sometimes it's only your crotch."

Did it depend sometimes on what was *out* of reach, a stance neither political nor Manichaean but essentially one of show-business strategy, and safe?

"Oh, sure, when it's not the one it's certainly the other. Or a car wash. Or a banana split."

If it was true that "The Beatles and The Stones are for blowing your mind, The Doors are for afterward, when your mind is already gone," then why the "staggering horrors" people saw in him: because body can't get lost with mind?

"No, because mind can't get lost with vodka. Because take enough vodka to lose mind you simultaneously lose body. For good. Horror that'll give you blind staggers every time is physiology. All this stuff you've bedded in and have to give top billing. It's f—ing humiliating, always being spear carrier to your meat. Who the f— it thinks it is, forever barking orders. That's the best reason I know for drinking, to shut it up for a minute. But, oh, next morning, how it barks."

We came to the core matter. It had been suggested that he was unique in the rock world as a "troubadour of Oedipality." By this reading, most of the rage and lust in the songs, the rageful lust, lustful rage, was a displacement into "girls" and "friends," peer sex objects, of strong sentiments originally directed toward the "Ogress of the Nursery," mother. With the bulk of the lyrics it could be argued either way, the wordings were so cryptic. But certainly *The End,* one of the most emotional of his offerings, was a wild outburst of Oedipal passions: Pop is mowed down and Mom is taken over.

"Absolutely. Unless you see it as Mom being mowed down and Pop taken over. Or Mom being exhaled and Pop inhaled. Or Mom being deposed and Pop installed. Or both being kissed off and the snotty kid going off to hit the road. Listen, real poetry doesn't say anything, it just ticks off the possibilities. Opens all doors. You can walk through any one that suits you."

The doors that were said to be opened in that particular lyric were two quite unambiguous ones, that to Pop's room, for purposes of killing, that to Mom's quarters, with an intent taken by most listeners to be physical possession. On the premise of this interpretation, the most popular, we were up against a paradox. Freud's early assumption was that of all the layers in the unconscious the Oedipal was the deepest and the most energetically repressed. More recent psychoanalysts saw a theoretical problem when, as in Stendhal's autobiographical novel, patricidal attitudes toward the father and incestuous urges toward the mother were hauled into the open and elaborately dwelled upon: how do such profoundly buried materials, such prime guilt-laden "secrets," come to the conscious surface so readily? Did he see this contradiction in some of his own writings? How would he explain these bottommost "criminal" appetites rising so spiritedly and with no hampering to the top? His own lyrics made it clear that he was with the more traditional Freudians in regarding incest as the most awful of all the transgressions, the taboo against it as the mightiest of the admonitions—could he then explain his straightforward confession, very much in public, bellowingly in public, to the primal crime?

"It's only a song, man, five minutes of tickling the public, not a signature on a police blotter."

But the song had a content. He was the one who had put it there. It was apparently his thought that such content would tickle people. It was hard to believe that the judgment was purely strategic, other-directed. What the artist intuits will tickle people often tickles him, too.

"I know what you're working up to. The new orality psychology stuff. I've read some of Melanie Klein and the others. The idea that the Oedipal layer *isn't* as deep as people used to think, that it gets deposited when the kid goes into the genital period and a whole lot of stuff has come together in his head before this, below it, when he was all mouth and no muscle or genitals. I know the whole line of thought, man. That there was just oral passive helplessness and bawling for Big Ma before the kid began to grow muscles and came to see his genitals as muscle and could counter his ache for Ma's shelter with a little genital aggression, at least in his fantasies. Deny yearning mouth with blustering phallus. I *know* this—there's a whiny toddler inside every growling rapist school."

He did indeed. His summary of the logic was flawless.

"Sure. By this reasoning it's easy to make a big red badge of your Oedipality and wear it on your sleeve. It's closer to the surface and you can dredge it out a lot faster than the worse Ma-cuddly stuff under *it*. Use the one to hide the other. What do they call that dodge? The lesser crime. Cop out to the Oedipal sin because it's nowhere near as bad as the oral ones that lie deeper. The crimes of the sucking baby wanting to hold tight to Mamma and go on sucking forever, and feeling abandoned by the old biddy because first she ejected him, then shoved him aside, cut him off. Anybody'd rather own up to fantasy crimes of muscle than those of the blobby and flabby. That's what you're accusing me of, right?"

No accusation involved. What was held to be the human being's most guilty secret he had publicized as a headline, a slogan, a street cry; we were trying to find the explanation for that.

"That's what's behind your sneaky questions about why my snake has to be seven miles long, right? The insinuation that it's an inchworm? Well, poetry's my business, not nit picking, and this kind of nit picking is death to poetry. There's a misunderstanding here. I agreed to be interviewed by you. I did *not* agree to be psychoanalyzed. I certainly did not agree to let you examine my poetry with a tape measure."

I said there was indeed a misunderstanding. My intention was least of all to psychoanalyze him. I had neither the credentials nor the commission to do so. There was Oedipal content in his lyrics. It was identified as such by people other than myself. I was curious as to *how* it came to be there; I assumed my readers shared that curiosity; there was no way to find out except by going to the sources. I wanted to print his comments on this matter, not mine. There was no malice in my question as to why his snake had to be elongated as he had made it. He had to admit that a seven-mile-long snake was a rarity and an attention-getter. He was responsible for its dimensions. He couldn't say he'd stretched them so *just* because he felt they'd tickle the public. Any light he might care to shed on the origins of his titanic vision I'd be happy to transmit to The *Times* audience. I agreed that poetry did not have to explain everything but now and then poets were friendly enough to add some illuminating footnotes.

"We can't do this talking in a bar. When I'm asked questions like these I want time to think them out. Why don't you write your questions out exactly and in detail on paper, and I'll study them and give you my answers in writing."

I sent him several pages of questions. Some days later he delivered to me five pages of typewritten notes which he explained he's extracted from his notebooks because he thought they were pertinent to my interests. They covered a wide range of subjects, from voyeurism, seance, archaic drama, cinema, gambling, vertigo, ecstasy, dancing, possession, shamanism, the birth of cities, comedy, tragedy, to certain practices of the old Tsars and the concept of God as a hermaphrodite, and were in no way pertinent to my interests, my questions, or my assignment. Three lines were underlined in red: "But most of the press were vultures descending on the scene for curious America aplomb. Cameras inside the coffin interviewing worms."

That was the last time I saw him. I told The *Times* editors that Morrison and I had not found a way to talk with each other fruitfully. I would be satisfied if The *Times* would finance a month's stay for me in a rustic rest home, if we could find one that required a vow of silence from its guests. I needed a period of quiet in which to renew my faith in the power of words to generate something more than decibels. I did not feel that I was in the main a linguistic positivist but it was my suspicion that if language got *entirely* reduced to noise something might be lost.

Morrison called me a few times after that, usually to give me further thoughts he'd had on the role of the shaman, the function of cinema, the stance of the spectator. I acknowledged that all of his ideas were interesting and well-formulated even though I was not competent to judge because I was remote from shamanism, knew little about movies and less about spectator sports. His last call, in March of 1969, had more topical import: some days before at the Dinner Key Auditorium in Miami, he'd been arrested for "exposing his private parts" before twelve thousand young fans and "simulating masturbation and oral copulation." It was this event he wanted to talk about. "You may look at things but not taste them. You may caress the mother only with the eyes . . . The theory is that birth is prompted by the child's desire to leave the womb. But in the photograph an unborn horse's neck strains inward w/legs scooped out. From this everything follows: Swallow milk at the breast until there's no milk. . . ."

"I guess you heard what happened in Miami." I'd gathered from the papers that at eleven p.m. on March 7 his vinyl pants had become unbearably tight. "I can guess what you're thinking." He was the one facing a felony charge in Dade County so his thoughts were to the point, not mine. "Don't you want to know why I did it?" It might be of interest to know why he thought he'd done it. "I suppose the way you see things it looks like I had to establish for a barnful of eyes that the snake is seven miles long." Had he established it? "The cops sure took it for seven miles long, the way they came down on me." What had he established for himself, except that to make your private parts public, whatever their proportions, is a good and speedy way to get arrested? "That it's very, very hard to just get up on a stage and sing a song when you're a sex symbol. They didn't come to hear my mouth, they were ogling my pants. The way they refuse to grant your mouth when they've been taught you're all below the waist is very frustrating for a poet. You come forth with your fine words and they keep on staring at your pants. I decided for once to give them what they were in the market for. The cops just don't understand the democratic process. They are just not attuned to the will of the people." Well put: now did he want to talk about why he opened his pants, aside from wanting to demonstrate how blind to democratic procedures the cops are? "You've got to get this through your head. Once and for all, man. Six inches isn't going to establish you're finally disentangled from the Ogress.

Seven miles just barely might." Had he done this to his own satisfaction in Miami? "The cops helped . . . Plenty. Six measly inches couldn't cause *that* amount of commotion." Had he, like the scrappy kids he theorized about, been pleased that the cops were present, and in strength? "They're not so strong. They had the muscle to book me but I've got the money to beat this." What would that prove, except that he had an awful lot of money? "Money, I've heard it said, is the longest snake of all, the oldest, the coldest. Rides you to the rarest lakes. Nice talking to you." (Months later he was acquitted on the felony charge. Somebody must know what it cost but the information is not available.)

There was one more transaction between us: when his poems and notes were published, he sent me a copy, without comment. Representative lines from the collection, without comment:

"More or less, we're all afflicted with the psychology of the voyeur. Not in a strictly clinical or criminal sense, but in our whole physical and emotional stance before the world. Whenever we seek to break this spell of passivity, our actions are cruel and awkward and generally obscene, like an invalid who has forgotten how to walk . . . The voyeur, the peeper, the Peeping Tom is a dark comedian. He is repulsive in his dark anonymity, in his secret invasion. He is pitifully alone. But, strangely, he is able through this same silence and concealment to make unknowing partner of anyone within his eye's range. This is his threat and power . . . Film spectators are quiet vampires . . . Peep show . . . imitates the keyhole or voyeur's window without need of color, noise, grandeur . . . The appeal of cinema lies in the fear of death . . . The voyeur is masturbator . . . Imagery is born of loss . . . The breast is removed and the face imposes its cold, curious, forceful and inscrutable presence. . . . You may enjoy life from afar. You may look at things but not taste them. You may caress the mother only with the eyes . . . The theory is that birth is prompted by the child's desire to leave the womb. But in the photograph an unborn horse's neck strains inward w/legs scooped out. From this everything follows: Swallow milk at the breast until there's no milk. . . ."

Sherry's dream came true: Morrison finally noticed her, they began a tangled, sometime relationship. Her retrospective:

"This isn't easy to write about but I'll do it. They're talking up a Jim who's a complete stranger to me, some pink-cheeked Little Fauntleroy of rock. The kids should get one long hard look at him without the velvet suit and lace collar. . . . He struck two notes when we started seeing each other. 'You're nice to look at and you're bright. I can use you. Just get straight on this, you're mine, you belong to me, you're my property, you do what I want.' And 'I know how to handle you, keep you dangling. Trust me, I know what I'm doing.' . . . He wanted dirty talk from me, it excited him. 'Act like a bitch in heat, that's all you are.' 'You have to beg me for it, say please.' . . . The sadomasochistic games. Always spanking me. 'You've been a bad girl, haven't you. You want to be punished. Come on, cry. I want you to cry, I want to hear you crying. Answer me. Say yes, say yes, sir.' . . . He wanted mostly to be the passive one. . . . I had to do things to do. He was mostly impotent, sometimes it would take hours. Sometimes when it didn't work, no matter how I tried, he'd turn violent. Very. Choke me and beat me. I had a lot of black and blue marks to explain. Twice I think I was very close to getting killed, had to run. . . . Remember when he wrote about seeking to break the spell of passivity with actions cruel and awkward. He knew what he was talking about. After hours of being inert and giving orders, being catered to, he could be cruel, oh yes. . . . Big problem of impotence. Most of the time with me he never had an orgasm, gave up. A few times he acted as though he did but I sensed it was an act. I never had a full response and it would drive him wild, he thought I was holding out on purpose, he'd squeeze my windpipe hard. . . . The brute and the baby. His oscillation between the two. A lot of roughing up, then the sudden collapse, whimpering, 'I need somebody to love me, please take care of me, please don't leave me.' . . . The mouth vs. phallus business really bugged him. Once I said to him, 'You said you're all phallus, but really you're all mouth. Your biggest games are talked. You talked your old man dead, but the rear admiral's still in the Pentagon. You talked a triumph over your old lady but she's still serving the rear admiral breakfast every morning, unmolested as always.' For once I was smart. I said it over the phone from a place five miles away. . . . My stomach turned when I read Michael McClure's recollections. How he found Jim sitting in his room holding the first copy of his book, crying and saying, 'This is the first time I haven't been f—ked.' Who f—ked him? The kids who made him rich for telling them everything but the plain truth? The cops he could always buy off? . . . The time I read him the report on a new study of incest in the United States. Statistics that showed it was a pretty common practice. I said, 'You're not as avant-garde as you thought, Jim. A lot of people seem to have gotten there before you. With more than their mouths.' I wasn't so smart that time. I was in the same room with him. I had the bruises for days afterwards. . . . The way they're all quoting that phony explanation for Miami he once gave a reporter, 'I think that . . . was the culmination, in a way of our mass performing career.

Subconsciously, I think it was trying to get (that point) across in that concert. . . . I was trying to reduce it to absurdity, and it worked too well.'

"I saw him right after that bust. He wasn't talking about reducing anything to absurdity or anything else. He said, 'Off the fuzz. All pigs the wall. They had me in their greasy hands and I'm going to slip right out. While we're at it, off the Joint Chiefs of Staff too.' The kids will remember him as tough, brutal, bestial, savage. The image I keep is a different one."

Another dream has become actuality for the girl here called Sherry: a producer has an option on her screenplay, she's moved into her own place. She writes she's revising her script:

"My producer and I agree that the public has had it with rock stars. I don't want to be accused of being behind the times, so I'm changing my central character entirely; now he's a young New Left politician, I think that's a very fresh approach, politics is really in now and the younger dudes getting into it show up very sexy. . . ."

JIM MORRISON—BOZO DIONYSUS A DECADE LATER
LESTER BANGS

We seem to be in the midst of a full-scale Doors Revival. It had been picking up steam for a while, but when Jerry Hopkins' and Daniel Sugerman's biography of Jim Morrison, *No One Here Gets Out Alive,* became a Number One best-seller last year, all the Doors' LP product began to move in a big way again. Now there is the inevitable talk of a movie of Morrison's life, with (shudder) perhaps equally inevitable hints that John Travolta might have the starring role. The first question that would occur to anyone might be that asked by the first person I told I was doing the article: "Yeah, just why *is* there this big Doors fanaticism all over again, anyway?" The answer to that is not so hard to find, though in the end it may be questionable just how much it really has to do with the Doors. I'm reminded of the younger brother of an old girlfriend—he recently graduated from high school, and still lives with their parents in Detroit, and when she told me he was playing in a rock band and I asked who his favorite artists were, she said: "His three favorite groups are the Yardbirds, Cream and the Doors."

Think about that for a minute. That kid is now entering college. The Doors broke up ten years ago this July—well, okay, Morrison died then, and if you want to call the trio that went on after his death the Doors, you can, but nobody else did—and Cream and the Yardbirds have been dead since '68–'69. Sure all three of them were great groups, but were they all that epochal that somebody who was in elementary school when they scored their greatest triumphs should look back to them like this, to be holding on to them after that many years? Yeah, the Beatles were one thing, but *Cream*?

Perhaps a more apposite question, though, might be: can you imagine being a teenager in the 1980s and having absolutely no culture you could call your own? Because that's what it finally comes down to, that and the further point which might as well be admitted, that you can deny it all you want but almost none of the groups that have been offered to the public in the past few years begin to compare with the best from the sixties. And this is not just sixties nostalgia—it's a simple matter of listening to them side by side and noting the relative lack of passion, expansiveness and commitment in even the best of today's groups. There is a half-heartedness, a tentativeness, and perhaps worst of all a tendency to hide behind irony that is after all perfectly reflective of the time, but doesn't do much to endear these pretenders to the throne. Sure, given the economic climate alone as well as all the other factors it was a hell of a lot easier to go all-out, berserk, yet hold on to whatever principles you had in the sixties—today's bands are so eager to get bought up and groomed and sold by the pound it often seems as if even the most popular and colorful barely even exist, let alone stand for anything.

So what did the Doors stand for? Well, if I remember correctly, back in 1968 when I was living in a hippie crash pad in San Diego, California, all my roommates used to have earnest bull sessions far into the night about the "Death Trip" the Doors were supposedly on. Recall this one guy used to sit there all day and night toking on his doob and intoning things like "*Genius* . . . is *very* close to . . . *madness* . . ." instead of doing his homework, and he had a high appreciation of the Doors' early work. Me, I always kind of wanted Morrison to be better than he actually was, like I wished all his songs could have had the understated power of, say, "People Are Strange" ("Faces look ugly when you're alone/Women seem wicked when you're unwanted . . ."), and, like many, it was only after being disappointed that I could learn to take the true poetry and terror whenever it could be found and develop an ever-increasing appreciation for most of the rest of Morrison's work as prime Bozo action.

As for the Poet himself, Hopkins' and Sugerman's book is primarily interesting for what it apparently inadvertently reveals. In the foreword, on the very first page of the book, Sugerman lets go two sentences which have stopped more than one person of my acquaintance from reading any farther: "I just wanted to say I think Jim Morrison was a modern-day god. Oh hell, at least a lord."

It was never revealed whether Hopkins shares this assessment, but the authors then go on for almost four hundred pages, amassing mountains of evidence almost all of which can for most readers point to only one conclusion: that Jim Morrison was apparently a nigh compleat asshole from the instant he popped out of the womb until he died in that bath-tub in Paris (*if* he did indeed die there, they rather gamely leave us with). The first scene in the book takes place in 1955, when Jim was twelve years old, and finds him tobogganing with his younger brother and sister in the snowcapped mountains outside Albuquerque, New Mexico. According to Hopkins and Sugerman, Jim packed his two moppet siblings in front of him in the toboggan so they couldn't move, got up a frightening head of downhill steam and aimed the three of them straight for the broadside of a log cabin:

> The toboggan was less than twenty yards from the side of the cabin on a certain, horrifying collision course. Anne stared dead ahead, the features on her face numbed by terror. Andy was whimpering.
>
> The toboggan swept under a hitching rail and five feet from the cabin was stopped by the children's father. As the children tumbled out of the sled, Anne babbled hysterically about how Jim had pushed them forward and wouldn't let them escape. Andy continued to cry. Steve and Clara Morrison tried to reassure the younger children.
>
> Jim stood nearby looking pleased. "We were just havin' a good time," he said.

Surely an auspicious episode with which to begin recounting the life of a god. But it is only the beginning. Later we will see Jim's little brother breathing heavily at night due to chronic tonsillitis, and the future Lizard King sealing his mouth with cellophane tape and laughing at his near-suffocation. Or ridiculing a paraplegic. Or, at the age of seventeen, rubbing dogshit in his little brother's face.

What the book makes clear is that this sort of thing was no different in kind from later Doors-era antics like covering an entire recording studio (when they first went in to cut "The End") in chemical fire extinguisher foam, or dragging a cab full of people up to Elektra Records president Jac Holzman's apartment in the middle of the night, where Jim ripped out massive amounts of carpet and vomited all over the lobby. Yet this was the sort of thing that not only the authors but his friends and fans from the sixties seemed to admire, even encourage. On one level it's just another case of a culture hero who by now you may not be so surprised to learn you would never have wanted to be around. On another, though, it's just more sixties berserkitude of the kind that piddles down to pathetic sights like Iggy Pop walking through a song called "Dog Food" on the *Tomorrow* show in 1981 and then telling Tom Snyder that he represents the "Dionysian" as opposed to "Apollonian" type o' performer. But there was a time that was true for both Iggy and Jim, though one must wonder just what the creepily conservative teenagers of these supremely Apollonian times might see in this kind of behavior which if anybody they knew was imitating would probably cause them to immediately call the cops. These kids would feel threatened by any performer who came out today and started acting like Morrison did, so is it only the remove of a decade that allows them to feel safe enjoying his antics? Or is it that, just like they could conceivably march happily off to get shot to pieces in El Salvador or Afghanistan to the tune of "The Unknown Soldier" without perceiving any irony, so they can take the life and death of Jim Morrison as just one more TV show with a great soundtrack? And could it be that they are right? If Jim Morrison cared so little about his life, was so willing to make it amount to one huge alcoholic exhibitionistic joke, why should they or we or anybody finally care, except insofar as the scamy details provide trashy entertainment? Or do they, like Danny Sugerman, take exactly these rantings and pukings as evidence he was a "god" or at least a "lord"?

Similarly, in the legendary Miami "cock-flashing" incident, the book reveals that likely all that really happened was he made a fool out of himself, moving entertainingly if not smoothly from "Ain't nobody gonna love my ass" to "You're all a bunch of fuckin' idiots," surely an appropriate *homage* to the Living Theatre's *Paradise Now.* When you're reading all of this stuff, one emotion you may well feel is *envy,* like, *I too* would like to be able to have a fullblown temper tantrum whenever I pleased, and not only get catered to by everybody around me but called a genius and an artist for letting myself act out this way. Or actually, any of us who aren't catered to in this way can count ourselves lucky, because it's supremely unhealthy. In a way, Jim Morrison's life and death could be written off as simply one of the more pathetic episodes in the history of the star system, or that offensive myth we all persist in believing which holds that artists are somehow a race apart and thus entitled to piss on my wife, throw you out the window, smash up the joint and generally do whatever they want. I've seen a lot of this over the years, and what's most ironic is that it always goes under the assumption that to deny them these outbursts would somehow be curbing their creativity, when the reality, as far as I can see, is that it's exactly such insane *tolerance* of another insanity that also contributes to their drying up as artists. Because how can you finally create anything real or beautiful when you have absolutely zero input from the real world, because everyone around is catering to and sheltering you? You can't, and this system is I'd submit why we've seen almost all our rock'n'roll heroes who, unlike Morrison, managed to survive the sixties, end up having nothing to say. Just imagine if he was still around today, 37 years old; no way he could still be singing about chaos and revolution. There are some people who think that everything he'd been through had finally wrought a kind of hard-won wisdom in him that, had he lived, would have allowed him to mellow into perhaps less of a cultural icon and a better poet.

There is another school of thought, though, which holds that he'd said it all by the first Doors album, and everything from there on led downhill.

My response is somewhere in between. I never took Morrison seriously as the Lizard King, but I'm a Doors fan today as I was in 1967; what it came down to fairly early on for me, actually, was accepting the Doors' limitations and that Morrison would never be so much Baudelaire, Rimbaud and Villon as he was a Bozo Prince. Surely he was one father of new wave, as transmitted through Iggy and Patti Smith, but they have proven to be in greater or lesser degree Bozos themselves. One thing that can never be denied Morrison is that at his best (as well as perhaps his worst, or some of it at any rate) he had style, and as he was at his best as a poet of dread, desire and psychic dislocation, so he was also at his best as a clown. So it's no wonder our responses got, and remain, a little confused.

Certainly there are great Bozo moments scattered through the Doors' records: the mock-portentousness of the "Do you remember when we were in Africa?" coda to "Wild Child"; the drunken yowling sermon "Yew CAN-*NOT* pe-TISH-SHON the Lo-WARD with PRAY-yer" at the beginning of "The Soft Parade"; the whole idea of songs like "Five to One" and "Land Ho," extending to the rhythmic bounce of the latter. Hopkins and Sugerman point out the line "I see the bathroom is clear" in "Hyacinth House," and of course there are many here among us who always thought "The End" was but a joke, not to mention the scream of the butterfly. I recall sitting in another hippie pad, in Berkeley during the Summer of Love, when one night in our dope-smoking circle on the floor we were not at all nonplussed to hear the FM deejay take off "The End" halfway through and bury it with snide comments before returning to his fave rave Frisco group; admittedly there was probably some Frisco vs. L.A. chauvinism at work there, but we laughed right along with him and at this "masterpiece." Finally, the Bozo Classic to end 'em all was probably *Absolutely Live,* which included such high points as Morrison stopping "When the Music's Over" to scream at the audience to shut up; the way he says "Pritty neat, pritty neat, pritty good, pritty good" before "Build Me A Woman," which begins with the line, "I got the poontang blues;" the intro to "Close to You:" "Ladies and gentlemen . . . I don't know if you realize it, but tonight you're in for a special treat"—crowd cheers wildly—"No, No, not that not that . . . last time it happened grown men were weeping, policemen were turning in their badges . . ."; and, best of all, the (almost certainly improvised) sung intro to "Break on Through #2:" "Dead cat in a top hat/suckin' on a young man's blood/wishin' that he could come . . . thinks he can kill and slaughter/thinks he can shoot my daughter . . . dead cats/dead rat/thinks he's an aristocrat/that's *crap* . . ."— true street poetry indeed. Plus the bonus of a brief reprise of the "Petition the Lord with prayer" bit, in which this time he sounds like no one so much as Lenny Bruce doing Oral Roberts in his "Religions, Inc." routine—listen to 'em and compare.

In the end, perhaps all the moments like these are his real legacy to us, how he took all the dread and fear and even explosions into the seeming freedom of the sixties and made them first seem even more bizarre, dangerous and apocalyptic than we already thought they were, then turned everything we were taking so seriously into a big joke midstream. Of course, there are still the other songs too, which will always be starkly poetic in their evocations of one "gazing on a city under television skies," perhaps the best conjurings of the L.A. myth in popular song: "End of the Night," "Moonlight Drive," "People Are Strange," "My Eyes Have Seen You," "Cars Hiss By My Window," "L.A. Woman," "Riders on the Storm." But even in these there are lines, all the "Mr. Mojo Risings," that give away his own sense of humor about, if not his talents as a poet, certainly his own persona and even the very real way in which he let his pop stardom lead him unto a betrayal of his poetic gifts. And perhaps what we finally conclude is that it's not really necessary to separate the clown from the poet, that they were in fact inextricably linked, and that even as we were lucky not to have been around any more than our fair share of "Dionysian" infants, so we were lucky to get all the great music on these albums, which is going to set rock 'n' roll standards for a long time to come.

A damsel with a dulcimer
In a vision once I saw:
It was an Abyssinian maid,
And on her dulcimer she played,
Singing of Mount Abora.
Could I revive within me
Her symphony and song,
To such deep delight 'twould win me,
That with music loud and long,
I would build that dome in air,
That sunny dome! those caves of ice!
And all who heard should see them there,
And all should cry, Beware! Beware!

—*from "Kubla Khan,"* SAMUEL TAYLOR COLERIDGE, *1798*

One story about Nico and Jim Morrison has passed into rock legend: *Jim and Nico are staying at The Castle that summer. They are both naked. They are both stoned on acid and drink and hashish. Jim takes Nico up the tower. Jim jumps on to the parapet and looks down to the deep drop below. Nude, he walks along the thin parapet, risking his life. He shouts to Nico to follow him. She refuses. He begs her. She declines. He commands her. She disobeys. He risks everything. She risks nothing.* That is how the story has been passed down from Doors biography to Doors biography. It came first from the lips of Danny Fields and Jack Simmons, who were on the spot, and today it is a renowned image of rock mythology to set aside Jimi Hendrix igniting his guitar and Jerry Lee Lewis smashing his piano: the he-man, the cave man, the strutting cock, disobeying death.

But nobody bothered to ask Nico for her side of the story: 'Everybody says it is true and they saw this thing we did,' she reflected in 1985, 'but I remember something they never say. That I argued with Jim. He asked if I would walk along the edge. I said to him "Why?" and he couldn't answer. It was not a positive act, and not a destructive act; it didn't change anything. So why should I do something that is so vain, just to follow him? It was not spiritual or philosophical. It was a drunk man displaying himself. Did they tell you that about the story? I don't think so.'

Danny Fields once told a journalist that 'Jim and Nico got into this fight, with him pulling her hair all over the place—it was just this weird love making, between the two most adorable monsters, each one trying to be more poetic than the other.' Nico stressed, again in 1985, 'I like my relations to be physical and of the psyche. We hit each other because we were drunk and we enjoyed the sensation. We made love in a gentle way, do you know? It was the opposite to Brian Jones. I thought of Jim Morrison as my brother, so we would grow together. We still do, because he is my soul brother. We exchanged blood. I carry his blood inside me. When he died, and I told people that he wasn't dead, this was my meaning. We had spiritual journeys together.' When asked to clarify this, Nico declared, 'We went into the desert and took drugs.'

Nico wanted Jim Morrison to join her brotherhood, and he obliged. They cut their thumbs in the desert with a knife and let their blood mingle. Such a ritual form of devotion appealed to their shared sense of theatre, but Nico wanted even more. She wanted Morrison to share not just her blood but her son. One night she decided that they should be married, to test if he was stringing her along or serious. As the drunken boor in front of her had offered little more than literary discourse and downright lust, she suggested to him that he might like to propose marriage to her. He laughed himself off his chair. She hit him, they fought and when they got tired, they made up. That was the routine nature of their alliance, day after day—affection-argument-rancour-resolution: 'I was in love with him and that is how love goes, isn't it? He was the first man I was in love with, because he was affectionate to my looks and my mind. But we took too much drink and too many drugs to make it, that was our difficulty. Everything was open to us; there were no rules. We had a too big appetite.'

During their time together in California, between the months of July and August 1967, they often drove out of Los Angeles and into the desert. Morrison found the cactus buttons called peyote, which they picked off and ate. 'Peyote was a spiritual drug. We were in the middle of the desert and everything was natural, you know, in the open air, nature all around, not a hotel room or a bar. And the cactus was natural. You did not buy it from somebody on a street corner. We had visions in the desert. It is like William Blake. Jim was like William Blake; he would see visions like Blake did, angels in trees, he would see these, and so would I. And Jim showed me that this is what a poet does. A poet sees visions and records them. He said that there were more poets in the Comanches than there were in bookstores. The Comanches took the cactus, too. We were like the Indians who lived in this way for thousands of years, before the Christians and as long as the Jews.'

Jim Morrison recorded his psycho-chemical visions and dreams. His notes often comprised the raw material for his poems and songs. He considered that this was how the opium-addicted Coleridge worked, a model good enough for him; one Coleridge poem he read to Nico was titled 'Kubla Khan, or a Vision in a Dream'. Nico just once offered an example of the peyote visions she endured with Morrison: 'The light of the dawn was a very deep green and I believed I was upside down and the sky was the desert which had become a garden and then the ocean. I do not swim and I was frightened when it was water and more resolved when it was land. I felt embraced by the sky-garden.' Soon after, she started to write a song lyric, possibly her first, titled 'Lawns of Dawns', which contained lines such as these:

He blesses you, he blesses me
The day the night caresses,
Caresses you, caresses me,
Can you follow me?

I cannot understand the way I feel
Until I rest on lawns of dawns—
Can you follow me?

The cross-eyed, internal rhymes come directly from Jim Morrison, who wrote 'The west is the best' and even other lines less elegant ('Your milk is my wine/your silk is my shine'). He showed her how he worked on his poems, and in doing so offered her a model. She was reluctant to write anything down, however. It was a major step, to talk about words and then to write them (especially in a foreign language, Nico liked to remind her fans). 'Jim gave me permission to be a writer,' Nico claimed. 'He said to me one day, "I give you permission to write your poems and compose your songs!" My soul brother believed I could do it. I had his authority. And why not? His song was the most popular song in America.' At the time, this was strictly true. The Doors' single 'Light My Fire' had been released in early June, and by the end of July it attained the number one position for three weeks. Nico spent her nights in the desert with the nation's number one pop star who told her to write songs and read to her Coleridge, Shelley and Blake. No wonder she stayed faithful to her boozy, conceited soul brother, when he was the first fuckable man to acknowledge her mind as much as her face.

Nico told him that she did not know how to compose. She could not follow the mechanics of writing. He told her to write down her dreams, literally, write down the images she remembered. This would provide her raw material. He admitted to her that he started by imitating other writers, Céline and Blake for instance, but then he realized that they were writing down their dreams, and so it would be more creative for him to do the same. The songs would be her recounting of her visions, and that was enough. But then she asked him where the melodies came from, and he gave the stock answer he had ready whenever the subject was raised: 'The music came first, and then I'd make up some words to hang on the melody, because that was the only way I could remember it, and most of the time I'd end up with just the words and forget the tune.' The music, then, was the melody, and all the rest was *arrangement*. Nico felt that she had finally passed an examination.

Their affair, a torrid mixture of drinks, drugs, fights and poetry readings, lasted little more than a month before this Adam and Eve left the Garden of Eden without any god's bidding and drifted down their separate roads to hell. They were tired of each other, little more than that; they were exhausted by each other's titanic demands. Aside from the authority she had received to compose, and the slanted introduction to English poetry, she kept two prevailing souvenirs of her liaison: his blood in hers, and red hair. 'He had a fetish for red-haired shanties, you know, Irish shanties. I was so much in love with him that I made my hair red after a while. I wanted to please his taste. It was silly, wasn't it? Like a teenager.' She kept her hair tinted a pale red until he died.

JIM MORRISON PLAYS HIMSELF
RICHARD GOLDSTEIN

Jim Morrison had a myth problem. In life, the artist was always being swallowed up by the sex symbol. In death, his music was appended to the carnage in Vietnam. It isn't Jim's fault that the scariest moments of *Apocalypse Now* are set to songs by the Doors. No doubt he meant "The End" to conjure up Oedipus Rex, not My Lai. But our memory of Morrison has been permanently scarred by napalm. His sexiest lines became an accompaniment to slaughter.

How fitting that Oliver Stone, official auteur of the Vietnam experience, should now attempt to bring the myth to a generation too young to have known the man. Stone's film, *The Doors,* opens March 1, and the director has been none too shy about mining the Morrison mystique. "I think he was a Dionysian figure," Stone told one journalist. "Remember, Dionysus was a god who came to earth to play and tease, to seduce and drive the women mad. Many of Morrison's performances resemble the bacchanals. . . . So I would associate Jim more with a pagan spirit. I think he had a problem with the Christian-god concept. I think he knew god. He read and adored Nietzsche. But he combined his philosophy with an Indian spirit, a sense of a pre-Christian god. Riding the snake, animist . . . Like, do you know he married a Celtic witch in New York? We re-create that."

Oliver Stone has been an acolyte since, fresh from Vietnam and wearing only black, he made the shaman scene on the Lower East Side. "I believed in Morrison's incantations," the director said recently. "Break on through. Kill the pigs. Destroy. Loot. Fuck your mother. All that shit. Anything goes. Anything." That, of course, is precisely what Morrison preached: utter abandon, total will. He wasn't just talking about sex; he meant desire in the broadest, most troubling, sense—as in *beyond good and evil.* No wonder he became an emblem of Vietnam. No wonder his persona remains compelling to a generation whose fantasies have been subordinated by sexual anxiety and terminal upward mobility.

Now, there's a new occasion for the Morrison myth, a new war waged under such a tarmac of denial that no one need face its horror—or capacity to arouse. As the flags fly and the yellow ribbons wave, we desperately need a god of the Great Refusal. Can Morrison fill that bill, or will his languid, writhing body come to signify everything in the American character we're trying to obliterate with Operation Desert Storm? Can Oliver Stone get the *Top Gun* generation to embrace the Lizard King?

Perhaps the harder question is: Can Stone rescue Jim from the iconography that haunted him in life and death? In order to accomplish that, he will have to do what Morrison could not: shatter the myth.

The shaman—he was a man who would intoxicate himself. See, he was probably already an, uh, unusual individual. And he would put himself into a trance by dancing, whirling around, drinking, taking drugs—however. Then he would go on a mental travel and, uh, describe his journey to the rest of the tribe.

This is Jim Morrison talking into my tape recorder. I've been granted an audience with the shaman of Sunset Strip at the peak of his power. A rock critic can still get time alone with a musician—even a superstar. No fleet of flacks, no conference calls with the record label's holding company in Tokyo: just Jim and me on a balmy day in L.A.

Before the Doors, all the heavy hair was flying upcoast, in San Francisco. L.A. stood for everything the counterculture despised, but I was convinced The Revolution would ultimately depend on the dream machine. So I spent a lot of time in that city of "plastic people," and many evenings in the company of world-weary folkies or warlocks with flames shooting from their hair. A friend in the industry, who managed several such acts with the faith of Broadway Danny Rose, suggested I see a band fresh from the boho enclave of Venice. The Doors were being championed by the Zappa/Beefheart contingent of industry intelligentsia, and they'd been signed by a hip label (Elektra) for a modest $5000. I remember less about that night's performance than about the audience, which was riveted on the lead singer, a cherubic rocker in black ringlets who could act out every position in the Kama Sutra with his lips alone.

He had a great rock 'n' roll mouth, and I wrote a rave review. A few months later, I got to preview the first Doors album, in a chamber furnished with mega-speakers, soft chairs, and a complimentary block of hash tucked discreetly in an ornamental box. This time, the music got to me. I loved the blend of blues and beat poetry, and wrote a column predicting great things for the album (carping, with my usual acumen, about its only weak cut: "Light My Fire"). When the hype came true, I had all the access an English major with a boner for rock could hope for.

I got to hang out with Jim Morrison while the forces that would eventually destroy him were still in check—when his creative juices were flowing freely, drinking hadn't destroyed his ability to function, and his relationship with the band was still intact, though barely. At the time, the most self-destructive parts of Morrison's personality seemed groovy—like, break on through to the other side. No one believed superstars were mortal. And, since we all thought show business was dead, no one noticed the time-honored ritual of celebrity sacrifice that was about to claim Jim.

It's necessary now to revise the '60s, even as we attempt to revive them. So I've reconsidered my original piece about meeting Jim. The scenes are described as I witnessed them, and all dialogue is reproduced as I heard it. But the original account celebrated the myth of Morrison; this version is informed by the rage and regret of an older man, whose memory resists the dream machine.

He picks me up at my hotel, settles me in the back seat of his convertible, and drives toward the beach. There's a woman with him, introduced as the Old Lady. (It wouldn't have been customary to mention her name.) She's in advertising, and she'd invented a major marketing concept—the blahs—on acid. Her voice has the flat beatific tone of someone under the lysergic spell. Jim himself seems vague yet animated; my drugometer tells me he's on several substances, at least one of them controlled. But driving around with stoned rock stars was an occupational hazard of countercultural journalism, and compared to some, he seems genuinely connected—to her, to me, to the day.

Jim drops the Old Lady off in Venice and drives us to his favorite setting for an interview: an ashram called the Garden of Self-Realization. We are sitting crosslegged on the ground (as rock writers and their subjects often did), not far from an urn certified to contain Mahatma Gandhi's ashes. Music oozes from speakers hidden in a spray-painted cupola. I make a note of the earthworms surfacing around Jim's hands. He picks one up and examines it as I set the mike in place.

"When you started, did you anticipate your image?"

He answers in a slithering baritone. "Nahh. It just sort of happened . . . unconsciously."

"How did you prepare yourself for stardom?"

"Uh, about the only thing I did was . . . I stopped getting haircuts."

"How has your behavior changed onstage?"

"See, it used to be . . . I'd just stand there and sing. Now, I . . . uh . . . exaggerate a little bit."

I'm too intimidated to raise the questions that preoccupy me: Why is this vision of freedom so violent? Does he really have the fantasies he sings about? How does it feel to throw so many people into a frenzy? How can he possibly live up to his image in bed? But the message I get from Morrison is to keep away from the truly personal or risk an elliptical answer. He would prefer that I believe his persona has everything to do with the Dionysian principle in art and consciousness, and nothing to do with his father (the navy's youngest admiral). He discusses his childhood in Promethian tones. "You could say I was ideally suited for the work I'm doing," he told one journalist. "It's the feeling of a bow string being pulled back for 22 years."

I was used to rock star rhetoric: bombast laced with contempt. But the vibe I got from Jim had an unexpected edge of doubt. It threatened his image, and that made both of us nervous. I thought: What if under the leather beats the heart of a nerd? Morrison strained to cover his tracks with quotability.

"I'm beginning to think it's easier to scare people than to make them laugh. . . ."

"I wonder why people like to believe I'm high all the time. I guess maybe they think someone else can take their trip for them. . . ."

"A game is a closed field—a ring of death with, uh, death at the center. Performing is the only game I've got, so I guess it's my life. . . ."

"They claim everyone was born, but I don't remember it. Maybe I was just having one of my blackouts."

Jim wasn't content to play the suffering artist. He wanted to be an avatar—and not just Elvis in love beads. He filled my tape with breathy hyperbole about the nature of myth. Twenty years later, such speculation would be fodder for Bill Moyers on PBS. Back then, Jim had to make do with a film student's knowledge of the boho pantheon: Artaud, Nietzsche, Rimbaud.

"There's this theory about tragedy," Jim expounds as the sun sets over the Garden of Self-Realization, "that Aristotle didn't mean catharsis for the audience, but a purgation of emotions for the actors themselves. The audience is just a witness to the events taking place onstage." What makes the ruminations bearable is Morrison's insistence on relating every high concept to the body—his body.

"See, singing has all the things I like," he says. "It's involved with writing and music. There's a lot of acting. And it has this one other thing . . . a physical element . . . a sense of the immediate. When I sing, I create characters."

"What kinds of characters?"

"Oh . . . hundreds. Hundreds of 'em."

Of course, next to Axl Rose or even Neil Young—who once told me that when the Revolution came, he'd die defending his swimming pool— Jim was tenured faculty. Whatever his limits, Morrison was engaged in the same struggle radical intellectuals were waging: to confront both the banality of mass-culture and the sterility of art. He saw sex—we all did then—as the point of connection between pleasure and politics. "Think of us as erotic politicians," he once said, utterly earnest about the liberation agenda of the '60s (and utterly oblivious to its limits). In the end, it was much easier for Morrison to project his sexuality than his sensibility. The world wanted, and still wants, to think of Jimbo the way groupie-turned-belle lettrest Pamela Des Barres described him: "He defied the system with his dick."

Morrison will always be remembered for the moment when he whipped it out onstage. I regard that incident as a gesture of desperation. He was being eaten alive by his own erotic mystique, and may finally have decided to make it literal. Miami was the beginning of the end for the Doors, and, literally, for Morrison. Along with placing him in psychic peril, it must also have forced him to confront the bind of the radical entertainer. Not even Lenny Bruce had the weight of superstardom on his back.

Jim was still keeping his dick in his pants when I met him, but I well remember, some months later, standing backstage as the Doors made their network debut, on *The Ed Sullivan Show* no less. When I got there, the band was bitching about the stage set: a grouping of pasteboard doors. On TV, nothing could be left to the imagination. Huxley's vision of a mind/body utopia; Artaud's theater of cruelty; Nietzsche's new man—all beside the point. Dionysus was just another show biz act, slotted between Van Cliburn and the Flying Walendas—something hairy and horny to bring in the kids. Jim seemed dejected. I thought it was the set, but unbeknownst to me, there had been a heated discussion backstage: could Dionysus please not sing the word *higher* in "Light My Fire"? (He did.)

The spirit of his songs, and their integrity as art, survived such insults, as well as Jim's own pretensions. That's because their power doesn't spring from the myths Jim draped around him like a cloak, but from the anguish he kept hidden. It lodged in the corners of his lyrics, and informed his every scream. Morrison's Oedipal passions seem forced next to John Lennon's, his rage against women far more prosaic than Bob Dylan's ice pick of misogyny. But his ballads of living on the edge are utterly authoritative, perhaps because Morrison believed, above all else, that "people are strange." He was far more eager to expound on theories of the unconscious than to explore his own psyche. But he was too vulnerable—and perhaps in too much pain—to control what he revealed about himself, even when asked to explain the central metaphor in one of his lyrics.

"See, this song is called 'Horse Latitudes,' because it's about the Doldrums, where sailing ships from Spain would get stuck. In order to lighten the vessel, they had to throw things overboard. Their major cargo was working horses for the New World. And this song is about that moment when the horse is in the air. I imagine it must have been hard to get them over the side. When they got to the edge, they probably started chucking and kicking. And it must have been hell for the men to watch, too. Because horses can swim for a while, but then they lose their strength and just go down . . . slowly sink away. . . ."

Jim was a blues singer wailing from behind a scrim of sound and light, movement and poetry. But bereft of his props, he looked less like his persona than any performer I'd ever met. The face was prematurely puffy, the gaze uncertain. I'd never be able to think of Jim Morrison as a sex symbol, despite his iconic looks. Under the snakeskin, I saw a slippery kid—and a fragile man. Even in the mock-sylvan setting of the Garden of Self-Realization, with film-school bromides flying fast and thick, I sensed that he was saying more than he had to, giving me more time than he should. If I stuck around long enough, he might let me see it all.

> Robby and I were sittin' on a plane an' like it's first class, so you get a couple a drinks, an' I said to Robby, "Y'know, there are Apollonian people . . . like, very formal, rational dreamers. An' then there's this Dionysian thing . . . the insanity trip . . . way inside. You're an Apollonian, y'know . . . an' you should get into the Dionysian thing." An' he looks up at me an' says, "Oh yeah, right Jim."

The Lizard King slithers down Sunset Strip in full snakeskin and leather tights. He moves past ticky-tacoramas and used-head shops into the open arms of recording studio B, where his subjects wait. I realize instantly that Jim is loaded. Juiced. Showing his traditional side, in this age of any-drug-but-booze. He deposits a half-empty quart of wine on top of the control panel and downs the remnants of somebody's beer. "Hafta break it in," he mutters, caressing the sleeves of his jacket, which sits green and scaly on his shoulders, crinkling like tinfoil whenever he moves.

Behind a glass partition, the other Doors hunch over their instruments, intent on a rhythm line. The gap between Morrison and the band is more evident in the studio than onstage, where cohesion is mandatory. You can do things in pieces in the studio. Here, in the realm of the overdub, the band takes on a methodical sobriety that Jim would call "Apollonian." When he is drinking, the others work around him, tolerating his presence as a pungent, if necessary, prop.

"I'm the square of the Western hemisphere," he fumes. "Man . . . whenever somebody'd say something groovy, it'd blow my mind. Now, I'm learnin'. You like people? I hate 'em . . . screw 'em . . . I don't need 'em. Oh, I need 'em . . . to grow potatoes."

Morrison walks into the glass booth used for recording vocals, and accosts a vacant mike. Between belches, he gazes out at us, smirking. Paul Rothchild, the group's producer, takes action, cutting off Jim's mike to assure concentration on the riff at hand. From behind the glass, Morrison looks like a silent movie of himself, speeded up for laughs. He teeters about, writhing frantically. The idol has turned into an ordinary alcoholic whose family has learned to tune him out. I'm horrified by his helplessness. Years later, I would realize that the other musicians are also horrified and helpless in the face of an old friend's self-destruction. Their indifference is actually a desperate attempt to repress their desire to bolt from his sight. But they need him—we all do. The myth of the Lizard King is too important for any of us to face the facts about where it's leading Jim and America—to the brink.

Now it's time for the vocal. Morrison turns out the lights in the recording chamber, fits himself with earphones, and begins to sing. Crescendos of breath between the syllables. Every guzzle and belch is audible. His voice is half threat, half plea. . . .

Suddenly, he emerges from his formica cell, inflicting his back upon a wall. He is sweat-drunk but still coherent, and he mutters so everyone can hear: "If I had an ax . . . man, I'd kill everybody . . .'cept . . . uh . . . my friends." Now, there is no avoiding him. We all sit frozen, waiting for some cataclysmic note to drop. Instead, he bleats: "Ah, I hafta get one o' them Mexican wedding shirts." A long pause, then Robbie Krieger's Old Lady takes him on: "I don't know if they come in your size."

"I'm a medium . . . with a large neck."

"We'll have to get you measured, then."

"Uh-uh. I don't like to be measured." His eyes glow with sleep and swagger.

"Oh Jim, we're not gonna measure all of you. Just your shoulders."

THE END
ALBERT GOLDMAN

Jim Morrison's death—in Paris on July 3, 1971—was kept so quiet that it took two days for even a rumor of the event to reach his manager in Los Angeles. When the phone awoke Bill Siddons and he got the word from London, he didn't take it seriously. Why should he? Reports of Morrison's death were as common as UFO sightings. One day he was rumored blind or dead of OD; the next day he had been killed in a car crash or locked up in a lunatic asylum or was in a hospital with both legs amputated. Those were the terrifying disasters his dangerous aura suggested, and the aura was reinforced by the way he lived, always dead drunk or wildly high, constantly falling out of windows or cracking up his car or proclaiming in some unmistakable fashion that he was hell-bent on dying. Yet as Siddons rolled over to go back to sleep, he found himself troubled by a worrisome impulse that finally compelled him to call the apartment in Paris where his star had been living for the past four months. Pamela Courson, Morrison's girlfriend, offered no explanations, but she told the manager, as if he lived around the corner, to come over immediately.

Three days later, Siddons addressed Morrison's fans in a prepared statement released through a public relations firm. "I have just returned from Paris," he announced, "where I attended the funeral of Jim Morrison. Jim was buried in a simple ceremony, with only a few close friends present. The initial news of his death and funeral was kept quiet because those of us who knew him intimately and loved him as a person wanted to avoid all the notoriety and circuslike atmosphere that surrounded the deaths of such other rock personalities as Janis Joplin and Jimi Hendrix."

Were the deaths of Joplin and Hendrix surrounded by a "circuslike atmosphere"? Not really. There was shock and horror, grief and curiosity, but the "notoriety" that enveloped those deaths was something again. It was engendered by their common cause—drug abuse. If the 27-year-old Jim Morrison had died as the press release asserted—"peacefully of natural causes . . . with his wife Pam," after seeing a doctor about a "respiratory problem"—why should there have been any fear of notoriety?

The truth is that there was a lot more to the death of Jim Morrison than could be inferred from Siddons's bland statement; in fact, nobody with any brains has ever believed that Jim Morrison died peacefully in his sleep from natural causes. Yet even today, nearly 20 years after the event, we still don't know exactly what happened. Though Morrison is currently enjoying one of those electric resurrections that have given many old rock stars a second life, though his albums are selling better than ever and his legend is being told and retold in a steady stream of new articles and books and he has now been enshrined in a major motion picture by Oliver Stone, we have yet to hear a convincing account of how he died. Nor is his death a matter of little consequence in comparison with his life; in fact, the two are one and the same thing, for no figure of the counterculture either in Jim's lifetime or before him had ever lived with the image of death fixed so firmly in his mental gaze.

From the beginning to the end of his brief but brilliant career, Jim Morrison wrote about death, talked about death, sang about death, and enacted death onstage. His masterpiece, the weird, shamanistic spirit voyage titled "The End," is entirely about death and its associations in his mind: patricide, maternal incest, drugs, love, and the end of the world.

Death not only looms up from his lyrics, but it sends its chilling breath out through the spooky music of the Doors, which often resembles a rock 'n' roll dance of death. Everybody who knew Morrison recognized that he was bound for an early grave, and this constant anticipation of his death finally translated itself into a wire dispatch on March 7, 1968, while the band was at the height of its fame. That day a news service flashed: "Jim Morrison dead—more later."

Morrison had a lot of reasons for his death obsession, and he was at pains to articulate them. Basically, he viewed life as a struggle to escape the deadening clutches of mindlessness and insensibility, the numbing effects of the routines into which we all sink after childhood. He found in the defiant and risky lives of such underground poets as Baudelaire and Rimbaud and in the nihilistic philosophy of Nietzsche chapter and verse for his instinctive conviction that the only way to break through to passion, illumination, and ecstasy was to live dangerously. One is free to accept his arguments as either courageous convictions backed by the authority of intellectual and artistic genius or as neurotic rationalizations for a self-destructive mania whose roots lay in his ill-reported childhood or perhaps in some anomaly of his biochemistry. The only thing that really matters is the recognition that Jim Morrison's life and art entailed a continuous dialogue with death; hence, the absurdity of treating his death, as some writers have done, as an unimportant or uninteresting event. The fact is that not knowing how Jim Morrison died is exactly like having a tragedy whose final act consists of nothing but rough sketches for a half-dozen possible endings.

This problem impressed itself strongly on Morrison's only authentic biographer, pop journalist Jerry Hopkins. His widely read book, *No One Here Gets Out Alive* (which bears the name of Danny Sugerman as coauthor), was designed originally to be printed in two alternate versions, one concluding with Morrison's death, the other with his escape from fame after staging a fake demise, these being the basic alternatives. Naturally, the publisher rejected such a preposterous scheme, which was simply a gimmick for making a virtue out of a failure in research.

The result is a biography that concludes in a hopeless welter of rumors and cockeyed speculations. Hopkins labeled the most plausible of these tales the "official" version without explaining what exactly makes it official. Apparently, this was the story that Pamela Courson told in the few years that intervened between Morrison's death and her own.

According to this account, Jim spent the early part of the evening of Friday, July 2, having supper on the terrace of a restaurant near his apartment with Pamela, his companion of five years—a pretty, freckled, inno-cent-looking girl from Orange County, California, with a bad heroin habit. They were accompanied by an old friend, Alan Ronay, a Paris-born film technician who lives in Los Angeles but was staying at the time with two well-known French filmmakers, Jacques Demy (director of *The Umbrellas of Cherbourg*) and his wife, Agnès Varda. After dinner Morrison went off alone to see a film that Ronay had recommended, Raoul Walsh's 1947 picture *Pursued,* a film-noir treatment of the tradi-tional Hollywood western, starring Robert Mitchum.

When Morrison returned to the flat late that night, he vomited a little blood. Pamela was not unduly concerned, because this had happened before without ill consequences. When he announced that he was going to take a bath, she went to sleep. At five in the morning, she awoke and found him in the tub, "his arms resting on the porcelain sides, his head back, his long, wet hair matted against the rim, a boyish smile across his clean-shaven face." At first Pamela thought he was playing one of his macabre jokes, but then she called the fire department's resuscitation unit.

Jerry Hopkins also possessed a far different and more interesting account to which he merely alludes, probably because he didn't place much faith in it. This reconstruction was the work of Hervé Muller, a French pop journalist who spent some time with Morrison in the last months of his life and actually phoned his apartment on the morning of his death, only to be told by Alan Ronay that the couple had gone out of town for the weekend. Subsequently, Muller published a book about Morrison, but he refrained from going into the details of his hero's death; not until March of last year did his findings appear, in the French maga-zine *Globe.*

According to Muller, Morrison had been waiting during the days that preceded his demise for a delivery of heroin from Marseilles (the head-quarters of the "French Connection"—i.e., the Corsican Mafia). Jim had bankrolled this buy, which was costly but justified by the fact that the dealer, whose nom de dope was "le Chinois," dealt only in the purest China White (highly refined heroin from Hong Kong). After the usual delays—accompanied doubtless by a lot of excuses from the connection's bag dealers in Paris and a lot of paranoia in the Morrison household—word came through that the smack could be picked up at Jim's customary hangout, the Rock 'n' Roll Circus.

The Circus was a vaulted *cave* at 57 rue de Seine in the student quar-ter of St.-Germaine. Decorated with huge blowups of rock stars dressed in circus costumes, it was meant to capture the atmosphere of trendy British clubs, like the Bag O'Nails. Its clientele was "restricted," its hours mid-night till way past dawn, its cuisine American soul food, the decor of its super-exclusive smoking room Moroccan, and its entertainment—apart from dancing to records—spontaneous jam sessions by visiting rock stars who wanted to stretch out after hours.

The former manager, Sam Bernett, recalls that Morrison came in every night. "He was always high or drunk, in an abnormal state." Few people recognized him because he had grown so fat that he appeared to be 40. One night he got rowdy and the bouncers, not knowing who he was, threw him out into an alley, where he was rescued by a French rock fan who carried him off to a friend's garret. After spending the night, Jim took everyone out to breakfast the next day at an expensive sidewalk restaurant. Another night Morrison tried to mount the stage at the Circus but was too drunk to perform. In his last days, he spent most of his time in the men's room, where the principal activity was scoring drugs.

It was in the men's room, according to Muller, that Morrison met on his last night a drug runner named "le Petit Robert." When Robert handed over the scag, he warned Jim, "This is very strong stuff." Jim promptly took a toot and collapsed in a coma. A couple of "Pam's friends," perhaps two of the club's husky bouncers, hauled Morrison out of the toilet (located upstairs in a quiet area) and through an adjacent fire exit that led into the kitchen of a glitzy transvestite cabaret, the Alcazar, which had shut down for the night. They carried him out of this club's entrance, which was on the opposite side of the block at 62 rue Mazarine. Here they put him into a car and carried him back to his apartment, where they immersed him a tub of cold water in an attempt to revive him.

Muller concedes when pressed that he is not totally persuaded of the accuracy of his account because his sources were shadowy junkies and small-time dealers with no reputation for honesty. Yet his story contains nothing inherently implausible. Though Morrison was not a junkie, he often bought heroin for Pam. (Scoring smack is a "man's job.") Michel Auder, former husband of Viva, the Andy Warhol "superstar," recalls encountering Jim on more than one occasion at the rooms of a heroin dealer in the Chelsea Hotel in New York. American disc jockey Cameron Watson recollects that a couple of weeks before Jim's death, he observed him sitting on the terrace of the Café de Flor with a photographer, who got up and approached Watson, whispering, "Jim Morrison wants to buy some smack. Do you know where he can get some?"

That Morrison himself would take a hit of something he had been warned against is perfectly in character. He would not have injected the drug, because he had a dread of needles. He would have sniffed it. And a couple of good snorts could have killed him, because nonusers lack the protective tolerance of the junkie. Though Muller's tale is not well-founded, it could be true, because it is true to "the life."

Confronted by two irreconcilable accounts of the same event, a biographer instinctively seeks a third source on which he can place greater reliance. But who would it be in this case? Clearly, there are a number of former intimates of Jim Morrison who know more about his death than they have ever divulged, but it is naive to assume that they would start talking after all these years unless they could be offered an inducement that would appeal to them, like an opportunity to appear in a major motion picture.

Lacking the ability to offer this resource, I decided to go after the files of the French police. Ostensibly, these reports are confidential and available only to family members or their authorized representatives, but past experience suggested that there might be some way to slip past the bureaucratic barriers.

Before I made the attempt, however, I decided to ask Jerry Hopkins what he thought of the approach. He assured me that there were no official records because no autopsy had been performed. This was clearly nonsense, because nobody can die in a city like Paris without the police making a record of the event. On the other hand, there was the possibility that the death of Jim Morrison had been covered up by the police for some mysterious reason, and in that case, there would be a record, but its value would be nothing.

As it turned out, retrieving the files from the archives was not so difficult as I had assumed. After going through the usual bureaucratic rigmarole and sweating out a period of anxious uncertainty, my Paris researchers, Martha Legace and Anne Souhrada, succeeded in extracting the relevant documents: the dossier of the criminal-investigation department of the French police and the report of an emergency-rescue team in the archives of the fire department.

The police report consists primarily of the transcript of an inquest held at the Arsenal police station on the afternoon following Morrison's death. Testimony was taken from the fire-department lieutenant commanding the rescue unit, the officer of the criminal-investigation department who inspected the premises (and who also presided over the hearing); the medical examiner who viewed the body; and the two chief witnesses, Pamela Courson and Alan Ronay.

Courson's testimony demands to be considered first because it offers what purports to be a complete account of Jim Morrison's last night. (Ronay acted as her interpreter, which means that the police did not question one witness independently of the other.) In the translation that follows, the word *ami* is rendered as "friend," although, of course, it can also mean "lover."

"I am the friend of Mr. Morrison," Pamela declared. "I lived with him as his wife for five years. I arrived in France with my friend last March. . . . He was a writer, but he lived on a private income. Before coming to live at [17] rue de Beautreillis [in the Marais district], we stayed for three weeks at the Hotel de Nice on the rue des Beaux Arts. There my friend became ill. He complained of having trouble breathing, and he also had coughing fits at night. I called a doctor, who arrived at the hotel and prescribed pills for asthma. My friend didn't like to go to doctors, and he never took care of his health. I can't say who the doctor was who looked after my friend, and I didn't keep the prescription. At the time of an earlier stay in London, my friend already had this same illness.

"Last night . . . my friend went alone to have dinner in a restaurant, undoubtedly in the neighborhood. When he returned from the restaurant, the two of us went to the movies to see *Pursued*. The movie house is near the Pelletier métro [in a sleazy commercial district in the ninth arrondissement]. It's called, I think, Action Lafayette.

"We returned from the movies [at] about one in the morning. I did the dishes and my friend showed home movies. He seemed to be in good health and very happy. But I must say that he never complained—it wasn't in his nature. Afterward, we listened to records in the bedroom. We listened lying together on the bed. I think we went to sleep around 2:30, but I can't say exactly. The record player stopped automatically.

"No, we didn't have sex last night.

"Around 3:30, I think—there wasn't any clock in the bedroom and I wasn't concerned about the time—I was awakened by the noise my friend was making breathing. . . . I had the impression that he was suffocating. I shook him and slapped him several times in order to wake him up. I asked him what was wrong. I wanted to call a doctor. My friend said that he felt fine and that he didn't want to see a doctor. He got up and walked around the room. Then he said that he wanted to take a warm bath.

"When he was in the bath, he called me and said that he was nauseated and wanted to vomit. As I went toward the bathroom, I took from the kitchen an orange pot. [He vomited into this pot.] It looked to me as though there was blood in his vomit. I emptied the pot. Then he vomited again into the pot—this time it was all blood. Then he vomited a third time, bringing up some blood clots. Each time I emptied the pot into the sink and rinsed it.

"Then my friend said that he felt 'bizarre,' but he said to me, 'I'm not ill. Do not call a doctor. I feel better. It's over.' He said to me, 'Go to sleep,' and added that when he had finished bathing he would rejoin me in bed. At this moment, it did seem to me that my friend was getting better, because since he had vomited, the color had come back into his skin. I went back to bed and fell asleep immediately because I felt reassured.

"I don't know how long I slept. I woke up with a start and saw that my friend was not next to me. I ran into the bathroom and I saw that he was still in the bathtub. His head was not in the water. He appeared to be sleeping. His head was resting on the edge of the tub. There was a little blood under his nostrils. I thought I could wake him. I thought that he was ill and unconscious. I tried to take him out of the tub, but I couldn't. At this moment I telephoned Mr. Ronay, another American, to ask him to call an ambulance.

"About a half hour later, Mr. Ronay came to my place. When Mr. Ronay arrived with his friend, Madame Agnès [Varda] Demy, they called, I believe, either the firemen or the police."

Ronay's testimony, predictably, corroborates Courson's in every detail save one:

"I have known Mr. Morrison since 1963. He is one of my friends. This morning around 8:30, I was awakened by a telephone call from Miss Courson, who asked for my help. She told me to come right away. She was crying. She said that her friend had lost consciousness. I got up and went at once to the rue de Beautreillis in the company of my friend, Madame Demy. [Jacques Demy was in London.] When I arrived, I saw the firemen in the street. I asked them what was happening. They didn't tell me. I went up to the apartment. I saw Miss Courson . . . who told me that her friend was dead. . . . He had already been removed from the bathroom and laid on the bed.

"My friend Morrison drank a lot and did not hold his liquor well.

"I am certain that my friend never used drugs. He often spoke about the folly of young people who used drugs and considered this a very grave problem.

"I saw Mr. Morrison yesterday afternoon around 6 P.M. I thought that he looked ill and told him. He replied that everything was going well. But

in any case, he never complained. I took a walk with him yesterday afternoon. He told me that he was tired. In the course of our stroll, he had an
attack of hiccups. This spell lasted, I think, for about an hour. At one point
he closed his eyes, and I noticed that his skin was gray. He told me that he
had closed his eyes to concentrate on getting rid of his hiccups. We also
carried up to his apartment some logs that were in the courtyard. My
friend was extremely tired by this exertion."

First, it will be observed that these statements differ at many points from
those in the so-called "official" version published in the Hopkins-
Sugerman biography. Second, there is a contradiction in Ronay's and
Courson's testimony. Ronay says that the firemen were at the building
when he arrived. But Courson, in her statement, translated by Ronay, says
that he and Varda summoned the firemen *after* they arrived. Assuming
Ronay's account to be true, who, then, *did* summon the firemen?

The most valuable professional testimony offered at the inquest was
provided by Lieutenant, now Colonel, Alan Raison, commander of the
fire-department rescue unit—ten men in a big truck—who were the first
people to come to Courson's aid. The lieutenant reported that he was
summoned at 9:20 by a report of an *"asphyxié,"* a person in a state of
suffocation. At 9:24 (the fire station was around the corner) he was met
at the door of the fourth-floor flat by a young woman whose nightgown
was damp and who did not speak French. She led him to the bathroom,
where he discovered a fat, naked man lying in the tub with his head
reclining on a pad and his right arm extended along the rim. The pale-
pink-tinged water in the tub was warm, as was the body, which was still
supple.

As a hot tub will not retain any noticeable heat for more than two or
three hours, it is clear that Jim Morrison drew the bath in which he died
at dawn, not in the middle of the night as Pam related. Nor could she have
discovered him dead at five o'clock.

The firemen removed the body from the tub and laid it on the bedroom floor to obtain the hard, unyielding surface required for heart mas-
sage. Soon they abandoned their efforts and, as the police arrived, they left
the premises at 9:47.

Upon their return to Sevigne Barracks, they filed a terse report. It
states that Morrison had become ill at 5:30 but had decided to take a bath
to make himself feel better. ("A neighbor"—i.e., Ronay—translated for

Courson.) His "wife" then fell asleep and did not awaken until 9:15, when she discovered him in the tub. She described Morrison as "writer, singer." Clearly, it was after the authorities had left and she had had time to discuss her predicament with Ronay and Varda that Pamela changed her tune and described Morrison as a writer living on a private income.

When quizzed about these events, Varda offered two explanations: (1) "It was not as a rock star that I loved him. Why should French policemen know that he was a famous rock star?" (2) "You have to be very careful when a foreigner is involved."

The report of the police investigator, Jacques Manchez, is interesting primarily for its misconceptions. After conferring with his colleagues from the fire department and after inspecting the body and the bathroom—where he measured the tub and the depth of its water—he went into the living room, where a patrolman introduced him to Courson, Ronay, and Varda. He was told—and the error went into the records—that *all three were Americans* and that only Ronay spoke French. Not only did he mistake an established French filmmaker for a foreigner, but—evidently because she gave the same home address as Ronay, on the rue Daguerre in Montparnasse—he described her as the latter's "concubine," the same term that he applied to Courson.

The most disappointing testimony was that furnished by the medical examiner, Dr. Max Vasille. He did not arrive at the apartment until six in the evening. The pertinent portion of his report offers no insight into the cause of death. "I note," the doctor attested, "that the body does not show, apart from the lividness of death, any suspicious signs of trauma or lesions of any kind. A little blood around the nostrils. The history of Mr. Morrison's condition, such as it was described to us by a friend on the premises [Ronay?], can be summed up thus: Mr. Morrison had been complaining for a few weeks of precordial [over the heart] pains with dyspnoea [difficulty breathing]. It was evidently coronary problems, possibly aggravated by abusive drinking. One can imagine that on the occasion of a change of outside temperature [a puzzling remark] followed by a bath, these troubles were suddenly aggravated, leading to classical myocardial infarction [blockage of a coronary artery], causing sudden death. I conclude from my examination that death was caused by heart failure (natural death)."

Under Article 74 of the French Penal Procedures Code, where there is "no crime or flagrant misdemeanor, the state prosecutor can charge a medical expert with the power of making an inquiry." When the doctor delivered his implausible but preemptive opinion that the deceased had died of natural causes, Captain Robert Berry, commander of the Arsenal

Precinct, closed the case and signed the report. Permission to bury the dead was granted.

The next steps were routine. During the afternoon, someone—most likely Alan Ronay, who describes himself at the conclusion of his deposition as being busy with the funeral arrangements—called a funeral home, Pompes Funébres Bigot at 8 rue du Cloître Notre-Dame. The director, Michel Gangenepain, made out the death certificate, and an undertaker was dispatched to the apartment. He cleansed the body, placing it in dry ice to prevent decomposition. It was then placed in an expensive oak casket lined with canvas. Bill Siddons saw the closed coffin when he arrived the following Tuesday. (It was the fact that Siddons did not see the corpse that gave rise to the rumors that the casket was empty and Jim was living happily in Africa, free of the burdens of fame.) Courson went, most likely with Ronay, to Père-Lachaise Cemetery—which Jim had visited recently to view the graves of the great—where she bought a double plot (one body laid atop another) for a moderate sum. No other kind of grave was available. The price of a funeral was controlled in those days by the government. The total cost, including four pallbearers and a hearse, was only 4,600 francs, about $830.

The funeral was held on Wednesday afternoon. No family members were invited, nor were any clergy involved. Those present were Pamela Courson, Alan Ronay, Agnès Varda, Bill Siddons, and Robin Wertle—a young Canadian woman who had acted as Jim and Pam's secretary in Paris. They read some verses and threw flowers on the coffin when it was lowered five meters into the earth.

That same day Courson filed the death certificate at the office of the American consul. The following day she and Siddons flew back to Los Angeles. Only then was the public notified of Morrison's death in a carefully contrived statement designed to quell suspicion.

On April 25, 1974, Pamela Courson, age 27, was found dead in her Hollywood apartment of a heroin overdose, shortly after receiving $20,000 in royalties as Jim Morrison's sole heir. She had celebrated by buying herself a yellow Volkswagen convertible, a monogrammed mink scarf, and an ounce of China White.

The testimony at the inquest and the statements—public and private— issued subsequently by Pamela Courson and Bill Siddons combine to create the impression that Jim Morrison died of a grave illness whose symptoms he stubbornly ignored. Yet when the basis for this opinion is sought, it all turns on the word of one drug-addicted woman with a notorious penchant for what is politely described as "fantasy."

Jim Morrison had no history of either heart disease or asthma before he left for Europe. He had done a lot of drinking and tried a lot of drugs, but he had never been seriously ill, nor had he exhibited any symptoms to anybody else, save for a heavy cough, doubtlessly aggravated by dragging deeply on three packs of cigarettes a day.

He had punctured a lung, however, early in March in a fall from the second floor of a Hollywood hotel. This is a self-healing injury from which he should have long since recovered. Even if he did vomit blood on his last night (note, by the way, how the violent hemorrhaging of the inquest shrinks to a "little blood" in the story that's quoted by Hopkins), the most likely explanation is that, like many drinkers, he had developed an ulcer that started bleeding when he started vomiting. He could have been nauseated because of something he ate for supper—or from snorting heroin.

Even a tiny amount of heroin can produce nausea in a nonuser, as Bill Siddons related when he returned from Morrison's funeral. He told the surviving members of the band, "Once, while alone in the living room [of Morrison's apartment], I opened a carved box on the coffee table and found white powder in a clear envelope. Pam was in the kitchen, so I decided to try a little and see what it was. It wasn't coke. Soon afterward I became nauseous and felt very sick. It sure was something that I'd never tried before."

The fact that Morrison insisted there was nothing wrong with him and that he did not want to see a doctor that night suggests he knew perfectly well what was wrong with him—and that it was not disease, but dope. His suggestion that Courson go to sleep while he remained in the bathroom, as well as the smile reported to have been on his face in the Hopkins biography, are further evidence that heroin was the cause of his death. People who die of myocardial infarction, which produces a crushing pain in the heart, do not die smiling.

Likewise, the behavior of Pam and her friends in concealing from the French authorities the real identity of James Douglas Morrison suggests that they had reason to fear the effects of such a disclosure. Clearly, if the police had known that the young man they had found dead at 17 rue de Beautreillis was an internationally famous American rock star, they would have examined his death more carefully and, suspecting it was due to drugs, ordered a post-mortem. If the autopsy had demonstrated the presence of heroin in his body, the investigation would have broadened to include Courson and her acquaintances. The police might have found her stash or they might have nailed her suppliers. Undoubtedly, the police had their eye on the Rock 'n' Roll Circus (which closed down shortly thereafter), where Jim and Pam probably scored some smack on the night of his death. Clearly, it was very important that Pamela Courson deceive the French police and get out of the country as quickly as possible.

When Captain Robert Berry, now 76, was quizzed recently about his involvement in the case, he confirmed that the police knew nothing of Jim Morrison's true identity. Asked if he thought that heroin could have been the true cause of death, he considered the question carefully and replied, "It is highly possible." Alan Ronay's vigorous denial that Jim Morrison ever took drugs shows where the shoe pinched. When Hervé Muller sought to question Agnès Varda about her role in *l'affaire Morrison,* she threatened to sue him.

That heroin was the cause of Jim Morrison's death is confirmed by information that has been available for four years but was published only recently in John Densmore's *Riders on the Storm.* When the Doors drummer raises the questions of Morrison's death, he remarks that he has known the truth since 1986, when he was interviewed on PBS by Roger Steffens, a well-known radio personality in Los Angeles. Steffens had objected to the widespread fantasy that Jim Morrison is still alive, remarking that he knew the people who had discovered his dead body. They were pop star Marianne Faithfull (who now denies ever having had any contact with Jim Morrison) and Jean DeBreteuil, the playboy son of a French count who until his demise owned most of the French newspapers in North Africa.

According to Steffens, on the night of Jim Morrison's death, Pam had called DeBreteuil, who was one of her lovers (Jim and Pamela had an "open" relationship), and told him, "Jim is in the bathroom. The door is locked. I can't get him out. Will you come over immediately?" DeBreteuil and Faithfull arrived shortly thereafter and managed to open the door. When they caught sight of Morrison stretched out dead in the tub, they went into shock. Both were heroin addicts, and in Jim's death, they foresaw their own. They were still agitated two days later when they recounted the story to Steffens and his wife of that time, Cynthia Cottle, a Vietnam War correspondent.

Prompted by this revelation, I got in touch with Steffens and Cottle, intent on putting the anecdote in context. Steffens told me that in 1971 he and his wife were living in Marrakech, where they had become acquainted wtih DeBreteuil through his widowed mother.

Jean had cut into the most closely guarded celebrity circles by handing out costly drugs as if they were party favors. He imported whole kilos of the finest Moroccan hashish via diplomatic pouch and had become a boot-and-shoot junkie—which was the bond that attached Pam to him. He had reached the apogee of his career as a superfan when he got tight with the Rolling Stones while working as a production consultant on a French TV show about the band.

Jean was staying at Keith Richards's flat in London when he fell in with Marianne Faithfull. The one-time pop star was so washed up by this point that she was virtually on the street. Naturally, she took up with the elegant young Jean, who was soon to inherit his deceased father's title and well-endowed with the medicine for all her ills. On their first day together, they bought a Bentley—and totaled it that night. Then they decided to get off the scene by shifting to Paris.

They had only just reached the city when they received Pam's desperate call. They described the scene in the bathroom with the floor littered with whiskey bottles.

That heroin was the cause of death is further substantiated by Danny Sugerman's account in *Wonderland Avenue* of a night spent snorting Brown Sugar (Mexican heroin) with Pamela after her return to Los Angeles. She is quoted as saying, "I killed him. It was my dope. . . . He found out I was doing dope, and of course, you know Jim, he just had to try it. And I gave it to him! He'd never done it before and I gave it to him. Then he said he didn't feel well. . . . I should have gone and checked on him, but I nodded out. . . . When I woke up at dawn . . . I went into the bathroom and there he was in the tub. . . . He was smiling . . . and I thought he was putting me on."

Clearly, DeBreteuil and Faithfull could not possibly have summoned the police. The scandal of two junkies—one bearing an aristocratic name, the other an international pop star—discovered at the site of another star's death of a drug overdose would have immediately enveloped them. They decided instead to flee the apartment and get out of the country fast.

The next day they flew to Tangier, and on Monday night, so stoned that they were weaving back and forth, they told their story to the Steffenses. Steffens recalls that Marianne Faithfull dropped her lit cigarette on her skirt three times that night and each time he had to beat out the fire as she stared at him with a startled expression that said, "Why is this man hitting me?" (The lesson of Morrison's death was wasted on Jean; a year later in Tangier, he, too, died of an overdose.)

Clearly, the gentlemanly Jean could not have left Pamela Courson in the lurch that morning on rue de Beautreillis. He and she must have racked their addled brains to come up with a convincing story. Once they had agreed to blame everything on Jim's health, the next task would be summoning the authorities. Jean would want to get clear of the apartment first. Pamela would need time to compose herself, to clear away the traces of drink and drugs, to hide her stash and get in touch with somebody respectable, like Varda and Ronay, who could aid her in her forthcoming confrontation with police—a frightening prospect. It's a safe bet that a lot of panicky work and worry went on that morning before anyone dialed 18, the emergency number, and reported a man having trouble breathing.

When Jean and Marianne left the Morrison flat, they must have gone straight to their connection and babbled out the story of Jim's death. Just before closing time at La Bulle, the hip new disco on Montaigne-St.-Genevieve, where deejay Cameron Watson was watching his last customers fade from the floor, two respectably dressed dope dealers walked up to his booth and one of them thrust his face into the observation window to confide, "Jim Morrison just snuffed it."

Watson switched on his P.A. mike and announced to the virtually empty club, *"Jim Morrison est mort!"*

INTERVIEWS WITH ALAIN RONAY AND AGNÈS VARDA
ALBERT GOLDMAN

Alain Ronay, his chum: "Paris did him good. He found himself again."

Jim Morrison had the reputation of being obsessed by death, but it is a subject that he rarely brought up with me. On that particular morning, however, this thought was in his mind. I had freed him (distracted him) from these somber thoughts by speaking to him of Oscar Wilde. A month earlier, when Jim and Pam had come to see me in London, I had booked them a room in the Cadogan Hotel near Sloane Square. In passing, I had informed them that Wilde had been arrested in that hotel. I also remembered another coincidence: In Paris, Jim and Pam had in fact stayed at the Hotel, in the rue des Beaux-Arts, where Oscar Wilde had lived. "I'm sure of it," I told him. "A plaque on the door mentions it. You've never noticed it?" Jim remained silent while I added, "Be careful, don't follow too closely in his footsteps . . . You'll end up dying like him."

On July 2, 1971, in Paris, we lunched together, and as we were about to go our separate ways, at a cafe in the Place de la Bastille, Jim said insistently, "Hey, Alain, stay! Stay and have a beer with me. Don't go. Stay. Do it for an old friend." A terrible attack of hiccups punctuated his entreaty, and I brought a chair over so he could sit down. I was confused and troubled by the inexplicable and sudden reversal of all the progress Jim had made in the past months. He had been so joyous, so calm, and so available. Paris had done him good. He had taken care of himself and found himself again. He wrote continually and had almost stopped drinking. He didn't take any drugs. Pam's vice hadn't got hold of him.

We ordered, and I asked the waiter to bring it quickly. Suddenly as Jim closed his eyes and threw his head back another attack of hiccups shook him. Looking at him, I noticed that his face had taken on the look of a death mask. This transformation disappeared when Jim opened his eyes again. He studied me, and, expecting a lie, asked me, "What did you see?" "Nothing, Jim, nothing." While he ordered another round of Kronenbourg, I quickly got up and said, "Terribly sorry, I've got to go now." I ran toward the entrance of the metro which was nearby. I stopped there and looked at Jim, to fix him in my mind. His face was in profile when suddenly, as though on signal, he turned to look at me. This lasted for several seconds, then I rushed down the stairs.

Agnès Varda raised her head from her desk impatiently and repeated, "So you thought you saw the face of a dead man, and then it disappeared?" "Not a face," I corrected her, "what I saw looked like a death mask."

On July 3—this would have been around eight in the morning, for I heard the mail drop into the letter box—the telephone rang. Usually, since I was a guest, I didn't pick up. It rang again. I picked up. It was Pam. She usually spoke so softly; now her voice was terrified. "Jim is unconscious, and bleeding. Call an ambulance! I don't speak French. Quick! I think he's dying!"

I rushed into the garden and knocked on Agnès's door. She woke immediately. I didn't know how to call for help with the complicated Paris telephone system, and asked Agnès to do it for me. "I don't know where Jim lives. Write his address on this paper. I'll take you. Take your passport, you'll need it to prove your identity." I begged Agnès not to give Jim's name to the police, but only his address and the floor of his apartment. She called the fire department (faster and more competent than the police).

In the car I couldn't hold back my question any longer: "Is there any medical reason for thinking that when you can't stop an attack of hiccups, it's a sign of imminent death?" "Where did you hear that?" "My father told me, when he was hiccuping badly in the hospital." "It's not true. Don't worry about it." "Well, he was dead a few hours later, and I've never known whether it was a coincidence. I didn't even think of it yesterday. Shit, if only . . ."

We saw the emergency vehicle in front of Jim's building. One of the men who was holding the crowd back escorted us to the main entrance. "Is he all right? I asked him. "Ask upstairs. I'll go with you."

The second floor was open. Pam was alone at the end of the entry hall, partly hidden by several firemen who were talking among themselves. They separated as I came down the hall and I rushed toward Pam, who told me that Jim was dead. "My Jim is dead, Alain. He has left us. He is dead." And as though speaking to no one in particular, she went on, "I want to be alone now. Leave me alone, please." I didn't know where to go, so I waited. I felt nothing, thought nothing. Time stood still. I saw Jim's boots in the other room, one a little in front of the other as though to walk.

Agnès was in the entrance and asked the fireman in charge, "Are you sure Jim is dead?" He replied that there had been nothing to be done, and that they had arrived at least an hour too late. I noticed that Pam was walking toward her bedroom. The idea of her staying alone in a room disturbed me, and I asked Agnès to stay with her.

The new arrival was a police inspector, to whom it was explained that Jim had been found dead in his bath, then how, since we had arrived, he had been taken into his bedroom.

"Give me your name and that of your friend, as well as his nationality and occupation," he asked. "Tell me also if he used drugs. In any case, we'll know when the medical examiner gets here."

"My friend's name is Douglas James Morrison. He was American, and a poet. He was an alcoholic, but he did not take drugs."

"In general, poets don't have much standing," the inspector went on. "How could he afford an apartment like this?"

"Listen, he was a poet with a personal fortune. He did lots of things . . ."

The inspector insisted: "Your friend Douglas was very young for a poet."

"Come on, Victor Hugo wasn't born with a white beard, and Rimbaud didn't have one when he was dead," I replied. "Could we stop for a moment? I'd like to stay with my friends."

"All right, that's all for now," agreed the inspector. "If the medical examiner files a satisfactory report, a death certificate and a burial permit will be delivered. But if he doesn't, in a case of suspicious death, other inspectors will come to make inquiries."

"How many?"

"A lot."

On the door of his room, Jim had pinned a hotel notice written in French and Arabic, "Please do not disturb." I looked at the doorknob for a long moment before deciding to push it. I did not want to see my friend dead. The last image I had had of him in the cafe was enough for a final portrait.

The firemen, who had left the room where Jim was lying had left the door open, and my friend's feet were the first thing I saw. This sad and final image projected toward the door replaced the banal image in the cafe. Pam gently took me by the arm. The white djellaba which she had put on made her look even paler than usual. I said to her, "I gave the name Douglas James Morrison instead of James Douglas to confuse them. But tell me quickly how he died. Tell us." Methodically fastening her sleeves, Pam began her story.

"Last night, we came straight back to the house after having gone to the movies. When we got back, we began sniffing heroin, and Jim listened to all the records he had made, one after the other. He put on 'The End,' of course, and we went to bed. We could hear clearly in the bedroom. Jim asked me for another sniff, and ended by taking more than I did, since he had already taken it several times during the day. Already, the night before, we had snorted some . . ." "Who had it? You, Pam?" Agnès asked. "Sure, I'm the one who keeps it," Pam replied before turning to me. "Alain, you haven't yet asked to see him! My Jim is so beautiful . . ." Then she went on, "We went to sleep. I don't know what time it was when Jim woke me. He was breathing very heavily. In fact, he was still sleeping, but he couldn't breathe normally, the poor baby! I tried to wake him, but didn't succeed. Then I panicked, shouted, and began hitting him. I hit him so hard. Again. Again. But it didn't do any good. Then I slapped him hard several times, and he finally came to, but he didn't seem to realize what was going on. I was very tired, but I took him into the bathroom."

There was a pause. Agnès had gone to make Pam some camomile tea. "Who ran the bath?" she asked. "I don't remember. But I woke up again later. I was really terrified. Jim wasn't in the bed. I found him in the bath-tub, unconscious. Blood was running from his nose onto his face and he had two red marks on the right side of his chest. Suddenly he began to vomit, and I rushed into the kitchen to find a pot. Three times I had to empty it, and the second time, I saw a clot of blood. I was so tired. He said he felt better, or something like that. I got back into bed and went back to sleep."

Agnès stroked Pam's hand and told her that Jim was dead at least an hour and a half before the firemen arrived. Pam didn't answer. She pulled some silk threads from her sleeve and resumed her story. "He seemed calm, his head was slightly bent, he was in the water up to his chest. He was smiling a little. If there hadn't been that blood around him . . ." "You know," said Agnès, "people who die losing blood don't suffer. He didn't know what was happening to him."

At that moment, the telephone rang. Pam took it in the other room, and we suspected that it was the young count whom she had been seeing. Jim was indifferent to this milieu, of Pam and dealers. One day he said to me, "There are only two choices to make: we have each made our own. You and I are on the side of life, she's on the side of death. We can't do anything for her. Don't worry about it." I stayed alone with Pam who was sorting papers. She had burned quite a few in the fireplace. She showed me their marriage application, filled out in Denver but never filed. "Do you think that the French will believe it's a marriage certificate? Yesterday evening we were looking at our 8 millimeter travel films. We sang an accompaniment for Morocco and Greece."

After that, I went out to buy some cigarettes and passing the crowd, I heard a few key words: "dead," "young," "foreigner." No one mentioned Jim's name or profession.

The medical examiner arrived. "Where is the body?" he asked. "In there," I said, indicating the bedroom. "Come, you must come and show me the body. That's how it's done," he said impatiently. "I don't want to see my friend dead. I don't want that to be my last memory of him. Do it yourself, please." Pam took him in. He was fast, and returned in a few minutes. "How old was he? Did he take drugs?" he asked Pam. I answered, "He was 27, and he absolutely did not take drugs. As a matter of fact, he never even smoked marijuana in Los Angeles, where it is as freely available as ordinary cigarettes. Oh, no! No chance that he took the slightest drug. In fact, only yesterday, he . . ." I was at the end of my rope. Why had the medical examiner spent so little time with Jim's body? Was it because he intended to close the file or because he wanted to carry his investigation further? Suddenly I said to him, "You ought to know that my friend was very pale when I saw him for the last time, several hours before he died. He'd had a terrible attack of hiccups, and he went to see a doctor last month, in London, who said . . ." with a gesture the medical inspector asked me to stop. "That's enough," he said, putting an envelope and an address in my hand. "Take that to the mairie of the sixth arrondissement and go to the window where they handle death certificates."

At the mairie, they told us that the certificate did not say, "natural causes," and a man in charge said to us, "You have ten minutes to return to the dead man's apartment." They took us once more to question Pam at the police station of the Arsenal district. Return to the apartment. Another medical examiner comes, goes briefly to Jim, then turns to Pam and takes her pulse. She weeps.

We decided to bury Jim in Père-Lachaise Cemetery, where Chopin, Delacroix, Piaf, and Isadora Duncan lie. We had to do it quickly before the press discovered the death of our friend. "Everybody wants to be in Père-Lachaise, and there's almost no more room," the funeral parlor man told us. "What did your friend do? He was a writer, wasn't he?" "Actually, he was a poet, a real poet." "In that case," replied the man, "you're in luck. Believe it or not, there's one place left near the grave of a famous American writer. His name is Oscar Wilde, have you heard of him?" "No, not near Mr. Wilde, please! Is there another place?" "There's one, but it's very badly situated," he said, pointing on the map. "Fine," I said to him. "That's settled. It will be fine. Thank you."

Agnès Varda:

A year (or more) after the death of Jim Morrison, I received several calls from the United States. They asked me if Jim was really dead, if I'd seen him dead, if it was really he . . . For certain of them were saying that he was still alive. I replied, "He is dead," and hung up. I say "certain," rather than "some," for these questioners had no reality, since I had really seen the memorable image, the scene of Jim dead in his bath, surrounded by the firemen whom I had summoned. (In fact, Alain, Jim's friend, was sleeping at our place and a call from Pam had awakened us, that July morning in 1971. It was about eight in the morning, or a little after. She had said to Alain, "Come quickly, I think Jim is dead." I thought it advisable to notify the fire department before going there. Too late—they were not able to revive him.

So I saw him dead. I saw the bathtub upon entering, in the end of the corridor. Jim's head was to the left, leaning onto the edge of the white enamel, and dark water covered his body like a cloth. A thread of blood had dried as it ran out of his nose, tracing an oblique line toward the corner of his mouth. I did not approach him, I was moved. I know that Alain and he had seen only a little while before a piece by Bob Wilson. Alain had described to me a scene with a man lying still in a bathtub, like the body of the assassinated Marat. It was only later that I remembered this account, thinking again of what I had seen, disbelieving what I had seen.

Stories went around, rumors are going around still, each person has his own investigation. Jim had fallen into a coma in a club or in the street and was brought back to his place and put into the bath the way someone else would have been put to bed. For myself, I know only what Pam told us. I scarcely knew her, but she spoke with conviction of the evening they'd spent and of Jim's being taken ill, deciding to take a bath in the middle of the night. Alain said that Jim was capricious, and also that he had had premonitions and moments of panic. Furthermore, he had had long attacks of the hiccups, like a motor making strange noises before it breaks down. I thought of something totally different, of those births presided over by Dr. Leboyer, in which the delivery ends in a half-light so that the infant, coming out of the dark, isn't traumatized by the sudden light. The newborn is immediately immersed in a bath, so that he can still feel himself for a little while in the dark waters of his mother. Candles are lit. Does the inverse exist of that experience? Jim, the poet of the Doors— was he seeking, as he dreamed in reverse, to remain for a moment in the night and the water, before entering the dry shadows where one dreams no more?

His grave is the most closely guarded in Père-Lachaise. Because Jim Morrison's fans—born, most of them, after his death—desecrated the neighboring sepulchers, but also because they are suspected of organizing "drug parties" on his grave, it has been placed under surveillance day and night by several electronic cameras. Modest and discreet, the grave is nevertheless the most visited in the whole cemetery, much more than those of Edith Piaf, Chopin, or Oscar Wilde. The easiest to find, as well—from the entrance the direction is indicated, tagged onto hundred-year-old graves. The fans sit right on Morrison's gravestone to listen to music and chat, as if they were visiting a friend. And instead of wreaths, girls lay photos and love letters on the grave.

July 28, 1992

Mr. Albert Goldman
New York, NY 10019

Dear Albert:

I'm sorry I took so long to respond. There is no obviously clear answer. Pam's versions would certainly indicate that he was snorting heroin although when he began and how often he did it (on July 2nd & 3rd) are unclear. It is possible that he did not have a great deal of tolerance and perhaps this latest material (China White or brown) was relatively pure. Three possibilities:
1) He died of heroin OD, while reclining in the tub, from an earlier dose.
2) He took more heroin after Pam left him and OD'd in the tub.
3) He bled to death.
The question you pose "people don't wake up, pronounce themselves improved and then relapse into a fatal coma," may make sense in the context of a nasal dose. Most described OD's occur in IV drug users who die (or become comatose) soon after injection. Some have been found with a needle still in the vein. However, a nasal or oral dose would delay the decline into respiratory death. Assume that he took a large nasal dose; Pam revived him and got him to the bath tub because the OD was indeed telescoped and prolonged. At the time she got him to the tub he may have still had material in his nose or the heroin/morphine concentration in his blood was still increasing. Remember that she woke because he was breathing noisily. I assume that the respiratory depression was "slow" in onset because the dose was nasal. Do you recall someone dying at a party with Cher (maybe a member of The Average White Band) who snorted heroin, thinking it was coke? I seem to recall that someone thought he was OK because of a temporary reviving from coma.

I don't think he bled to death, but the possibility exists. The presence of clots in vomitus signals that the bleeding was brisk. Young men have bled out from ulcers and this setting (alcohol & heroin) might have made it possible.

I believe he died of a nasal heroin OD and this led to the unusual pattern. I'll check around in the next couple of weeks and see if anyone else has noted the prolongation of OD from nasal use or if it is described in the literature. Write or call if you don't get a follow up note in a month.

Sincerely,
John P. Morgan, M.D.
Professor of Pharmacology

REVIEW OF *THE LORDS AND THE NEW CREATURES* BY JIM MORRISON

PATRICIA KENNEALY MORRISON

It would be one thing if this were a collection of notes (*The Lords: Notes on Vision*) and poems (*The New Creatures*) published by your typical struggling, insightful, young and hungry poet. But this is a collection of notes and poems published by a culture hero of the first water, a rock superstar who at the apex of his popularity deserved every bit of it, chief minstrel of the Doors, celebrated for, among other things, incisive lyrics and poetic rock drama, and as such, of course, it is quite another thing.

Therein, fellow Lit. majors, lies the rub.

The Lords, then, is a somewhat glib compendium of notes from Morrison's UCLA career as a film school problem child, and unfortunately does not amount to much more than a collation of determinedly minor observations that were apparently scribbled down in the margins of his notebooks during particularly dull lectures. *The Lords* abounds in neo-profundity and stream-of-consciousness overkill; some few of the would-be aphorisms might make first-rate essays for, say, *Cahiers du Cinéma,* had they been developed, but as small, hard, resolved, gemlike comments (which, judging by the presentation, is what I am assuming Morrison was trying for), they simply and sadly do not make it.

The New Creatures is another problem entirely, and its deficiencies are ultimately much sadder than those of *The Lords* because its scope, its potentiality and the poetic success that does break through are all so much larger than those of the other work.

Morrison is so economical, so splendidly spare and disciplined in his choice of words and structures when lyric-smithing for the Doors that the poems come as a vast disappointment for one who expected more of the same, only better (because Morrison was not here tied to the requirements of a melody line). A re-reading at the earliest opportunity of Aristotle's *Poetics,* or better, the Preface to the *Lyrical Ballads,* might assist to a re-establishment of poetic priorities sorely needed. Morrison is by no means a peon of the creative imagination, having the makings of a fine Irish poet of the old school—once he learns the rules.

His poetic style (undeniably poetic, even at his worst) demonstrates a buttery satisfaction; it is self-indulgent in the worst degree, because almost nowhere in all the poems does he attempt to bridge in any way the gap between his own experience and the reader's experiencing of that experience. The poems, especially the shorter ones, are stuffed with highly personal allusion, images and events that only Morrison himself, his wife and his press agent could possibly claim to understand: I am sure that a goodly percentage of even those poems could perhaps have meaning to others— if only we could grasp the hidden codebreaker. Morrison, however, whether through intent or carelessness, has failed to supply any poetic Rosetta Stone, and much of *The New Creatures* remains studiedly inaccessible, and tiring to try.

More's the pity, for Morrison does exhibit in his better moments the same evocative and expansive command of word tension and plasticity that makes his lyrics so superb. . . . The bulk of the poems, though, offer no such felicity of wedded word and mood. Morrison himself describes *The New Creatures* as having been patched together over a period of several years, and it is much to the volume's disadvantage that there was apparently no unifying factor but whim to tie the poems together.

If there are strange truths here, they are well concealed.

* * *

This was the review I wrote of the only two of Jim's published poetry books over which he had any editorial control—the others were edited and published years after his death. I had no business reviewing him at all at this point, since we had been romantically involved since September 1969, but hey, it was the Sixties! We did things like that! And too bad you missed it, it was big fun!

I was tough on Jim's poetry both in print and to his face: and the fact that I was said much for us both, and for the nature of our relationship. When unintelligent people are in love, they become indulgent and lax; but when smart people fall in love, they become more demanding and discerning, they ask *more* of the beloved, not less . . . I thought Jim could write such better things, and Jim knew I was right to think so.

Anyway, my first word on Jim's reaction to the review came in the form of a telegram reading in its entirety, "Thanks for the pat on the back. Jim." A few nights later I saw the Doors perform in Philadelphia, and talked at length with Jim backstage, afterwards. Much to my gratification, he was going around telling everybody about the review, saying with wonder that it was the first time anyone had ever reviewed his work and not just him.

A couple of days later, when he joined me in New York, Jim showed his appreciation by asking me to handfast him—probably the only time in literary history that a slap-on-the-wrist review occasioned a marriage proposal from subject to reviewer, proving that Jim Morrison was not only a man in love, and a man who could take constructive criticism, but a very brave man indeed.

You know

You know more
than you let on

Much more than you betray

Great slimy angel-whore
you've been good to me

You really have

been swell to me

Tell them you came & saw
& look'd into my eyes
& saw the shadow
of the guard receding
Thoughts in time
& out of season
The Hitchhiker stood
by the side of the road
& levelled his thumb
in the calm calculus
of reason.

Chronology

Time works like acid.
—Jim Morrison

THE DOORS

THE WORLD

1935 Feb. 12, Ray Manzarek born in Chicago, IL.

1943 Dec. 8, Jim Morrison born in Melbourne, FL.

1944 Dec. 1, John Densmore born in Los Angeles, CA.

1946 Jan. 8, Robby Krieger born in Los Angeles, CA.

1948 Antonin Artaud dies ten years after publishing *The Theater and Its Double.*

1954 Aldous Huxley takes mescaline and publishes *The Doors of Perception*.

1956 Allen Ginsberg publishes *Howl and Other Poems*.

1957 Jack Kerouac publishes *On the Road*. A year later he will see into print *The Subterraneans* and *The Dharma Bums*.

1959 William Burroughs publishes *Naked Lunch*.

1963 John F. Kennedy is assassinated in Dallas.

1964 Morrison enrolls in the film school at UCLA and meets Manzarek.

1964 North Vietnamese patrol boats are reported to have attacked a U.S. destroyer in the Tonkin Gulf. Morrison's father is in charge of a ship at this time in the Gulf. Congress passes the Tonkin Gulf resolution, which gives President Johnson power to employ the U.S. military in Vietnam. American planes bomb North Vietnam for the first time.

1965 Morrison meets Manzarek on the beach and Morrison sings him "Moonlight Drive." Manzarek brings in Densmore and Krieger, and they call themselves the Doors.

1965 Malcom X is shot to death in New York.
Operation Rolling Thunder, a program of prolonged and intense bombing of North Vietnam, begins.

THE DOORS

1966 The Doors are signed by Elektra and they get fired as the house band at the Whiskey a Go-Go after Morrison takes the entire audience on a ride through his subconscious during a performance of "The End."

1967 *Annus Mirabilis.* The Doors release their self-titled debut album at the beginning of the year. In July, "Light My Fire" is the biggest song in America. In September, the Doors appear on *The Ed Sullivan Show,* and they are asked not to sing a line from "Light My Fire": "Girl, we couldn't get much higher." The band agrees not to sing the line, but when on live TV, Morrison not only sings the line, he emphasizes it. In November, the band releases their second album, *Strange Days.* A day after his birthday, Dec. 9, Morrison becomes the first rock musician to be arrested on stage. He is charged with breach of the peace and resisting arrest, but the charges are later dropped. The Doors end the year headlining the Fillmore West.

1968 The Doors make a movie for "The Unknown Soldier" in which Morrison is shot to death by a firing squad. They play at the Hollywood Bowl and the concert is filmed. The Doors release their third album, *Waiting for the Sun.* "Hello, I Love You" becomes the band's second #1 single. A documentary of the Doors' visit to Britain, *The Doors Are Open,* is broadcast on British TV.

THE WORLD

1967 Protest against the war in Vietnam increases and is widely discussed in the media. American troops in Vietnam almost reach 500,000.

1968 Dr. Martin Luther King is assassinated in Memphis. Robert Kennedy is gunned down in Los Angeles after winning the California primary. Students and workers unite, riot, strike, and take over France for the summer. American police riot and attack protesters at the Democratic convention in Chicago. The Soviets invade Czechoslovakia. The Tet Offensive takes place in Vietnam, and at year's end, 540,000 American troops are stationed there. The My Lai massacre occurs, but it will not be revealed until a year later. Nixon is elected president.

THE DOORS

1969 On March 1, the infamous Miami show takes place. Morrison arrives at the show drunk, but a more serious factor in his behavior is that he spent the week before watching The Living Theatre perform their plays of global protest. No one can agree on what Morrison did during the show— some say he exposed himself, some say he tried to, some say he didn't, some say it was just a big joke. Manzarek believes that Morrison "instilled into that crowd a mass hallucination." The authorities don't believe in hallucinations, and they charge Morrison with lewd behavior in public. The ensuing media frenzy makes touring impossible. *The Soft Parade* appears and the homegrown documentary *Feast of Friends* is premiered. Morrison has two books of poetry, *The Lords: Notes on Vision* and *The New Creatures,* privately published. Morrison ends the year by being arrested again for "interfering" with a stewardess during a flight. He is faced with a serious federal charge, but the stewardess later withdraws her testimony and the charges are dropped.

THE WORLD

1969 Jack Kerouac and Ho Chi Minh die. Woodstock Music and Art Fair takes place, and Neil Armstrong walks across the surface of the moon. *Easy Rider* is premiered. The "Chicago Eight" are found innocent of inciting to riot after a trial that featured Abbie Hoffman coming into court in judge's robes, entering the courtroom doing somersaults, accusing the judge of being his natural father, and being bound and gagged. Hundreds of thousands of Americans take to the streets to protest the war in Vietnam. In August, the Manson murders occur, and the nation is stunned at the brutality of the killings. The first U.S. troops are withdrawn from Vietnam. Nixon begins secret bombing of Cambodia.

THE DOORS

1970 The Doors release their fifth album, *Morrison Hotel*. The album features the song "Peace Frog," which begins: "There's blood in the streets, it's up to my ankles." The double album *Absolutely Live* appears and features the first recorded version of the complete "Celebration of the Lizard." In court, Morrison is found guilty of the thing that nobody is sure of—indecent exposure—and found innocent of what he actually was guilty of—public drunkenness and lewd and lascivious behavior. He is sentenced to eight months' hard labor, 28 months of probation, and a $500 fine. He is free on bond while the sentence is appealed. To celebrate his 27th birthday, Morrison goes into the studio and records some of his poetry. The tapes of this recording session will be lost for several years, but when they are found, the surviving Doors put music behind his words to create *An American Prayer*. The Doors give their final performance in New Orleans. Something happens to Morrison on stage that signals the end; Manzarek described it as a loss of the spiritual power that had always been behind Morrison's words and performance: "He lost all his energy about midway through the set. He hung on the microphone, and it just slipped away. You could actually see it leave him." They all saw something leave him, so the remainder of the tour is canceled. Morrison feels the need to leave America and makes plans to move to Paris.

THE WORLD

1970 Across the U.S., 448 colleges and universities are closed or on strike in protest over the war. National guardsmen kill four students at Kent State University in Ohio. Lt. William Calley goes on trial for his leadership role in the My Lai massacre. Jimi Hendrix is found dead in London, and all the coroner can say is: "The question why Hendrix took so many sleeping tablets cannot be safely answered." Janis Joplin is found dead in her Hollywood apartment with $4.50 clenched in her fist.

THE DOORS

1971 Morrison moves to Paris with Pamela. He concentrates on his writing. *The Lords and The New Creatures* goes into paperback. The Doors' last album with Morrison, *L. A. Woman,* is released. A month after the album hits record stores, Morrison is found dead in his bathtub. Mysterious circumstances surround his death: no autopsy is performed, and the body is quickly and quietly buried in the Père-Lachaise Cemetery in Paris. Morrison's grave will soon become the most famous in a graveyard holding the remains of Oscar Wilde, Edith Piaf, Chopin, and Balzac. His grave becomes one of the most visited locations in Europe as tourists go to see the ancient shapes all around us. The surviving members of the Doors release *Other Voices,* the first album without Morrison.

1972 After releasing their final album, *Full Circle,* the surviving members of the band break up and the Doors are over.

1974 Pamela Courson Morrison dies from an overdose of heroin.

1979 *An American Prayer* is released. Francis Ford Coppola begins *Apocalypse Now* with "The End."

THE WORLD

1971 Lt. William Calley is convicted of premeditated murder of South Vietnamese civilians at My Lai. *The New York Times* begins to publish the Pentagon Papers.

1974 Faced with impeachment over the Watergate affair, Nixon resigns. President Gerald Ford pardons him for any crimes he "committed or may have committed."

1975 Ford calls the war in Vietnam "finished," and a week later Communist forces capture Saigon.

THE DOORS

THE WORLD

1980 Jerry Hopkins and Danny Sugerman publish *No One Here Gets Out Alive.* The biography of Morrison will eventually sell 5 million copies and rekindle the popularity of the band, and the myths surrounding Morrison.

1981 On the tenth anniversary of Morrison's death, the surviving Doors lead a graveside tribute to Morrison.

1988 Frank Lisciandro, Katherine Lisciandro, Columbus Courson, and Pearl Marie Courson are instrumental in getting *Wilderness: The Lost Writings of Jim Morrison* published. The poetry from this volume is taken from the notebooks and typescripts Morrison left with Pamela after his death. A second volume of "lost" writing is promised.

1990 John Densmore publishes *Riders on the Storm,* his account of his life with the band. It is a revealing portrait of what living with the band was like, but it seems to be mostly about Densmore's wish to talk to Morrison in a way he never did: "What was that big black Morrison cloud that hovered over your head? Anyone who came into contact with you found himself under the fringes of that darkness." *The American Night: The Writings of Jim Morrison* appears. It includes the screenplay "The Hitchhiker" that formed the basis for *HWY,* some of the poems he recorded on Dec. 8, 1970, and the last poems Morrison wrote under the title "Paris Journal."

1980 On Dec. 8, Morrison's birthday, John Lennon is shot to death in New York.

THE DOORS

1991 Oliver Stone's *The Doors* is premiered.

1992 Patricia Kennealy Morrison publishes *Strange Days: My Life With and Without Jim Morrison.*

1993 The Doors are inducted into the Rock and Roll Hall of Fame. At the ceremony, the remaining Doors perform two Doors songs with Eddie Vedder from Pearl Jam on vocals.

Selected Bibliography

Artaud, Antonin. *The Theater and Its Double.* Trans. Mary Caroline Richards. New York: Grove Weidenfeld, 1958.

Azerrad, Michael. *Come as You Are: The Story of Nirvana.* New York: Doubleday, 1994.

Balfour, Victoria. *Rock Wives.* New York: William Morrow & Co., 1986.

Bangs, Lester. *Psychotic Reactions and Carburetor Dung.* Ed. Greil Marcus. New York: Vintage Books, 1988.

Crisafulli, Chuck. *Moonlight Drive: The Stories Behind Every Doors' Song.* New York: MBS, 1995.

Dalton, David. *Mr. Mojo Risin': Jim Morrison, The Last Holy Fool.* New York: St. Martin's Press, 1991.

Densmore, John. *Riders On the Storm.* New York: Dell Publishing, 1990.

Des Barres, Pamela. *I'm with the Band.* New York: William Morrow and Co., 1987.

Didion, Joan. *The White Album.* New York: Simon and Schuster, 1979.

Doe, Andrew, and John Tobler. *The Doors in Their Own Words.* London: Omnibus Press, 1988.

The Doors. *The Doors: The Complete Illustrated Lyrics.* Compiled by Danny Sugerman. New York: Hyperion, 1991.

Fowlie, Wallace. *Rimbaud and Jim Morrison: The Rebel as Poet.* Durham and London: Duke University Press, 1993.

Goldstein, Richard. *Goldstein's Greatest Hits.* Englewood Cliffs, NJ: Prentice Hall, 1970.

Hopkins, Jerry. *The Lizard King: The Essential Jim Morrison.* New York: Simon and Schuster, 1992.

Hopkins, Jerry, and Danny Sugerman. *No One Here Gets Out Alive.* New York: Warner Books, 1980.

Jones, Dylan. *Dark Star.* New York: Viking, 1991.

Kennealy Morrison, Patricia. *Strange Days: My Life With and Without Jim Morrison.* New York: Dutton, 1992.

Kerouac, Jack. *On the Road.* New York: Viking, 1955.

Kostelanetz, Richard. *The Fillmore East: Reflections of Rock Theater.* New York: Schirmer Books, 1995.

Lisciandro, Frank. *An Hour for Magic.* New York: Delilah Books, 1982.

Lydon, John. *Rotten: No Irish, No Blacks, No Dogs.* New York: St. Martin's Press, 1994.

Marcus, Greil. *Lipstick Traces: A Secret History of the Twentieth Century.* Cambridge, Mass.: Harvard University Press, 1989.

———. *Mystery Train: Images of America in Rock 'n' Roll Music.* New York: E. P. Dutton and Co., Inc, 1975.

McNeil, Legs, and Gillian McCain. *Please Kill Me: The Uncensored Oral History of Punk.* New York: Grove Press, 1996.

Morrison, Jim. *The Lords and The New Creatures.* New York: Simon and Schuster, 1970.

———. *Wilderness: The Lost Writings of Jim Morrison.* Vol. 1. New York: Vintage, 1988.

———. *The American Night: The Writings of Jim Morrison.* Vol. 2. New York: Villard Books, 1990.

Nietzsche, Friedrich. *The Birth of Tragedy and The Case of Wagner.* Trans. Walter Kaufmann. New York: Vintage, 1967.

———. *The Will to Power.* Trans. Walter Kaufmann and R. J. Hollingdale. Ed. Walter Kaufmann. New York: Vintage, 1968.

Reynolds, Simon, and Joy Press. *The Sex Revolts: Gender, Rebellion, and Rock 'n' Roll*. Cambridge, Mass.: Harvard University Press, 1995.

Rimbaud, Arthur. *"Illuminations" and Other Prose Poems*. Trans. Louise Varèse. New York: New Directions, 1957.

Riordan, James, and Jerry Prochnicky. *Break On Through: The Life and Death of Jim Morrison*. New York: William Morrow & Co., 1991.

Savage, Jon. *England's Dreaming: Anarchy, Sex Pistols, Punk Rock, and Beyond*. New York: St. Martin's Press, 1992.

Sugerman, Danny. *The Doors: The Illustrated History*. New York: William Morrow & Co., 1983.

————. *Wonderland Avenue*. New York: William Morrow & Co., 1989.

Tytell, John. *The Living Theater: Art, Exile, and Outrage*. New York: Grove Press, 1995.

————. *Naked Angels: The Lives and Literature of the Beat Generation*. New York: McGraw Hill, 1976.

Witts, Richard. *Nico: The Life and Lies of an Icon*. London: Virgin Books, 1993.

Discography

As this book went to press, two new Doors CDs were released: *Greatest Hits* and *Absolutely Live* (this is the first time the latter has appeared on CD). Both have great sound but *Greatest Hits* has two provocative features: the version of "The End" is from *Apocalypse Now,* complete with surreal helicopter and insect sounds; and, what is even more interesting, the CD contains a video that can be played on a CD-ROM. The video is for "The Ghost Song" and it begins with a shaman conjuring up the remaining Doors, with a projection of Morrison on a screen in the middle of them. It is a fascinating montage of the three playing instruments with images of Morrison hovering around them.

Greatest Hits also has a book mark file for connection to the Official Doors Web site (http://www.thedoors.com). The Doors are all over the World Wide Web. Many of the sites are fan-driven—speculation on Morrison's hiding place while his coffin in Paris is filled with empty Jameson bottles, for example—but others are informative. The All Music Guide's site for The Doors (http://www.vis.colostate.edu/%7Euser1209/doors/doorsamg.html) lists all the Doors recordings and has a running commentary by Jeff Tamarkin and William Ruhlmann. The Doors FAQ site (http://www.vis.colostate.edu/%7Euser1209/doors/doorsfaq.html) has every piece of information you would ever want to know about the band and their records, while the The Doors Book Review site (http://www.seanet.com/~wors/library.htm) provides a good working bibliography. The Doors Mailing List Homepage (http://www.seanet.com/~user1209/doors/) has the most comprehensive and detailed list of Doors bootlegs I have ever seen. Most of these sites have links to the many other sites dedicated to the Doors.

January 1967	*The Doors*
October 1967	*Strange Days*
August 1968	*Waiting for the Sun*
July 1969	*The Soft Parade*
February 1970	*Morrison Hotel*
July 1970	*Absolutely Live*
November 1970	*13*
April 1971	*L. A. Woman*
November 1971	*Other Voices*
November 1971	*Weird Scenes Inside the Goldmine*
July 1972	*Full Circle*
September 1973	*The Best of the Doors*
December 1978	*An American Prayer*
October 1980	*Greatest Hits*

About the Contributors

Antonin Artaud (1896–1948) was an actor (he appeared in Gance's *Napoleon* and Dreyer's *The Passion of Joan of Arc*), poet, playwright, and theorist of the theater. His most famous book is *The Theater and Its Double*.

Lester Bangs (1948–82) was a great rock critic who, in his own words, "defined a style of critical-journalism based on the sound and language of rock 'n' roll which ended up influencing a whole generation of younger writers and perhaps musicians as well." Some of his most famous writing appears in *Psychotic Reactions and Carburetor Dung*.

Michael Cuscuna writes for *Down Beat*.

David Dalton is the author of *Mr. Mojo Risin': Jim Morrison, the Last Holy Fool*.

Joan Didion is an essayist and novelist whose work includes *Slouching Towards Bethlehem, Play It As It Lays,* and *The White Album.*

Albert Goldman (1927–94) was the author of hundreds of articles on music and books on Wagner, Disco, Elvis, and John Lennon. The last two biographies earned him the reputation as the most inflammatory figure in rock literature.

Richard Goldstein is executive editor of the *Village Voice*. He began writing about rock and the counterculture for the *Voice* in 1966 and his most recent book is *Reporting the Counterculture*.

Stephanie Harrington is a freelance writer.

Bruce Harris was director of advertising and publicity for Elektra Records.

Jac Holzman was the founder of Elektra Records and its chairman from 1950 to 1973.

Jerry Hopkins wrote the first biography of Elvis in 1971, and in 1980 he co-authored the book that rekindled the Morrison legend, *No One Here Gets Out Alive*. His *The Lizard King: The Essential Jim Morrison* is a provocative look back at his own writing and on the ever-growing myth of Morrison and the Doors.

Richard Kostelanetz is the author of over forty books on music, art, literature, and culture. He is a poet, holographic and video artist, and the editor of many groundbreaking anthologies of avant-garde art and literature. Two recent books are *The Dictionary of the Avant-Gardes* and *Writings on John Cage.*

Yasue Kuwahara is, the last I heard, in the Communications Department at Northern Kentucky University.

Tony Magistrale is an assistant professor of English at the University of Vermont. He edited a collection of writing on Stephen King called *The Shining Reader.*

Dr. John P. Morgan is currently Medical Professor in the Pharmacology Department at the CUNY Medical School and the City College of New York. Dr. Morgan has published more than one hundred articles and books on clinical pharmacology.

Patricia Kennealy Morrison was born in New York City and has lived there for most of her life. One of the first women rock critics, she was from 1968 to 1971 the editor-in-chief of *Jazz & Pop* magazine, and, as an advertising copywriter in the '70s, a two-time Clio nominee.

In January 1969 she met Jim Morrison in a private interview, and in June 1970 they were married in a Celtic handfasting ceremony. Her memoir, *Strange Days: My Life With and Without Jim Morrison,* was published in 1992; the New York *Daily News* called it "the first good book on Jim Morrison."

She is the author of the Keltiad science-fantasy series. Her eight novels include *The Hawk's Gray Feather, Blackmantle,* and the upcoming *The Deer's Cry.* Dame Patricia was knighted in Scotland in 1990.

She was a consultant to Oliver Stone's 1991 film *The Doors,* in which she also made a cameo appearance, performing her own wedding ceremony, and was herself portrayed by actress Kathleen Quinlan.

In 2021, to commemorate the fiftieth anniversary of Jim's death, she will publish *Fireheart: The True 'Lost Writings' of James Douglas Morrison,* an extensively annotated collection of the many love letters, poems, songs and drawings Morrison left her.

Arthur Rimbaud (1854–91) rebelled against everything he ever knew and wrote all of his poetry before he reached nineteen. His two important works that set the day on fire are *Une Saison en enfer* and *Les Illuminations.*

James Riordan and Jerry Prochnicky are the authors of the most detailed biography of Morrison to date, *Break On Through: The Life and Death of Jim Morrison.*

Richard Witts was asked by Nico to write her biography, and he wrote *Nico: The Life and Lies of an Icon.*

Bernard Wolfe is the author of twelve novels, among them *Really the Blues* (optioned by Paramount Pictures for a feature film) and *The Great Prince Died,* an account of his time as secretary and bodyguard to Leon Trotsky when he was in exile in Cocoacan, Mexico. Wolfe also wrote several screenplays, feature films, and numerous magazine articles. He is survived by his wife and twin daughters, Jordan and Miranda.

Permissions

Index

About the Editor

John Rocco teaches English at Queens College, CUNY. He has published essays on James Joyce, punk rock, Samuel Beckett, and anarchism; with Richard Kostelanetz, articles on rock music and literature. He is coeditor of *The Frank Zappa Companion* (Schirmer Books, 1997).